SUPERGIRL BEYOND GOOD AND EVIL

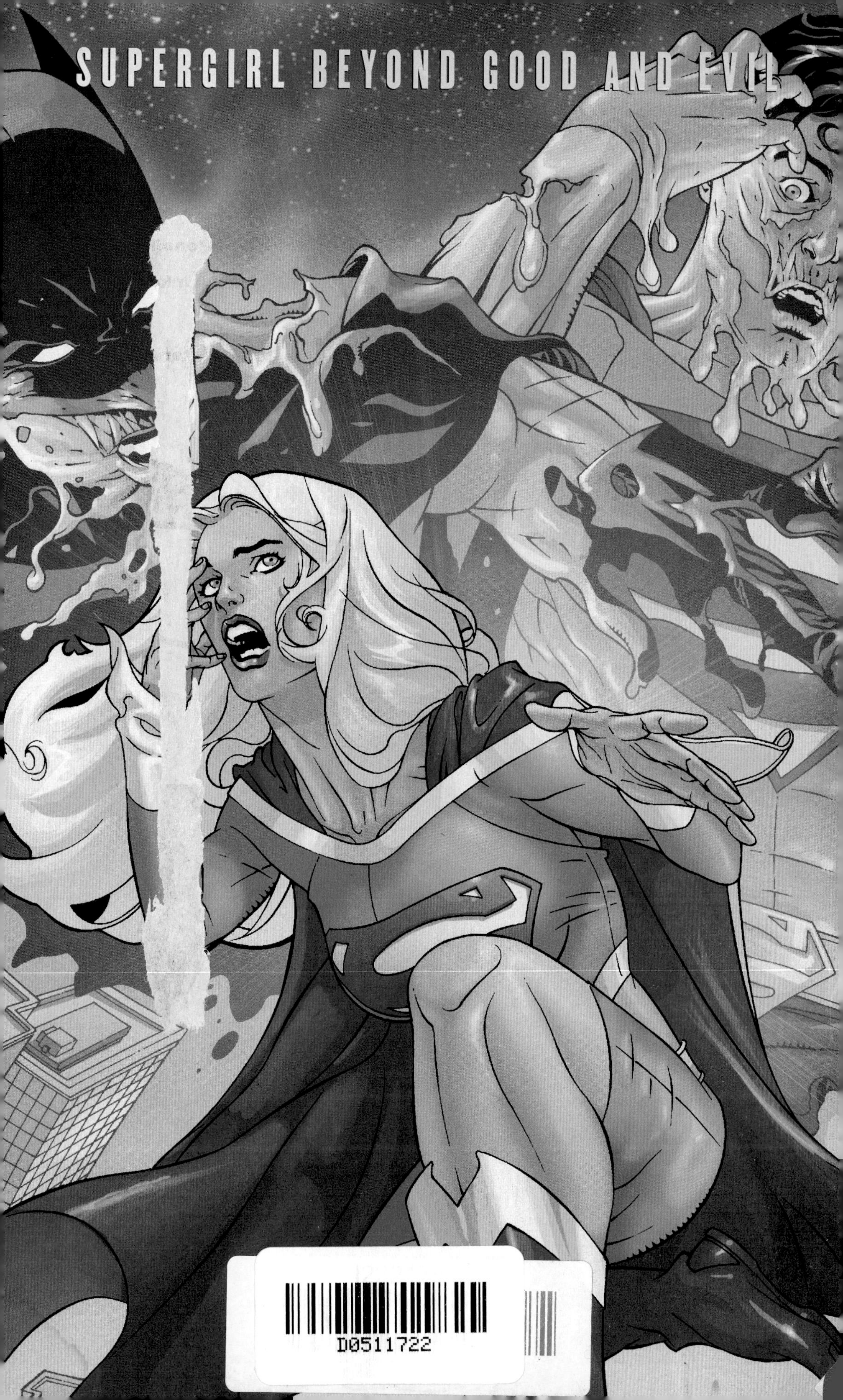

Kelley Puckett   Kurt Busiek   Fabian Nicieza   Geoff Johns Writers
Drew Johnson   Renato Guedes   Lee Ferguson   Rick Leonardi Pencillers
Ray Snyder   José Wilson Magalháes   Marc Deering   Dan Green Inkers
Brad Anderson Colorist
Rob Leigh   Jared K. Fletcher   Travis Lanham   Steve Wands Letterers

Superman created by Jerry Siegel and Joe Shuster

SUPERG

BEY
GOODA

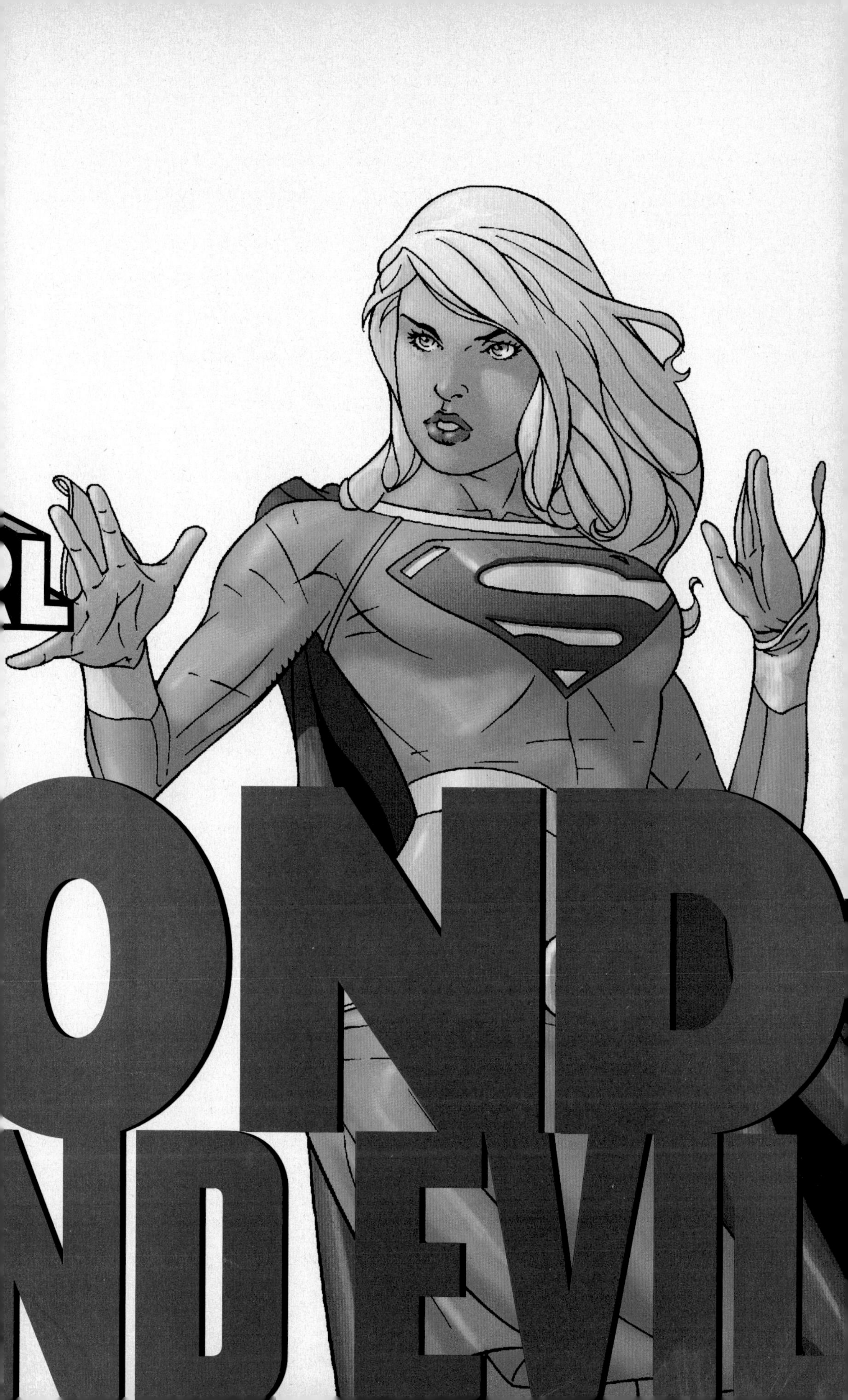
RL
OND
NDEVIL

Cover art by Renato Guedes

SUPERGIRL: BEYOND GOOD AND EVIL
Published by DC Comics.
Cover and compilation Copyright © 2008 DC Comics.
All Rights Reserved.

Originally published in single magazine form in ACTION
COMICS 850, SUPERGIRL 23-27 Copyright © 2007, 2008
DC Comics. All Rights Reserved. All characters, their distinctive
likenesses and related elements featured in this publication
are trademarks of DC Comics. The stories, characters and
incidents featured in this publication are entirely fictional.
DC Comics does not read or accept unsolicited submissions of
ideas, stories or artwork.

DC Comics, 1700 Broadway, New York, NY 10019
A Warner Bros. Entertainment Company
Printed in Canada. First Printing.

ISBN: 978-1-4012-1850-8

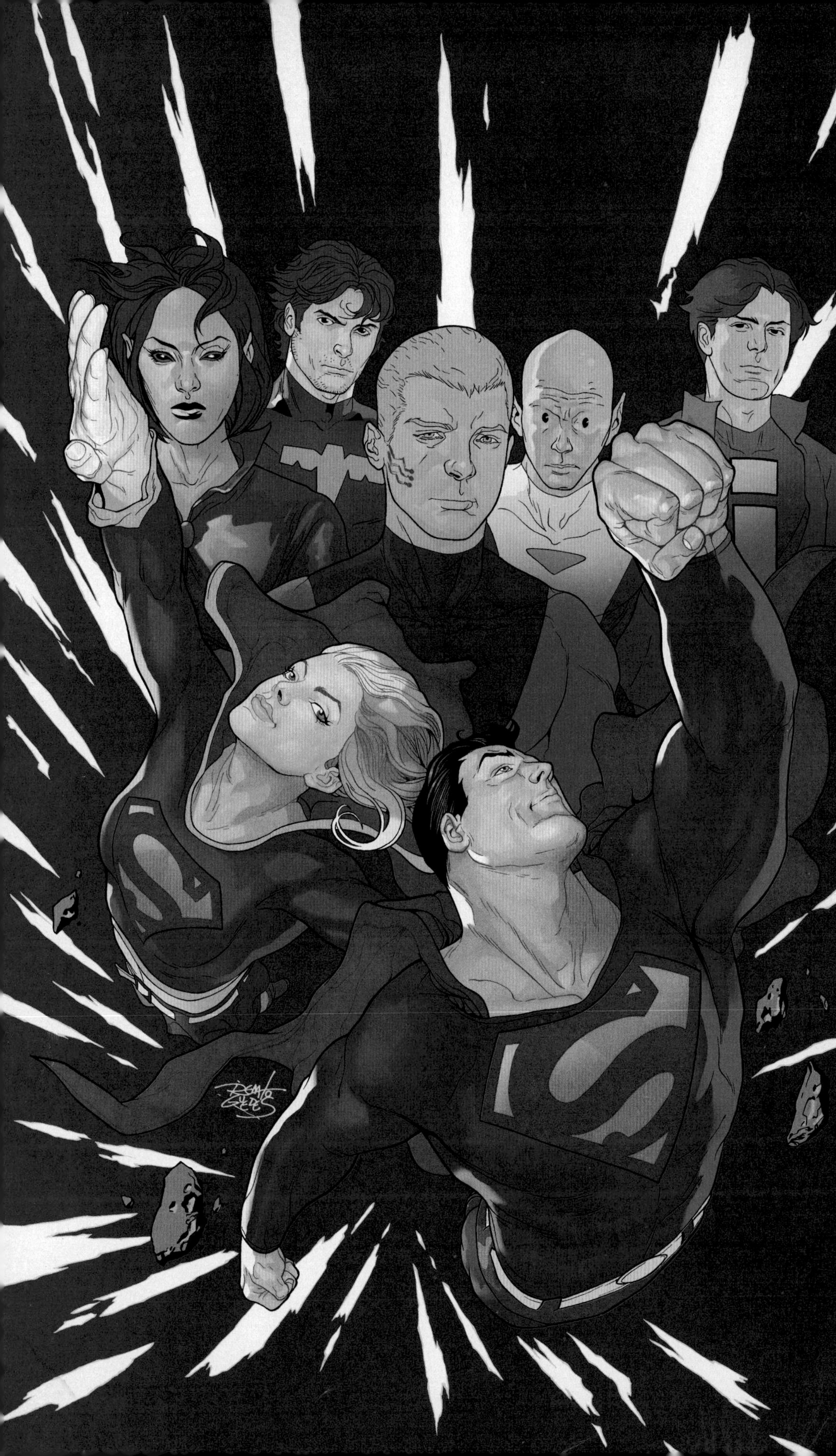

ACTION COMICS 850 Renato Guedes

SUPERMAN: FAMILY

KURT BUSIEK   FABIAN NICIEZA   GEOFF JOHNS   WRITERS
RENATO GUEDES   PENCILS & COLORS
JOSÉ WILSON MAGALHÁES   INKS

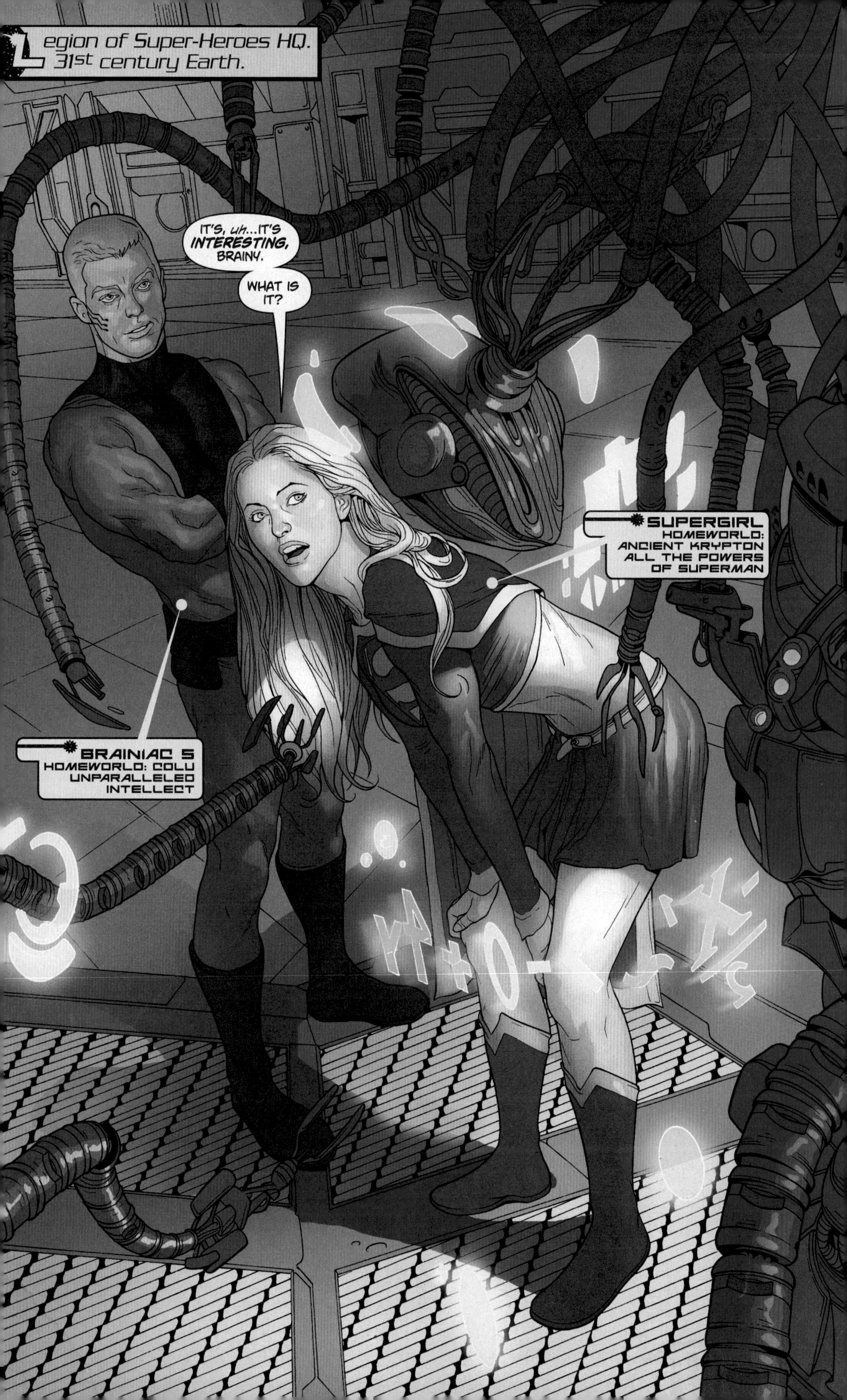

Legion of Super-Heroes HQ. 31st century Earth.
IT'S, uh...IT'S INTERESTING, BRAINY.
WHAT IS IT?
SUPERGIRL HOMEWORLD: ANCIENT KRYPTON ALL THE POWERS OF SUPERMAN
BRAINIAC 5 HOMEWORLD: COLU UNPARALLELED INTELLECT

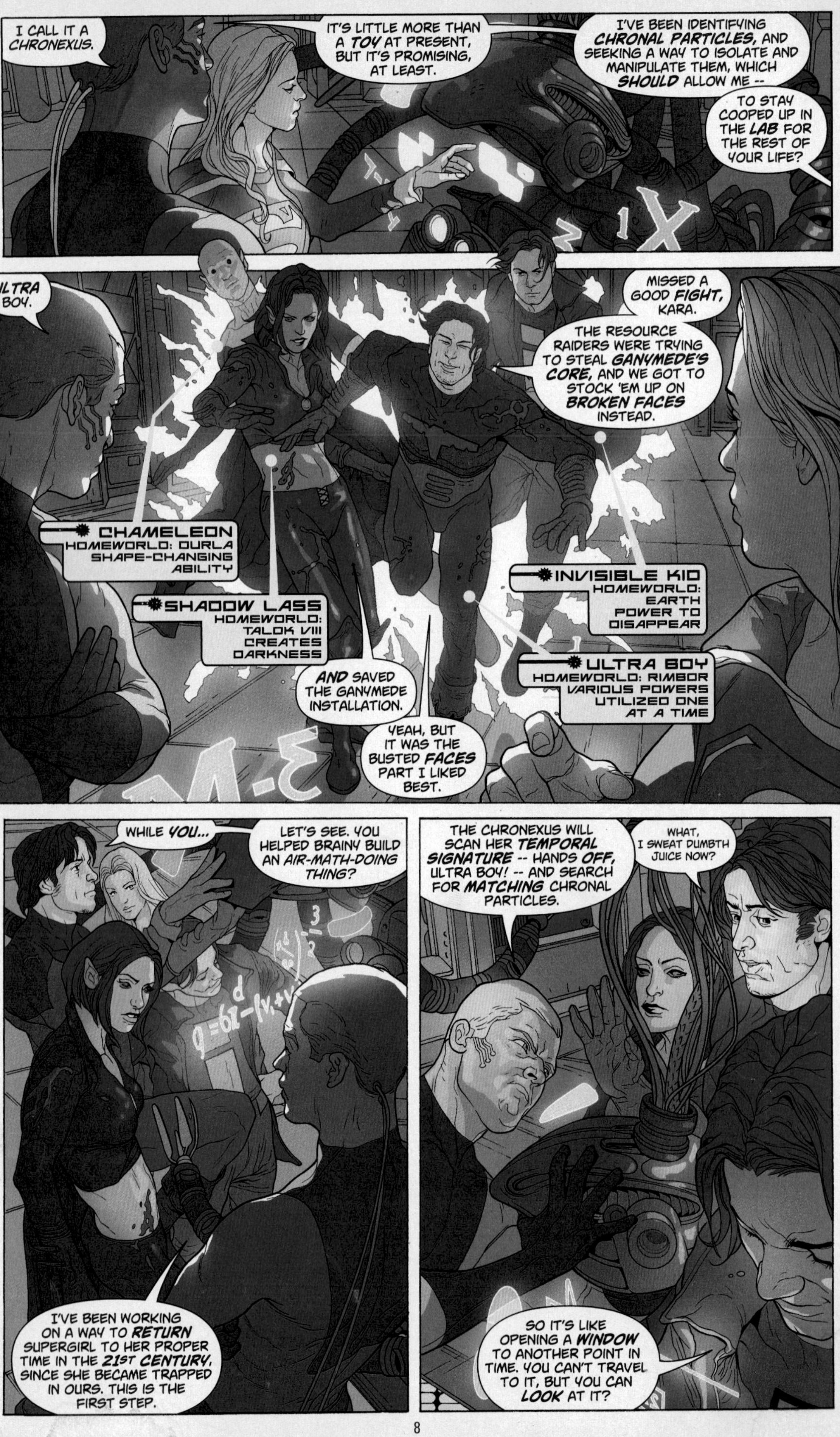
I CALL IT A CHRONEXUS.
IT'S LITTLE MORE THAN A TOY AT PRESENT, BUT IT'S PROMISING, AT LEAST.
I'VE BEEN IDENTIFYING CHRONAL PARTICLES, AND SEEKING A WAY TO ISOLATE AND MANIPULATE THEM, WHICH SHOULD ALLOW ME --
TO STAY COOPED UP IN THE LAB FOR THE REST OF YOUR LIFE?
ULTRA BOY.
MISSED A GOOD FIGHT, KARA.
THE RESOURCE RAIDERS WERE TRYING TO STEAL GANYMEDE'S CORE, AND WE GOT TO STOCK 'EM UP ON BROKEN FACES INSTEAD.
CHAMELEON HOMEWORLD: DURLA SHAPE-CHANGING ABILITY
SHADOW LASS HOMEWORLD: TALOK VIII CREATES DARKNESS
INVISIBLE KID HOMEWORLD: EARTH POWER TO DISAPPEAR
ULTRA BOY HOMEWORLD: RIMBOR VARIOUS POWERS UTILIZED ONE AT A TIME
AND SAVED THE GANYMEDE INSTALLATION.
YEAH, BUT IT WAS THE BUSTED FACES PART I LIKED BEST.
WHILE YOU...
LET'S SEE. YOU HELPED BRAINY BUILD AN AIR-MATH-DOING THING?
I'VE BEEN WORKING ON A WAY TO RETURN SUPERGIRL TO HER PROPER TIME IN THE 21ST CENTURY, SINCE SHE BECAME TRAPPED IN OURS. THIS IS THE FIRST STEP.
THE CHRONEXUS WILL SCAN HER TEMPORAL SIGNATURE -- HANDS OFF, ULTRA BOY! -- AND SEARCH FOR MATCHING CHRONAL PARTICLES.
WHAT, I SWEAT DUMBTH JUICE NOW?
SO IT'S LIKE OPENING A WINDOW TO ANOTHER POINT IN TIME. YOU CAN'T TRAVEL TO IT, BUT YOU CAN LOOK AT IT?

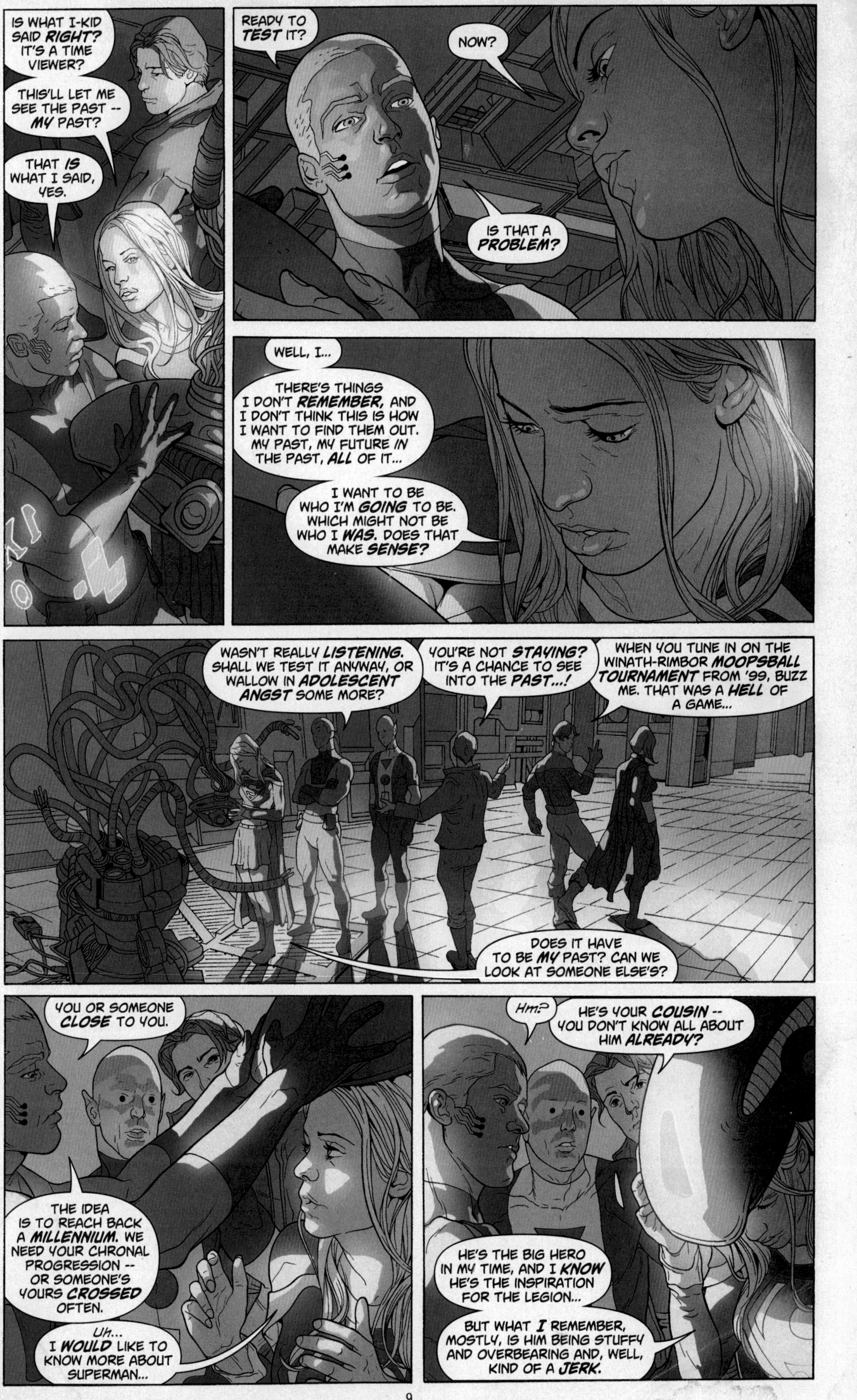
IS WHAT I-KID SAID RIGHT? IT'S A TIME VIEWER?
THIS'LL LET ME SEE THE PAST -- MY PAST?
THAT IS WHAT I SAID, YES.
READY TO TEST IT?
NOW?
IS THAT A PROBLEM?
WELL, I...
THERE'S THINGS I DON'T REMEMBER, AND I DON'T THINK THIS IS HOW I WANT TO FIND THEM OUT. MY PAST, MY FUTURE IN THE PAST, ALL OF IT...
I WANT TO BE WHO I'M GOING TO BE. WHICH MIGHT NOT BE WHO I WAS. DOES THAT MAKE SENSE?
WASN'T REALLY LISTENING. SHALL WE TEST IT ANYWAY, OR WALLOW IN ADOLESCENT ANGST SOME MORE?
YOU'RE NOT STAYING? IT'S A CHANCE TO SEE INTO THE PAST...!
WHEN YOU TUNE IN ON THE WINATH-RIMBOR MOOPSBALL TOURNAMENT FROM '99, BUZZ ME. THAT WAS A HELL OF A GAME...
DOES IT HAVE TO BE MY PAST? CAN WE LOOK AT SOMEONE ELSE'S?
YOU OR SOMEONE CLOSE TO YOU.
THE IDEA IS TO REACH BACK A MILLENNIUM. WE NEED YOUR CHRONAL PROGRESSION -- OR SOMEONE'S YOURS CROSSED OFTEN.
Uh... I WOULD LIKE TO KNOW MORE ABOUT SUPERMAN...
Hm?
HE'S YOUR COUSIN -- YOU DON'T KNOW ALL ABOUT HIM ALREADY?
HE'S THE BIG HERO IN MY TIME, AND I KNOW HE'S THE INSPIRATION FOR THE LEGION...
BUT WHAT I REMEMBER, MOSTLY, IS HIM BEING STUFFY AND OVERBEARING AND, WELL, KIND OF A JERK.

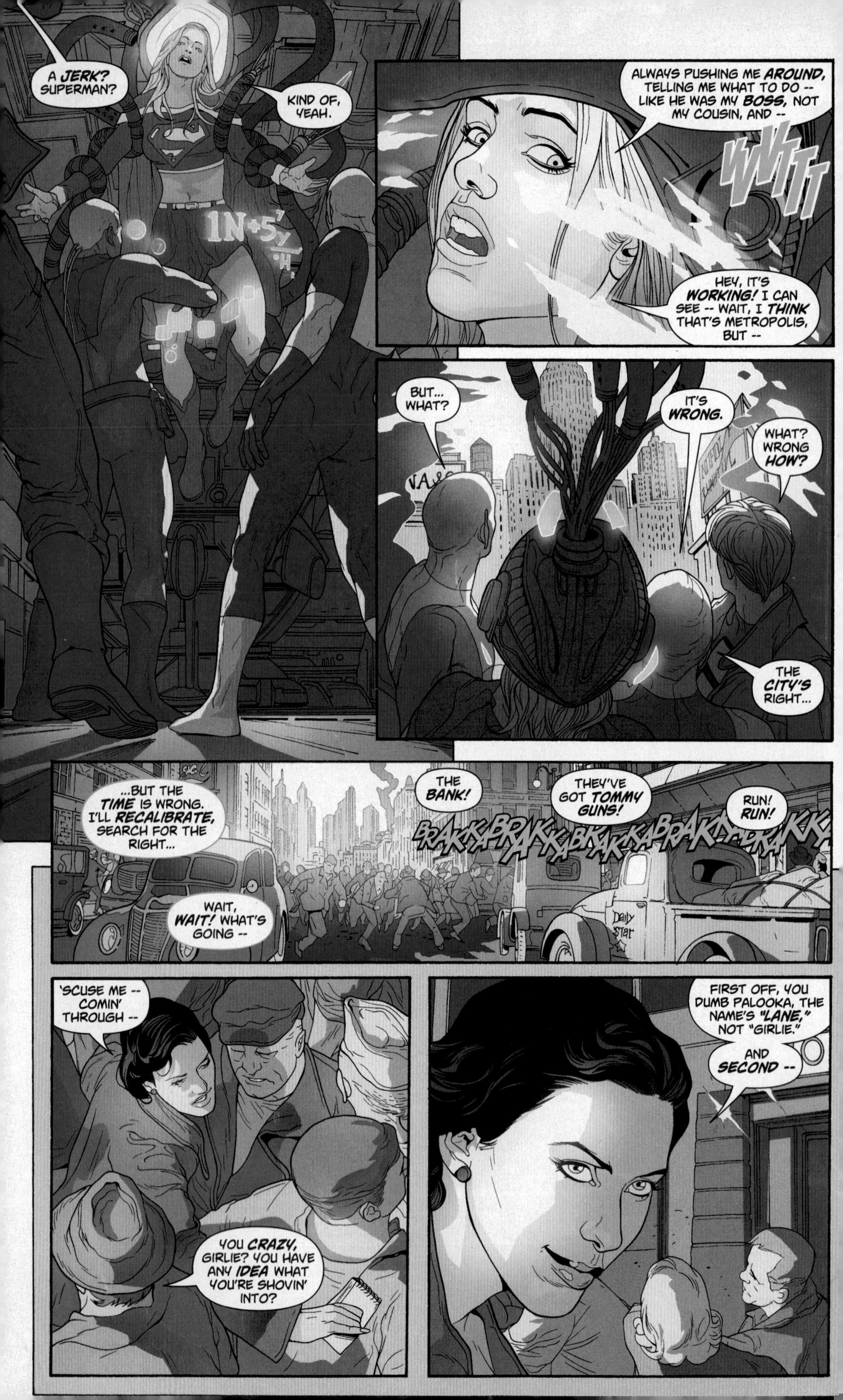
A JERK? SUPERMAN?
KIND OF, YEAH.
1N+5
ALWAYS PUSHING ME AROUND, TELLING ME WHAT TO DO -- LIKE HE WAS MY BOSS, NOT MY COUSIN, AND --
VVVTTT
HEY, IT'S WORKING! I CAN SEE -- WAIT, I THINK THAT'S METROPOLIS, BUT --
BUT... WHAT?
IT'S WRONG.
WHAT? WRONG HOW?
THE CITY'S RIGHT...
...BUT THE TIME IS WRONG. I'LL RECALIBRATE, SEARCH FOR THE RIGHT...
WAIT, WAIT! WHAT'S GOING --
THE BANK!
THEY'VE GOT TOMMY GUNS!
RUN! RUN!
BRAKKABRAKKABRAKKABRAKKABRAKKABRAKKA
Daily Star
'SCUSE ME -- COMIN' THROUGH --
YOU CRAZY, GIRLIE? YOU HAVE ANY IDEA WHAT YOU'RE SHOVIN' INTO?
FIRST OFF, YOU DUMB PALOOKA, THE NAME'S "LANE," NOT "GIRLIE."
AND SECOND --

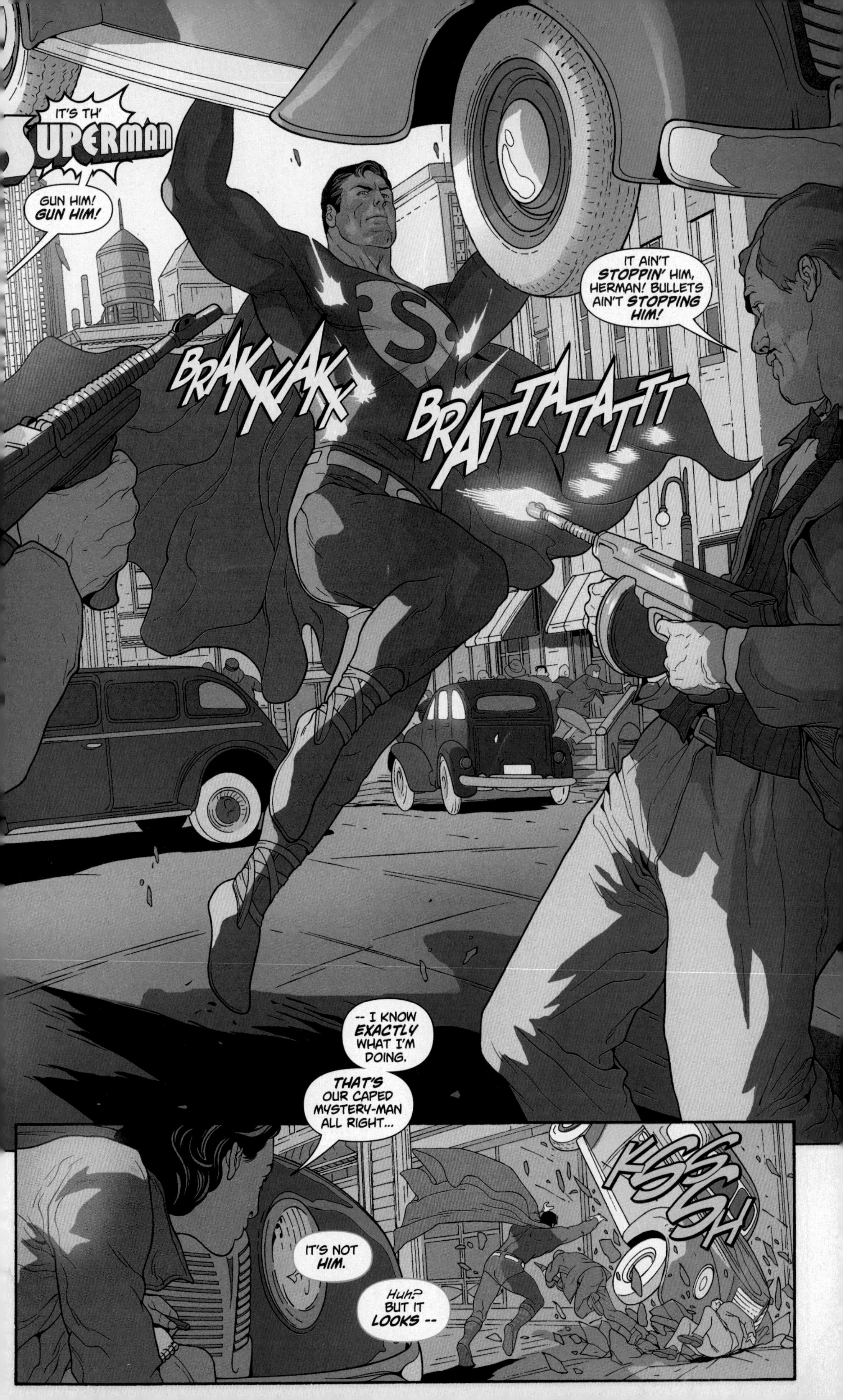

IT'S TH' SUPERMAN
GUN HIM! GUN HIM!
IT AIN'T STOPPIN' HIM, HERMAN! BULLETS AIN'T STOPPING HIM!
BRAKKAKKK
BRATTTATATTT
-- I KNOW EXACTLY WHAT I'M DOING.
THAT'S OUR CAPED MYSTERY-MAN ALL RIGHT...
KSSSH
IT'S NOT HIM.
Huh? BUT IT LOOKS --

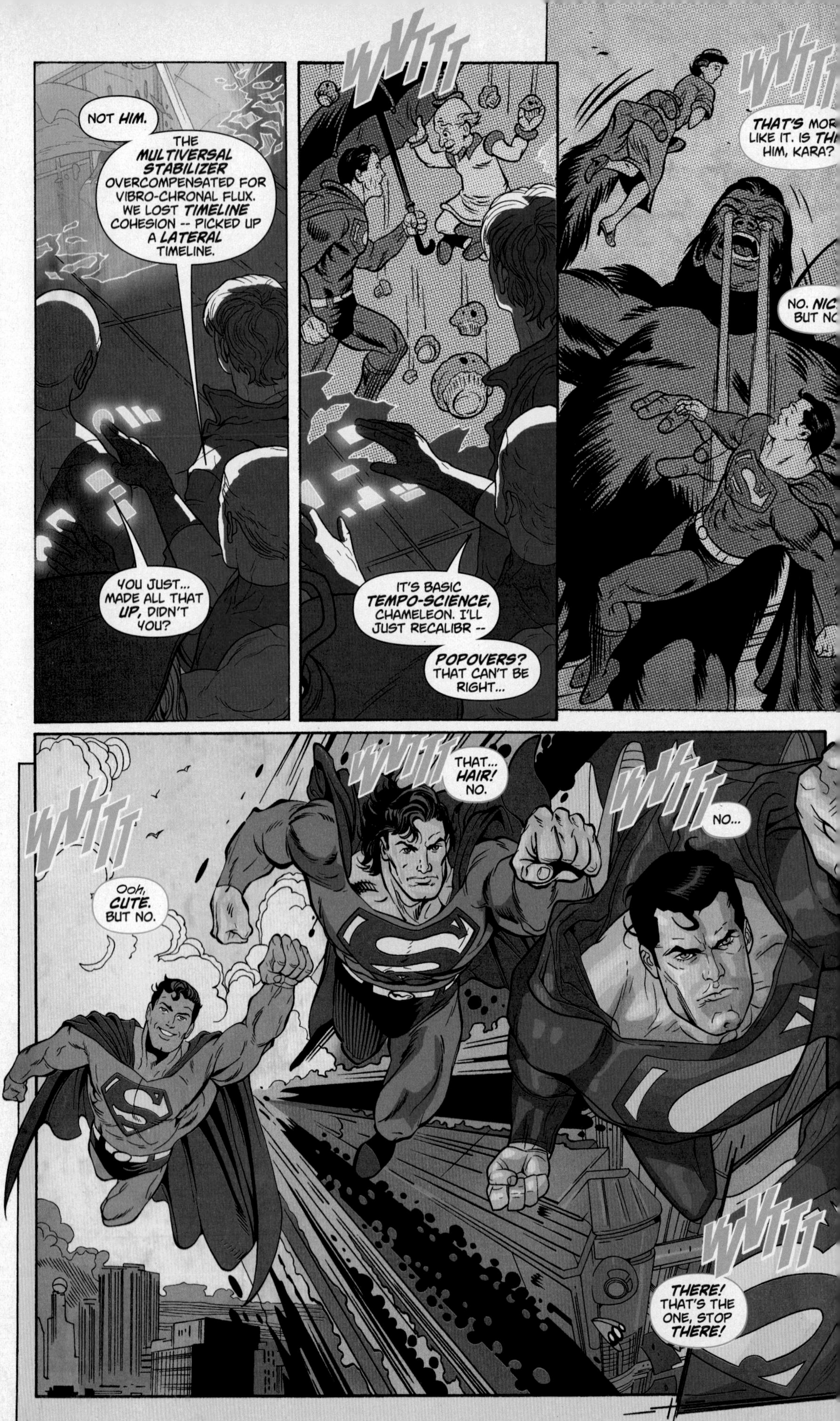
NOT HIM.
THE MULTIVERSAL STABILIZER OVERCOMPENSATED FOR VIBRO-CHRONAL FLUX. WE LOST TIMELINE COHESION -- PICKED UP A LATERAL TIMELINE.
YOU JUST... MADE ALL THAT UP, DIDN'T YOU?
IT'S BASIC TEMPO-SCIENCE, CHAMELEON. I'LL JUST RECALIBR --
POPOVERS? THAT CAN'T BE RIGHT...
THAT'S MOR LIKE IT. IS THI HIM, KARA?
NO. NIC BUT NO
Ooh, CUTE. BUT NO.
THAT... HAIR! NO.
NO...
THERE! THAT'S THE ONE, STOP THERE!

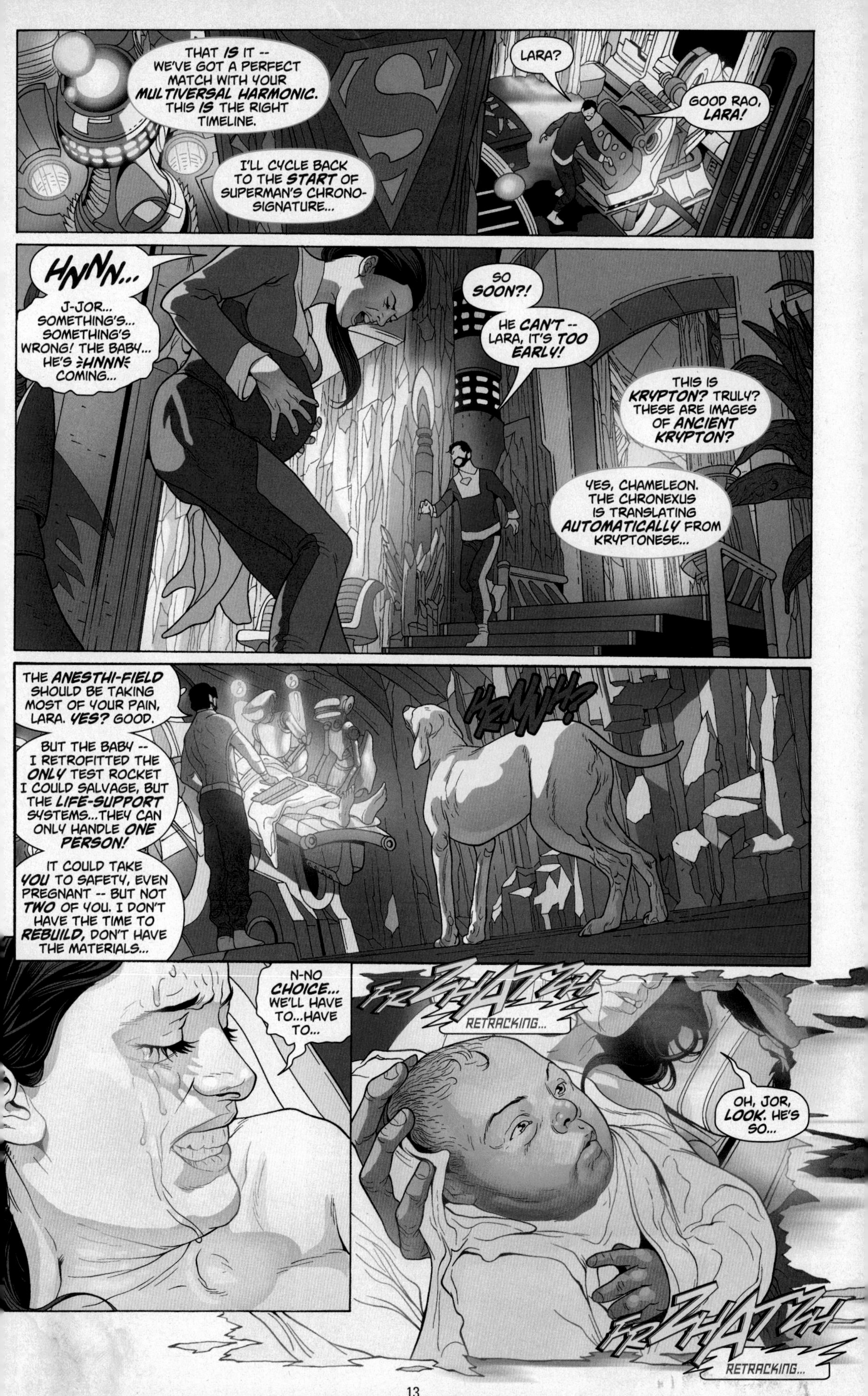
THAT IS IT -- WE'VE GOT A PERFECT MATCH WITH YOUR MULTIVERSAL HARMONIC. THIS IS THE RIGHT TIMELINE.
I'LL CYCLE BACK TO THE START OF SUPERMAN'S CHRONO-SIGNATURE...
LARA?
GOOD RAO, LARA!
HNNN...
J-JOR... SOMETHING'S... SOMETHING'S WRONG! THE BABY... HE'S HNNN COMING...
SO SOON?!
HE CAN'T -- LARA, IT'S TOO EARLY!
THIS IS KRYPTON? TRULY? THESE ARE IMAGES OF ANCIENT KRYPTON?
YES, CHAMELEON. THE CHRONEXUS IS TRANSLATING AUTOMATICALLY FROM KRYPTONESE...
THE ANESTHI-FIELD SHOULD BE TAKING MOST OF YOUR PAIN, LARA. YES? GOOD.
BUT THE BABY -- I RETROFITTED THE ONLY TEST ROCKET I COULD SALVAGE, BUT THE LIFE-SUPPORT SYSTEMS...THEY CAN ONLY HANDLE ONE PERSON!
IT COULD TAKE YOU TO SAFETY, EVEN PREGNANT -- BUT NOT TWO OF YOU. I DON'T HAVE THE TIME TO REBUILD, DON'T HAVE THE MATERIALS...
HRMNH?
N-NO CHOICE... WE'LL HAVE TO...HAVE TO...
FRZHATZH
RETRACKING...
OH, JOR, LOOK. HE'S SO...
FRZHATZH
RETRACKING...

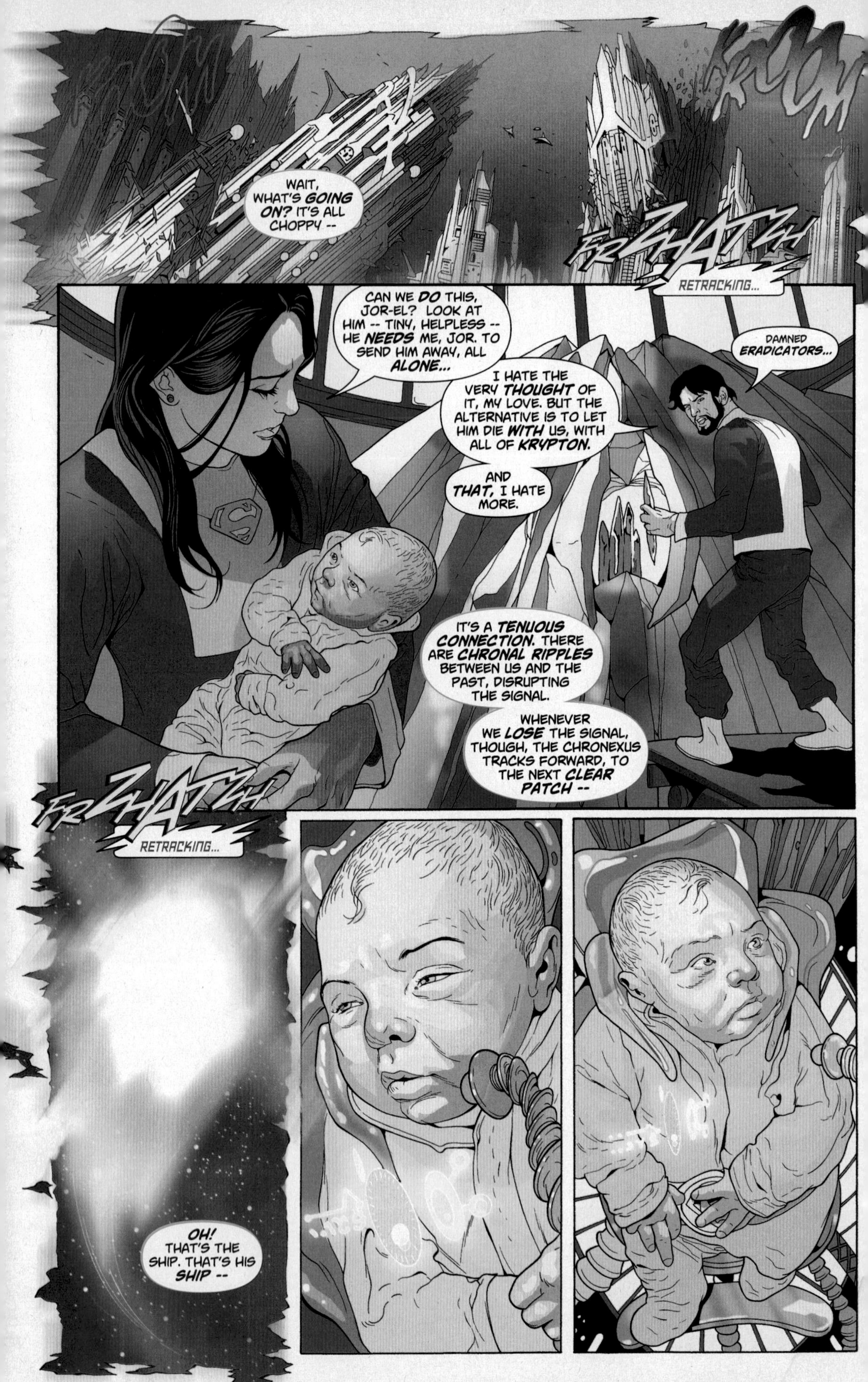
WAIT, WHAT'S GOING ON? IT'S ALL CHOPPY --
KROOM
FRZHATZH
RETRACKING...
CAN WE DO THIS, JOR-EL? LOOK AT HIM -- TINY, HELPLESS -- HE NEEDS ME, JOR. TO SEND HIM AWAY, ALL ALONE...
I HATE THE VERY THOUGHT OF IT, MY LOVE. BUT THE ALTERNATIVE IS TO LET HIM DIE WITH US, WITH ALL OF KRYPTON.
AND THAT, I HATE MORE.
DAMNED ERADICATORS...
IT'S A TENUOUS CONNECTION. THERE ARE CHRONAL RIPPLES BETWEEN US AND THE PAST, DISRUPTING THE SIGNAL.
WHENEVER WE LOSE THE SIGNAL, THOUGH, THE CHRONEXUS TRACKS FORWARD, TO THE NEXT CLEAR PATCH --
FRZHATZH
RETRACKING...
OH! THAT'S THE SHIP. THAT'S HIS SHIP --

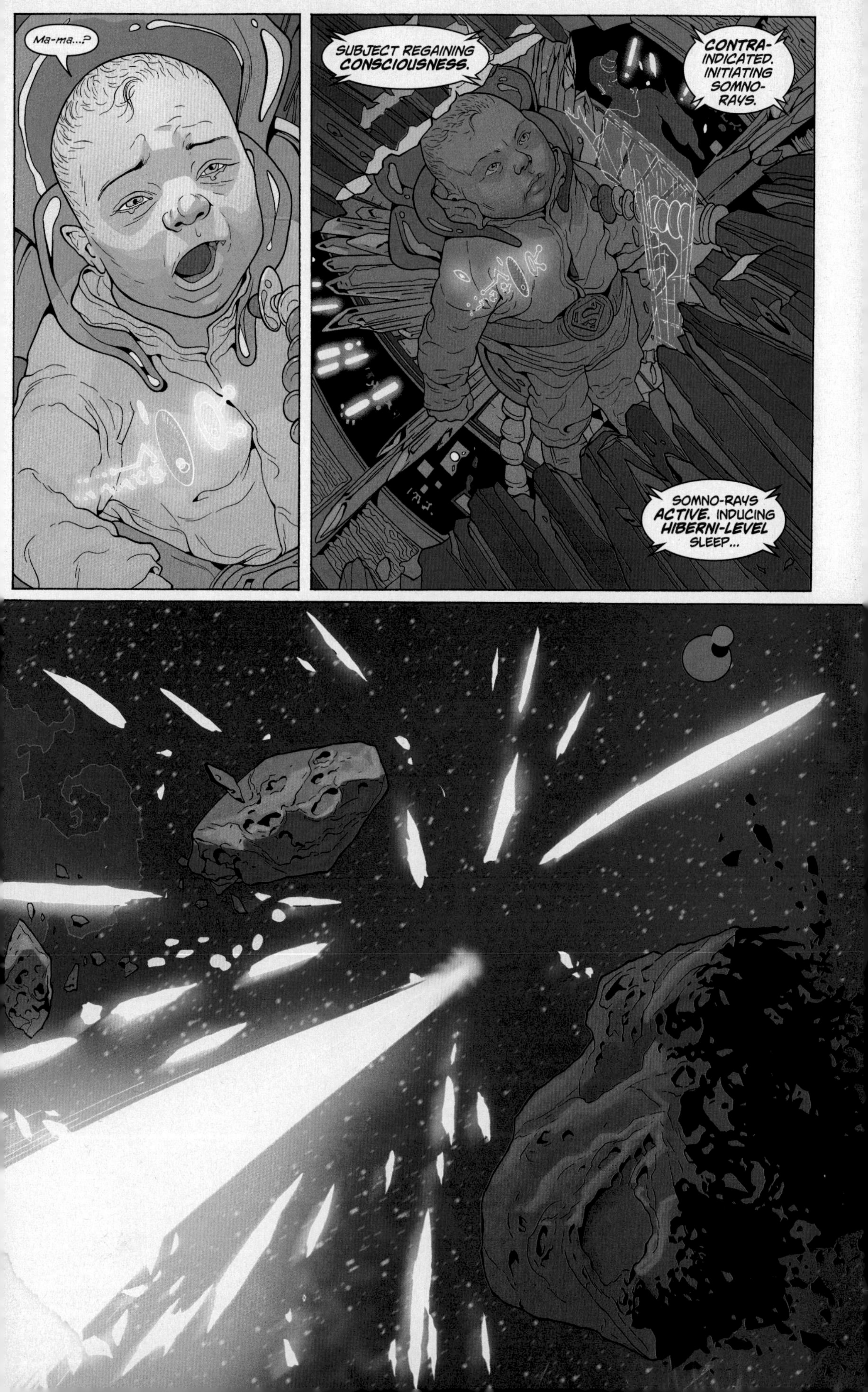
Ma-ma...?
SUBJECT REGAINING CONSCIOUSNESS.
CONTRA-INDICATED. INITIATING SOMNO-RAYS.
SOMNO-RAYS ACTIVE. INDUCING HIBERNI-LEVEL SLEEP...

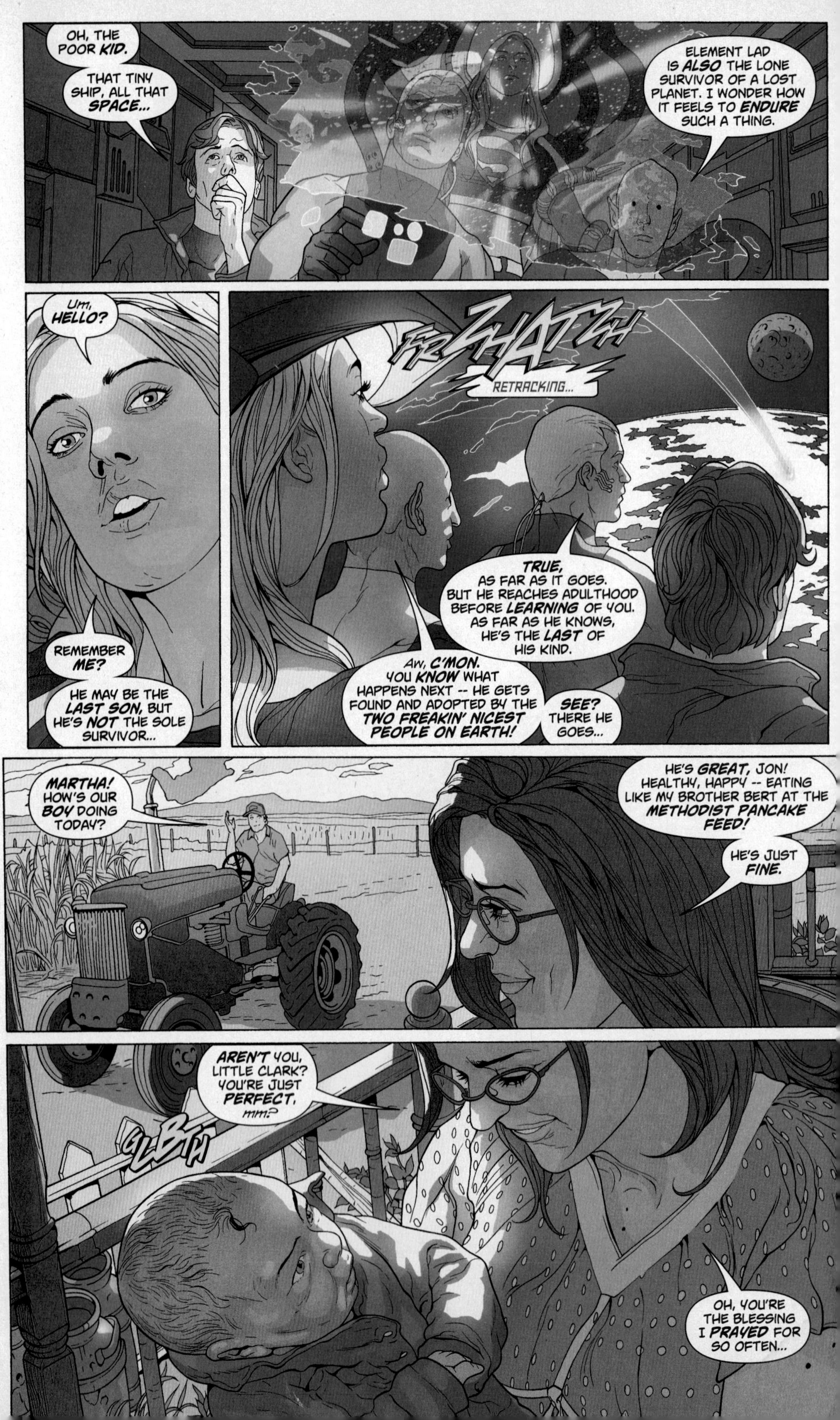

OH, THE POOR KID.
THAT TINY SHIP, ALL THAT SPACE...
ELEMENT LAD IS ALSO THE LONE SURVIVOR OF A LOST PLANET. I WONDER HOW IT FEELS TO ENDURE SUCH A THING.
UM, HELLO?
REMEMBER ME?
HE MAY BE THE LAST SON, BUT HE'S NOT THE SOLE SURVIVOR...
FRZHATZH
RETRACKING...
TRUE, AS FAR AS IT GOES. BUT HE REACHES ADULTHOOD BEFORE LEARNING OF YOU. AS FAR AS HE KNOWS, HE'S THE LAST OF HIS KIND.
AW, C'MON. YOU KNOW WHAT HAPPENS NEXT -- HE GETS FOUND AND ADOPTED BY THE TWO FREAKIN' NICEST PEOPLE ON EARTH!
SEE? THERE HE GOES...
MARTHA! HOW'S OUR BOY DOING TODAY?
HE'S GREAT, JON! HEALTHY, HAPPY -- EATING LIKE MY BROTHER BERT AT THE METHODIST PANCAKE FEED!
HE'S JUST FINE.
AREN'T YOU, LITTLE CLARK? YOU'RE JUST PERFECT, MM?
GLBTH
OH, YOU'RE THE BLESSING I PRAYED FOR SO OFTEN...

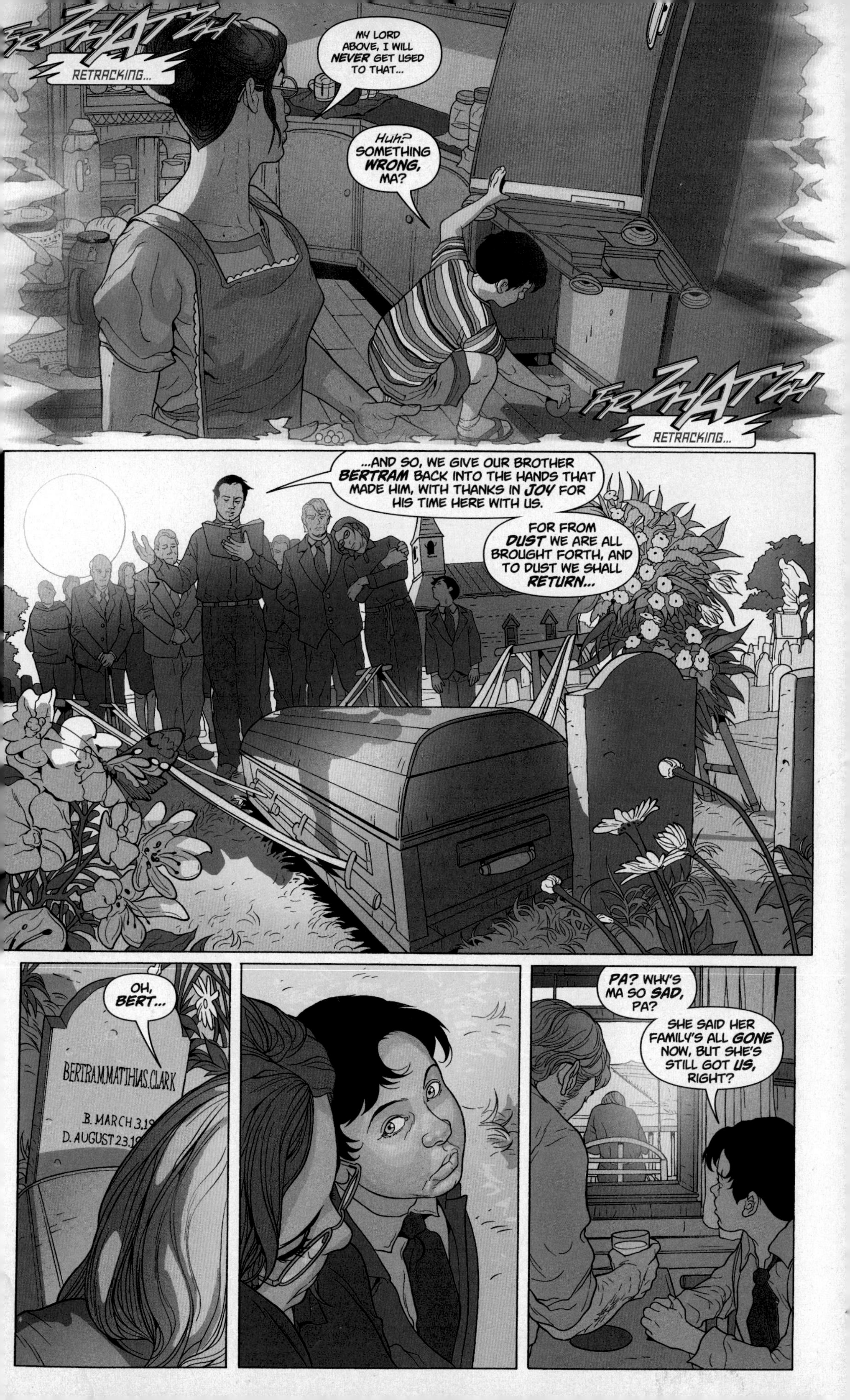
FRZHATZZH
RETRACKING...
MY LORD ABOVE, I WILL NEVER GET USED TO THAT...
Huh? SOMETHING WRONG, MA?
FRZHATZZH
RETRACKING...
...AND SO, WE GIVE OUR BROTHER BERTRAM BACK INTO THE HANDS THAT MADE HIM, WITH THANKS IN JOY FOR HIS TIME HERE WITH US.
FOR FROM DUST WE ARE ALL BROUGHT FORTH, AND TO DUST WE SHALL RETURN...
OH, BERT...
BERTRAM.MATTHIAS.CLARK
B. MARCH 3.19
D. AUGUST 23.19
PA? WHY'S MA SO SAD, PA?
SHE SAID HER FAMILY'S ALL GONE NOW, BUT SHE'S STILL GOT US, RIGHT?

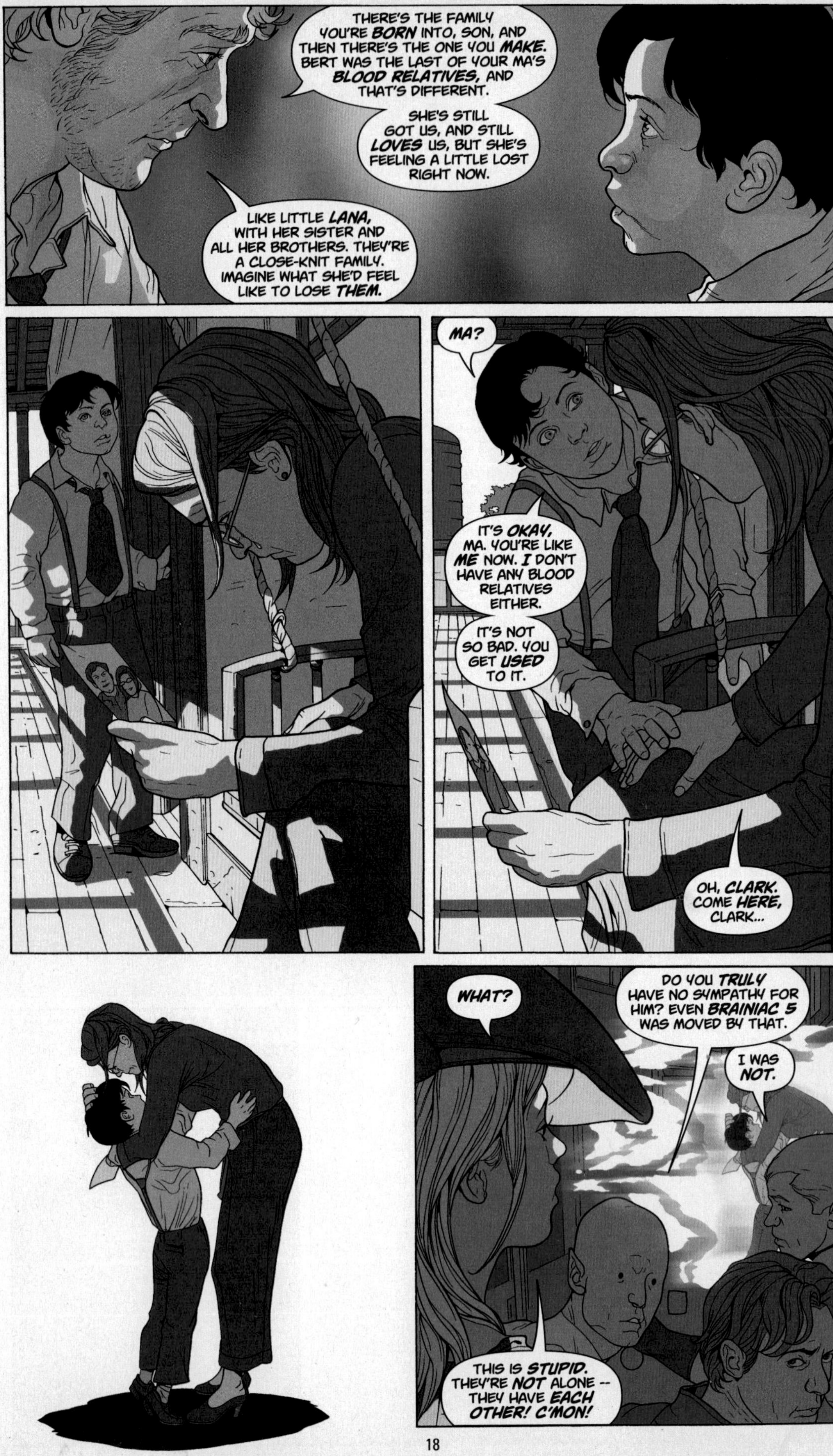
THERE'S THE FAMILY YOU'RE BORN INTO, SON, AND THEN THERE'S THE ONE YOU MAKE. BERT WAS THE LAST OF YOUR MA'S BLOOD RELATIVES, AND THAT'S DIFFERENT.
SHE'S STILL GOT US, AND STILL LOVES US, BUT SHE'S FEELING A LITTLE LOST RIGHT NOW.
LIKE LITTLE LANA, WITH HER SISTER AND ALL HER BROTHERS. THEY'RE A CLOSE-KNIT FAMILY. IMAGINE WHAT SHE'D FEEL LIKE TO LOSE THEM.
MA?
IT'S OKAY, MA. YOU'RE LIKE ME NOW. I DON'T HAVE ANY BLOOD RELATIVES EITHER.
IT'S NOT SO BAD. YOU GET USED TO IT.
OH, CLARK. COME HERE, CLARK...
WHAT?
DO YOU TRULY HAVE NO SYMPATHY FOR HIM? EVEN BRAINIAC 5 WAS MOVED BY THAT.
I WAS NOT.
THIS IS STUPID. THEY'RE NOT ALONE -- THEY HAVE EACH OTHER! C'MON!

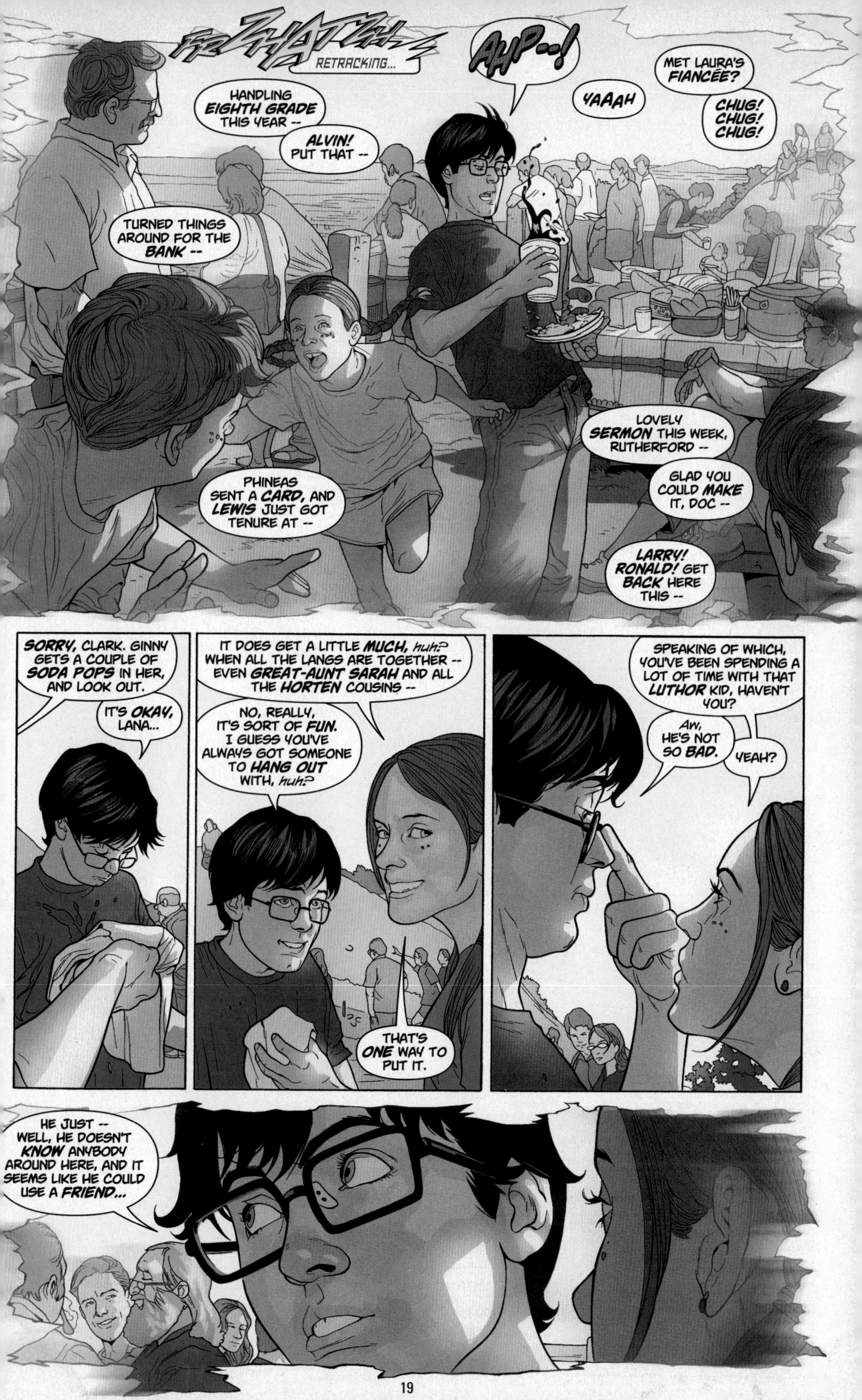

RETRACKING...
AHP--!
HANDLING EIGHTH GRADE THIS YEAR --
ALVIN! PUT THAT --
YAAAH
MET LAURA'S FIANCÉE?
CHUG! CHUG! CHUG!
TURNED THINGS AROUND FOR THE BANK --
LOVELY SERMON THIS WEEK, RUTHERFORD --
GLAD YOU COULD MAKE IT, DOC --
PHINEAS SENT A CARD, AND LEWIS JUST GOT TENURE AT --
LARRY! RONALD! GET BACK HERE THIS --
SORRY, CLARK. GINNY GETS A COUPLE OF SODA POPS IN HER, AND LOOK OUT.
IT'S OKAY, LANA...
IT DOES GET A LITTLE MUCH, huh? WHEN ALL THE LANGS ARE TOGETHER -- EVEN GREAT-AUNT SARAH AND ALL THE HORTEN COUSINS --
NO, REALLY, IT'S SORT OF FUN. I GUESS YOU'VE ALWAYS GOT SOMEONE TO HANG OUT WITH, huh?
THAT'S ONE WAY TO PUT IT.
SPEAKING OF WHICH, YOU'VE BEEN SPENDING A LOT OF TIME WITH THAT LUTHOR KID, HAVEN'T YOU?
Aw, HE'S NOT SO BAD.
YEAH?
HE JUST -- WELL, HE DOESN'T KNOW ANYBODY AROUND HERE, AND IT SEEMS LIKE HE COULD USE A FRIEND...

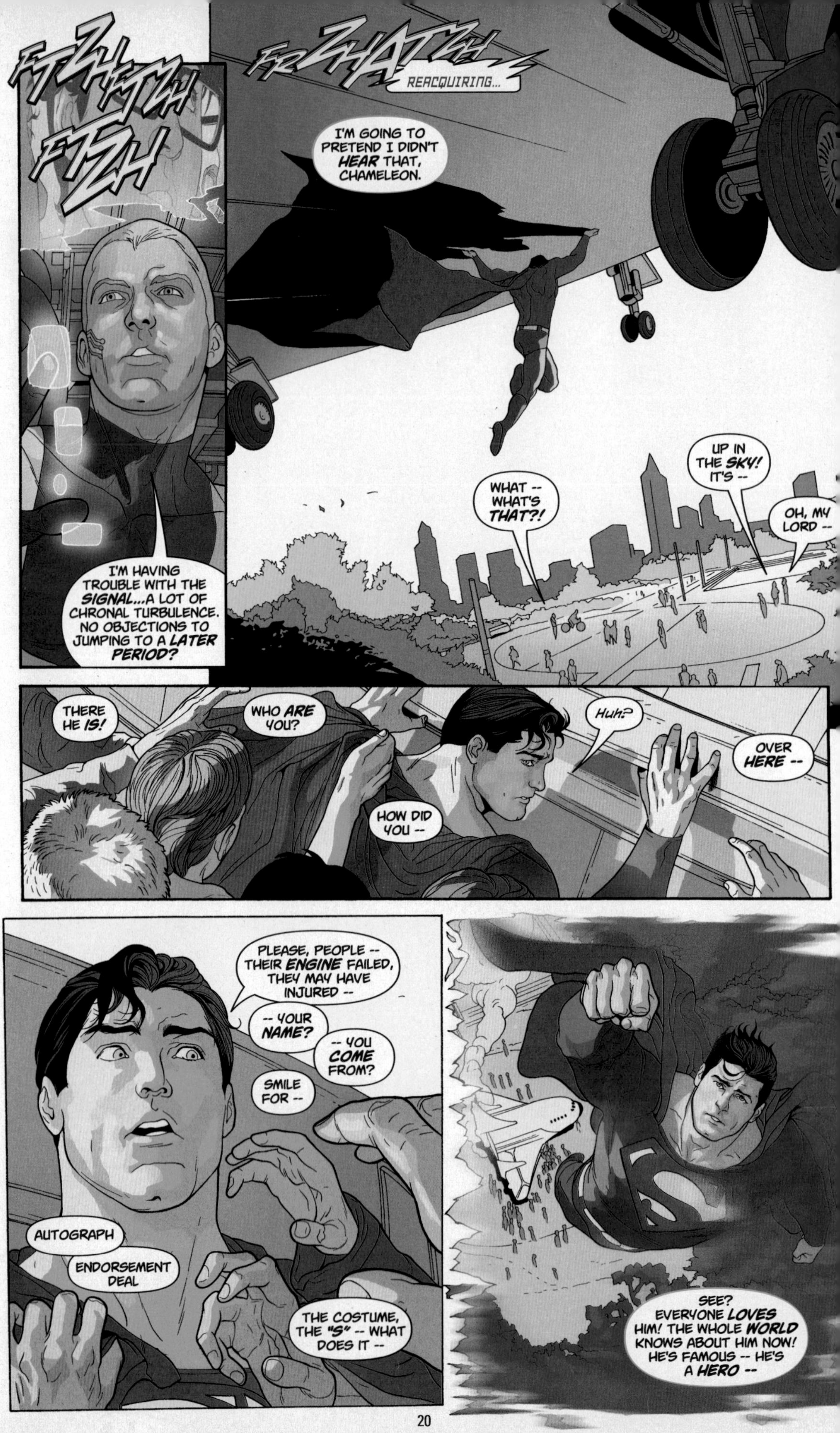
FTZH
FRZHATZH
REACQUIRING...
I'M GOING TO PRETEND I DIDN'T HEAR THAT, CHAMELEON.
I'M HAVING TROUBLE WITH THE SIGNAL...A LOT OF CHRONAL TURBULENCE. NO OBJECTIONS TO JUMPING TO A LATER PERIOD?
WHAT -- WHAT'S THAT?!
UP IN THE SKY! IT'S --
OH, MY LORD --
THERE HE IS!
WHO ARE YOU?
HOW DID YOU --
Huh?
OVER HERE --
PLEASE, PEOPLE -- THEIR ENGINE FAILED, THEY MAY HAVE INJURED --
-- YOUR NAME?
-- YOU COME FROM?
SMILE FOR --
AUTOGRAPH
ENDORSEMENT DEAL
THE COSTUME, THE "S" -- WHAT DOES IT --
SEE? EVERYONE LOVES HIM! THE WHOLE WORLD KNOWS ABOUT HIM NOW! HE'S FAMOUS -- HE'S A HERO --

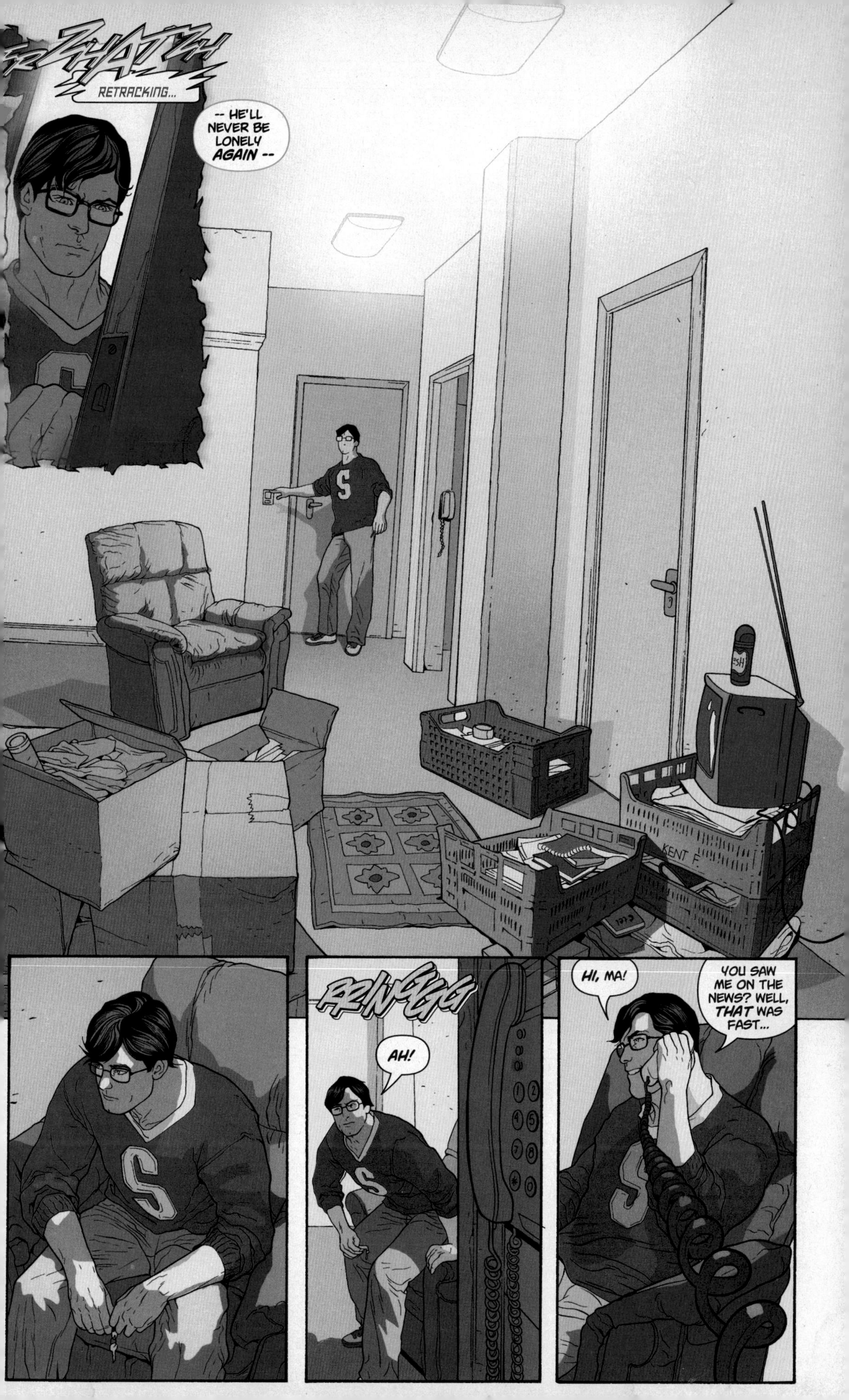
ZHATCH
RETRACKING...
-- HE'LL NEVER BE LONELY AGAIN --
KENT F.
RRINGGG
AH!
HI, MA!
YOU SAW ME ON THE NEWS? WELL, THAT WAS FAST...

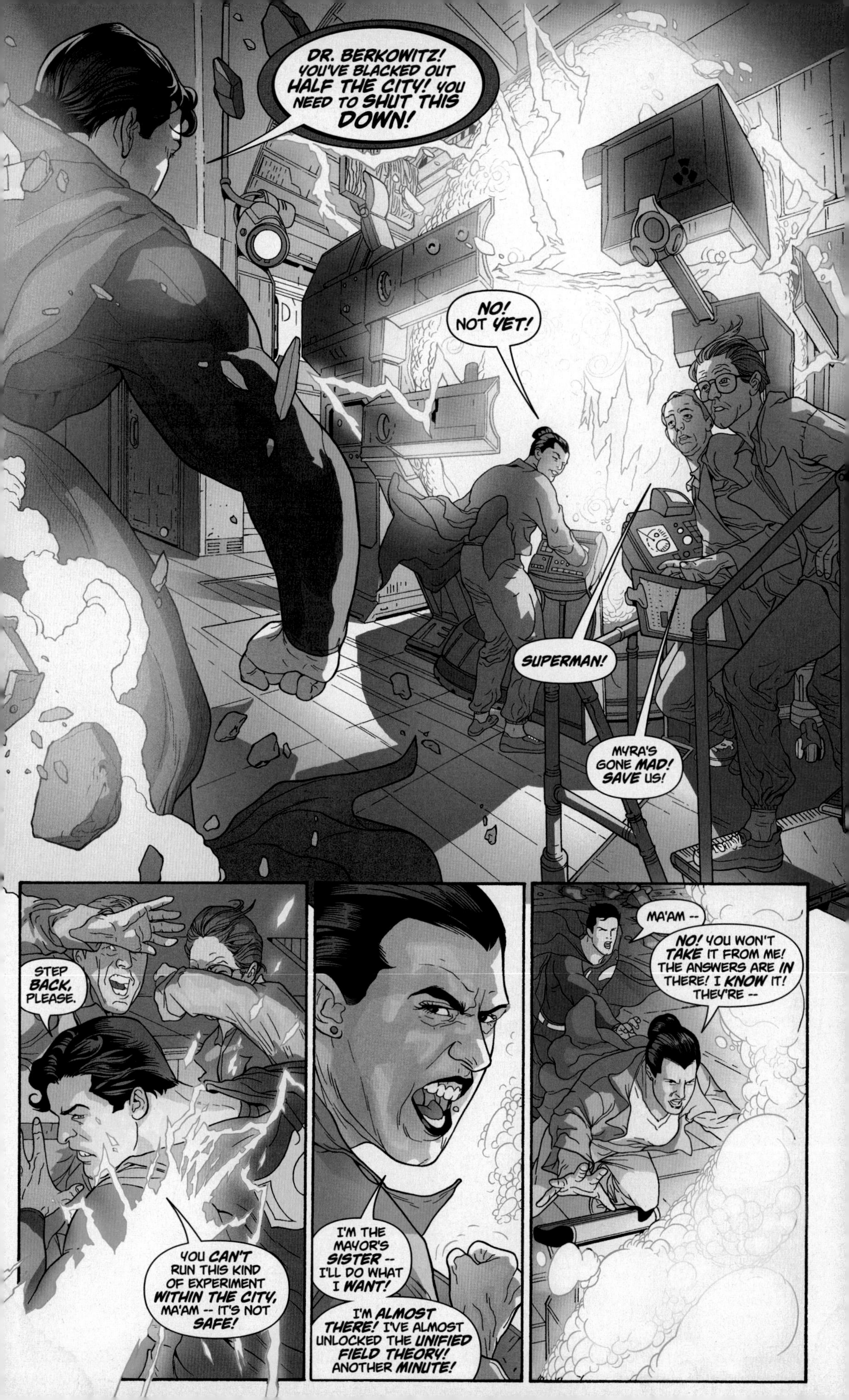
DR. BERKOWITZ! YOU'VE BLACKED OUT HALF THE CITY! YOU NEED TO SHUT THIS DOWN!
NO! NOT YET!
SUPERMAN!
MYRA'S GONE MAD! SAVE US!
STEP BACK, PLEASE.
YOU CAN'T RUN THIS KIND OF EXPERIMENT WITHIN THE CITY, MA'AM -- IT'S NOT SAFE!
I'M THE MAYOR'S SISTER -- I'LL DO WHAT I WANT!
I'M ALMOST THERE! I'VE ALMOST UNLOCKED THE UNIFIED FIELD THEORY! ANOTHER MINUTE!
MA'AM --
NO! YOU WON'T TAKE IT FROM ME! THE ANSWERS ARE IN THERE! I KNOW IT! THEY'RE --

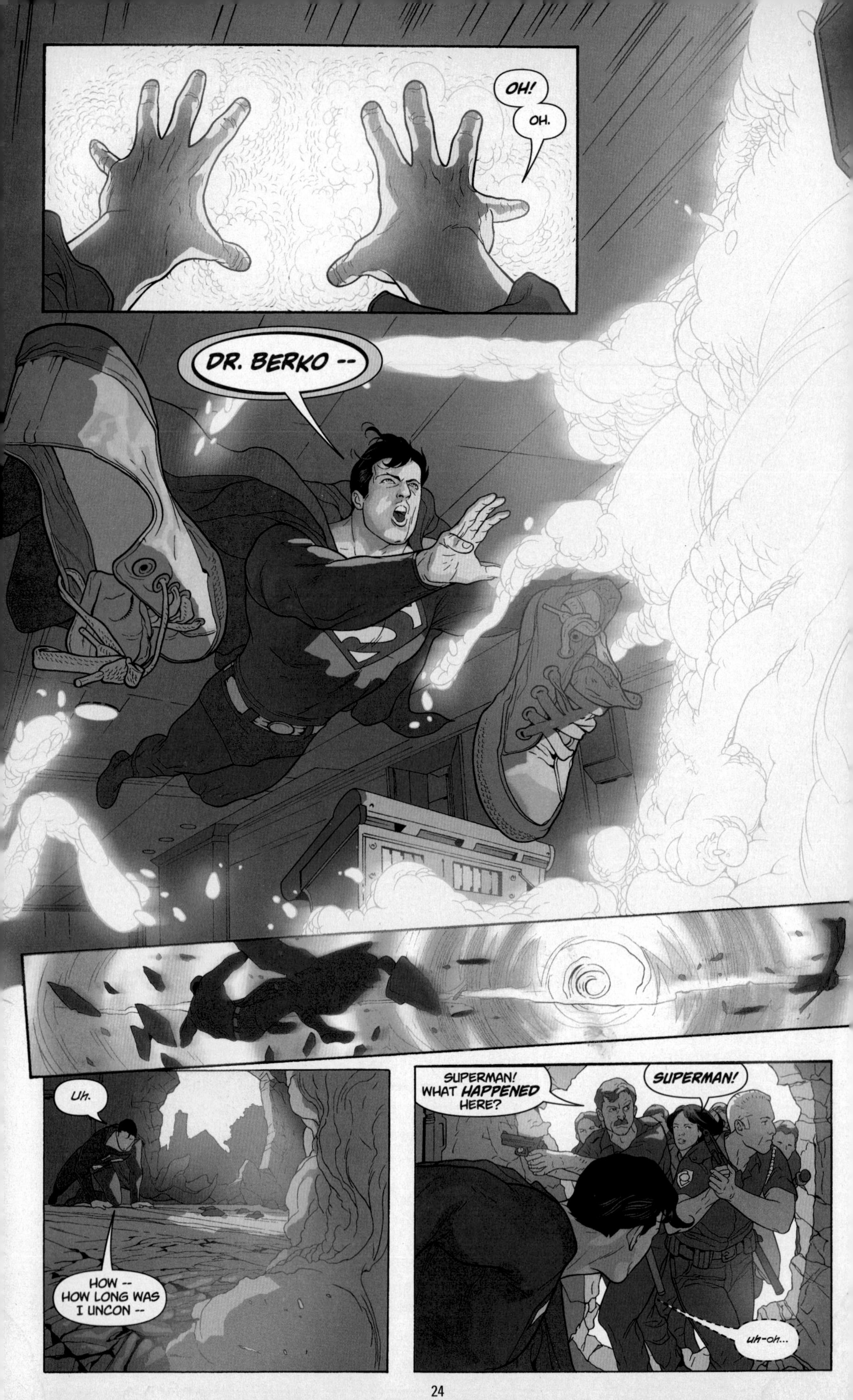
OH!
OH.
DR. BERKO --
Uh.
HOW -- HOW LONG WAS I UNCON --
SUPERMAN! WHAT HAPPENED HERE?
SUPERMAN!
uh-oh...

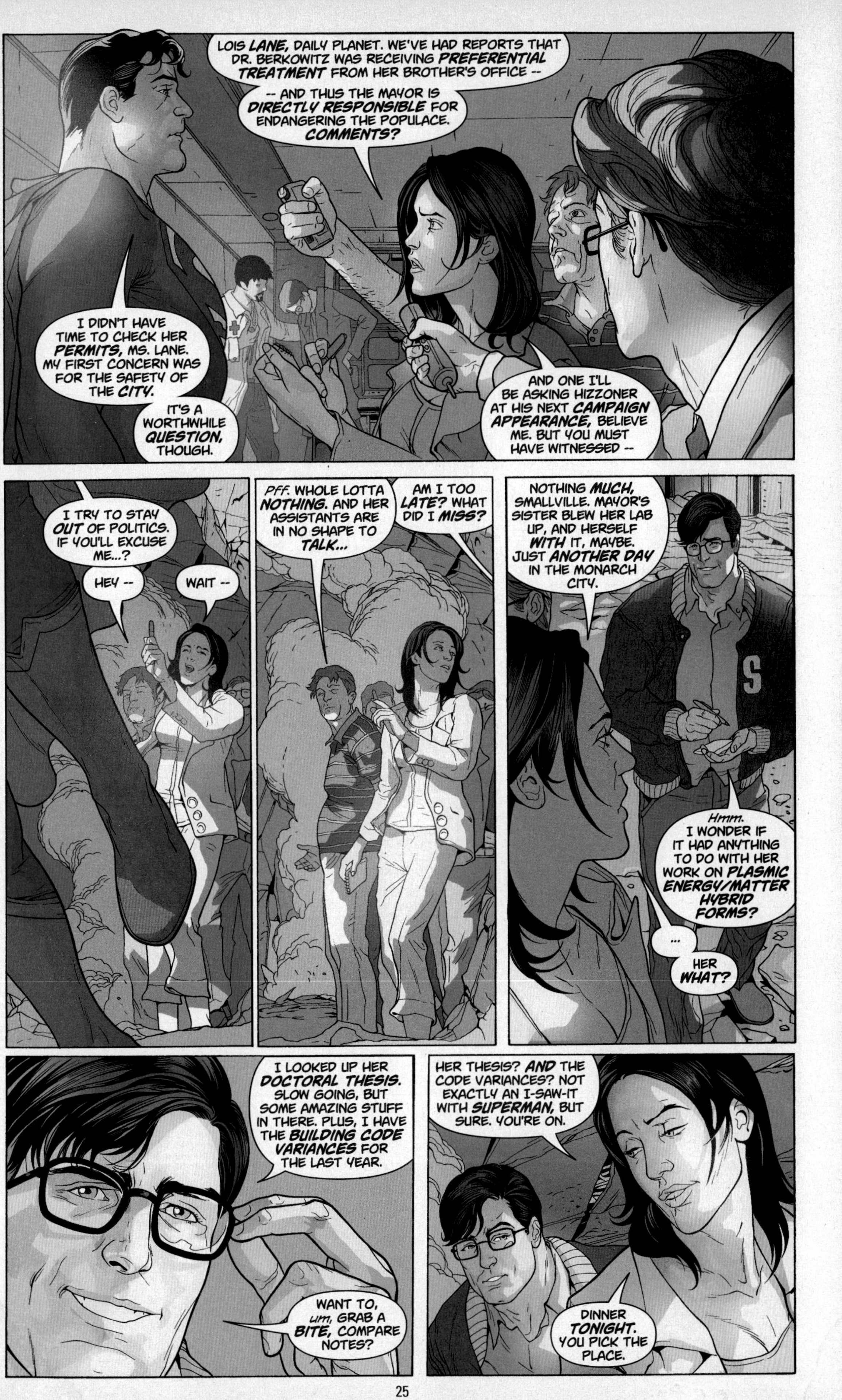
LOIS LANE, DAILY PLANET. WE'VE HAD REPORTS THAT DR. BERKOWITZ WAS RECEIVING PREFERENTIAL TREATMENT FROM HER BROTHER'S OFFICE --
-- AND THUS THE MAYOR IS DIRECTLY RESPONSIBLE FOR ENDANGERING THE POPULACE. COMMENTS?
I DIDN'T HAVE TIME TO CHECK HER PERMITS, MS. LANE. MY FIRST CONCERN WAS FOR THE SAFETY OF THE CITY.
IT'S A WORTHWHILE QUESTION, THOUGH.
AND ONE I'LL BE ASKING HIZZONER AT HIS NEXT CAMPAIGN APPEARANCE, BELIEVE ME. BUT YOU MUST HAVE WITNESSED --
I TRY TO STAY OUT OF POLITICS. IF YOU'LL EXCUSE ME...?
HEY --
WAIT --
AM I TOO LATE? WHAT DID I MISS?
Pff. WHOLE LOTTA NOTHING. AND HER ASSISTANTS ARE IN NO SHAPE TO TALK...
NOTHING MUCH, SMALLVILLE. MAYOR'S SISTER BLEW HER LAB UP, AND HERSELF WITH IT, MAYBE. JUST ANOTHER DAY IN THE MONARCH CITY.
Hmm. I WONDER IF IT HAD ANYTHING TO DO WITH HER WORK ON PLASMIC ENERGY/MATTER HYBRID FORMS?
...
HER WHAT?
I LOOKED UP HER DOCTORAL THESIS. SLOW GOING, BUT SOME AMAZING STUFF IN THERE. PLUS, I HAVE THE BUILDING CODE VARIANCES FOR THE LAST YEAR.
WANT TO, um, GRAB A BITE, COMPARE NOTES?
HER THESIS? AND THE CODE VARIANCES? NOT EXACTLY AN I-SAW-IT WITH SUPERMAN, BUT SURE. YOU'RE ON.
DINNER TONIGHT. YOU PICK THE PLACE.

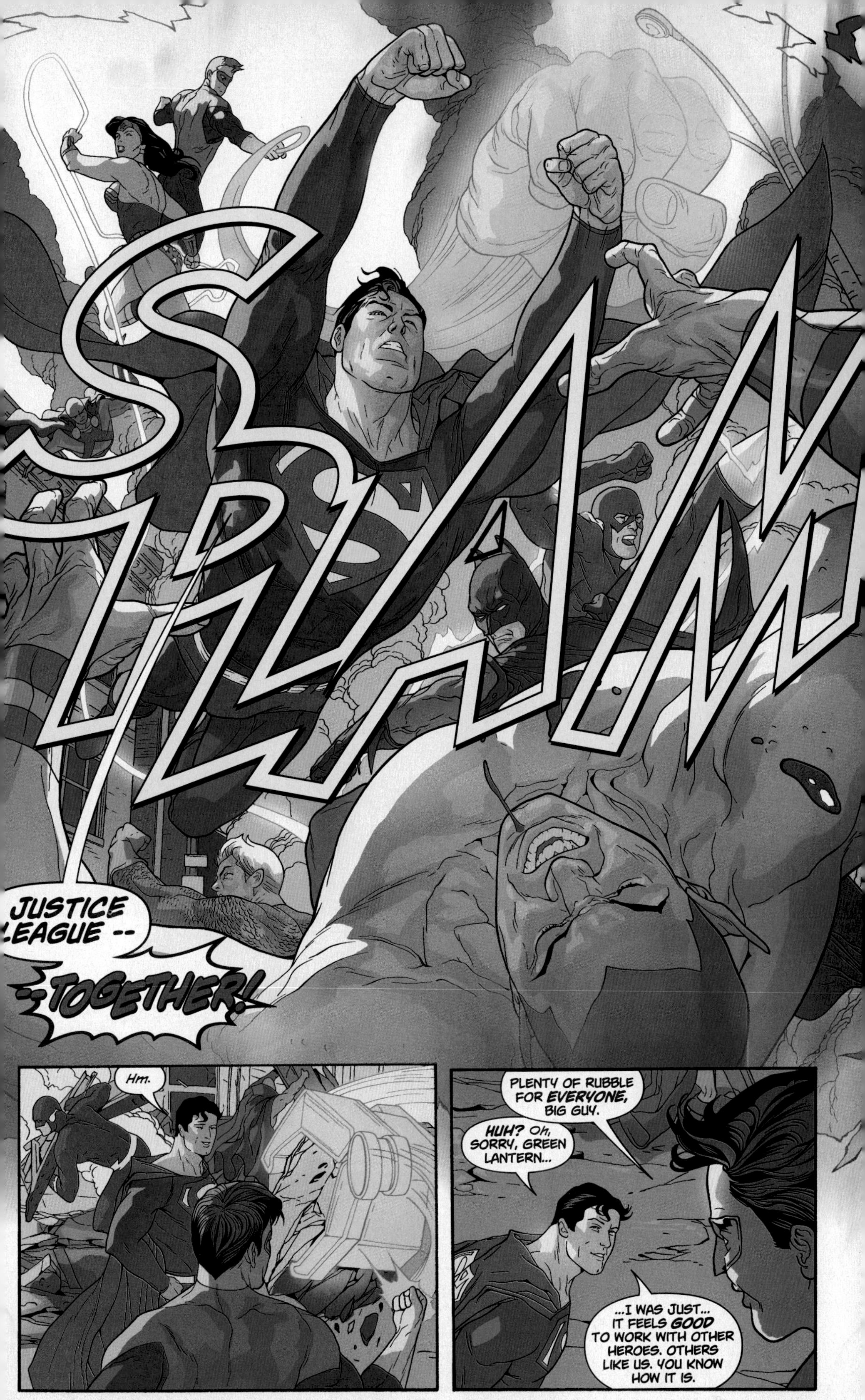
JUSTICE LEAGUE --
-- TOGETHER!
Hm.
PLENTY OF RUBBLE FOR *EVERYONE*, BIG GUY.
HUH? Oh, SORRY, GREEN LANTERN...
...I WAS JUST... IT FEELS *GOOD* TO WORK WITH OTHER HEROES. OTHERS LIKE US. YOU KNOW HOW IT IS.

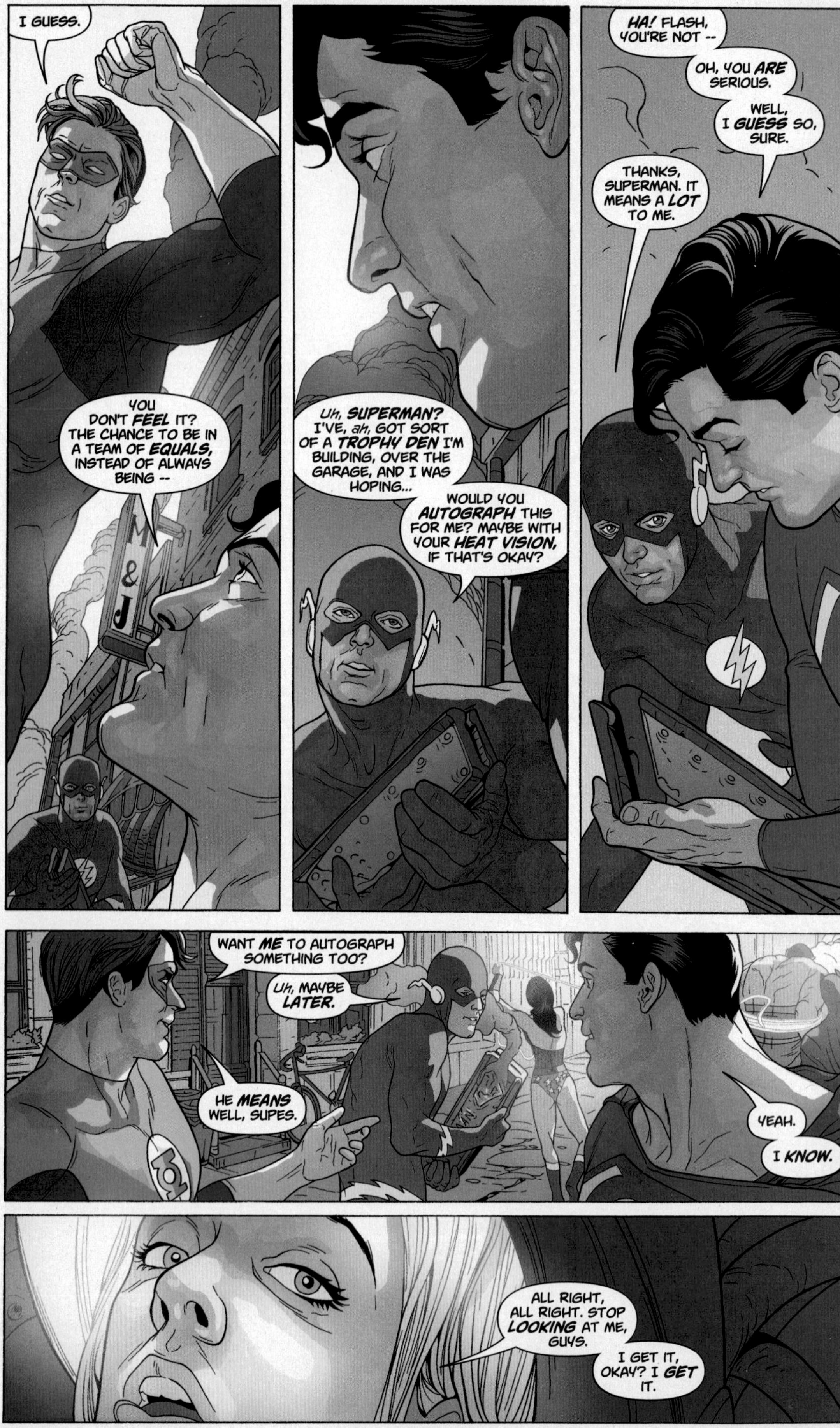
I GUESS.
YOU DON'T FEEL IT? THE CHANCE TO BE IN A TEAM OF EQUALS, INSTEAD OF ALWAYS BEING --
Uh, SUPERMAN? I'VE, ah, GOT SORT OF A TROPHY DEN I'M BUILDING, OVER THE GARAGE, AND I WAS HOPING...
WOULD YOU AUTOGRAPH THIS FOR ME? MAYBE WITH YOUR HEAT VISION, IF THAT'S OKAY?
HA! FLASH, YOU'RE NOT --
OH, YOU ARE SERIOUS.
WELL, I GUESS SO, SURE.
THANKS, SUPERMAN. IT MEANS A LOT TO ME.
WANT ME TO AUTOGRAPH SOMETHING TOO?
Uh, MAYBE LATER.
HE MEANS WELL, SUPES.
YEAH.
I KNOW.
ALL RIGHT, ALL RIGHT. STOP LOOKING AT ME, GUYS.
I GET IT, OKAY? I GET IT.

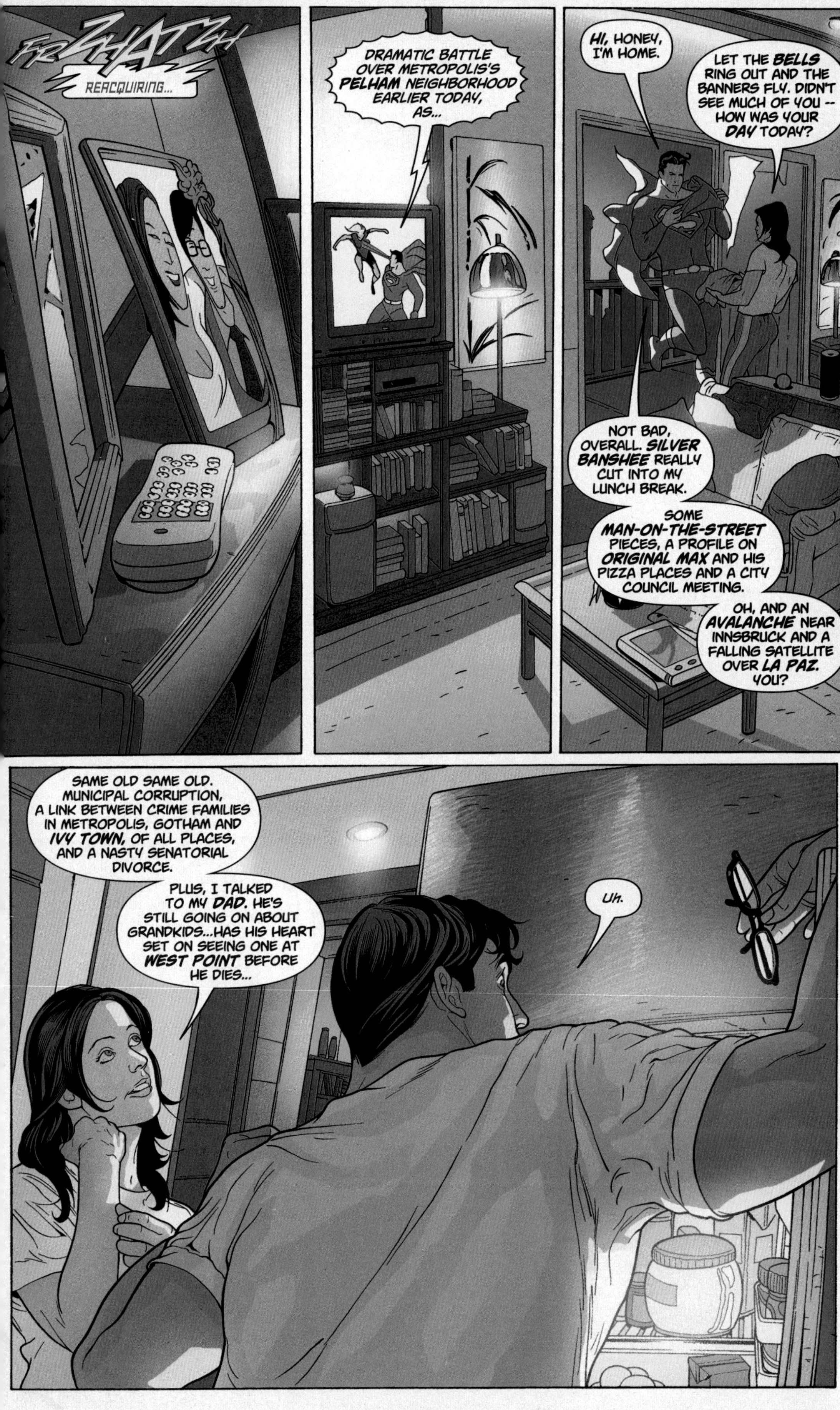
FRZHATZH
REACQUIRING...
DRAMATIC BATTLE OVER METROPOLIS'S PELHAM NEIGHBORHOOD EARLIER TODAY, AS...
HI, HONEY, I'M HOME.
LET THE BELLS RING OUT AND THE BANNERS FLY. DIDN'T SEE MUCH OF YOU -- HOW WAS YOUR DAY TODAY?
NOT BAD, OVERALL. SILVER BANSHEE REALLY CUT INTO MY LUNCH BREAK.
SOME MAN-ON-THE-STREET PIECES, A PROFILE ON ORIGINAL MAX AND HIS PIZZA PLACES AND A CITY COUNCIL MEETING.
OH, AND AN AVALANCHE NEAR INNSBRUCK AND A FALLING SATELLITE OVER LA PAZ. YOU?
SAME OLD SAME OLD. MUNICIPAL CORRUPTION, A LINK BETWEEN CRIME FAMILIES IN METROPOLIS, GOTHAM AND IVY TOWN, OF ALL PLACES, AND A NASTY SENATORIAL DIVORCE.
PLUS, I TALKED TO MY DAD. HE'S STILL GOING ON ABOUT GRANDKIDS...HAS HIS HEART SET ON SEEING ONE AT WEST POINT BEFORE HE DIES...
Uh.

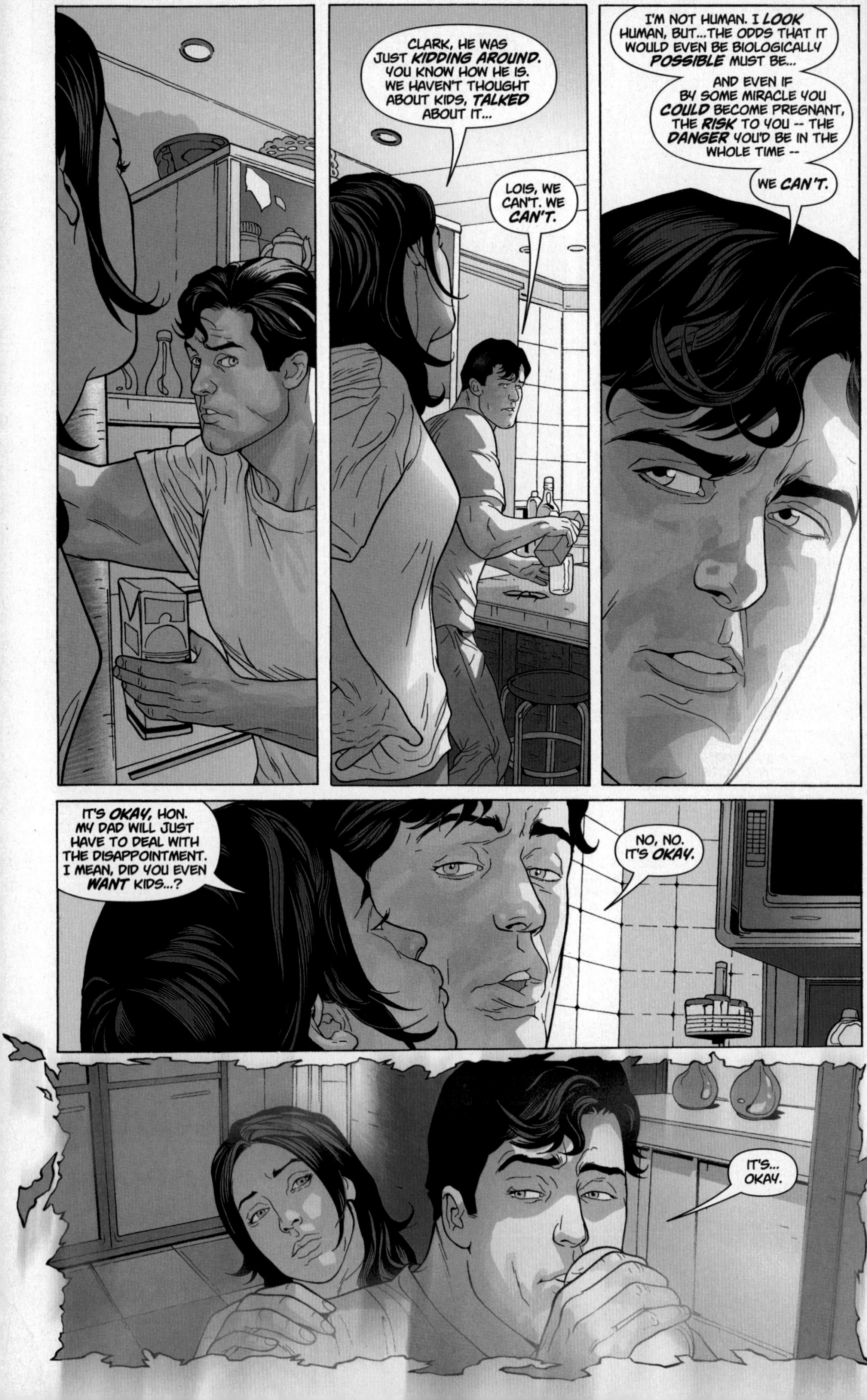
CLARK, HE WAS JUST KIDDING AROUND. YOU KNOW HOW HE IS. WE HAVEN'T THOUGHT ABOUT KIDS, TALKED ABOUT IT...
LOIS, WE CAN'T. WE CAN'T.
I'M NOT HUMAN. I LOOK HUMAN, BUT...THE ODDS THAT IT WOULD EVEN BE BIOLOGICALLY POSSIBLE MUST BE...
AND EVEN IF BY SOME MIRACLE YOU COULD BECOME PREGNANT, THE RISK TO YOU -- THE DANGER YOU'D BE IN THE WHOLE TIME --
WE CAN'T.
IT'S OKAY, HON. MY DAD WILL JUST HAVE TO DEAL WITH THE DISAPPOINTMENT. I MEAN, DID YOU EVEN WANT KIDS...?
NO, NO. IT'S OKAY.
IT'S... OKAY.

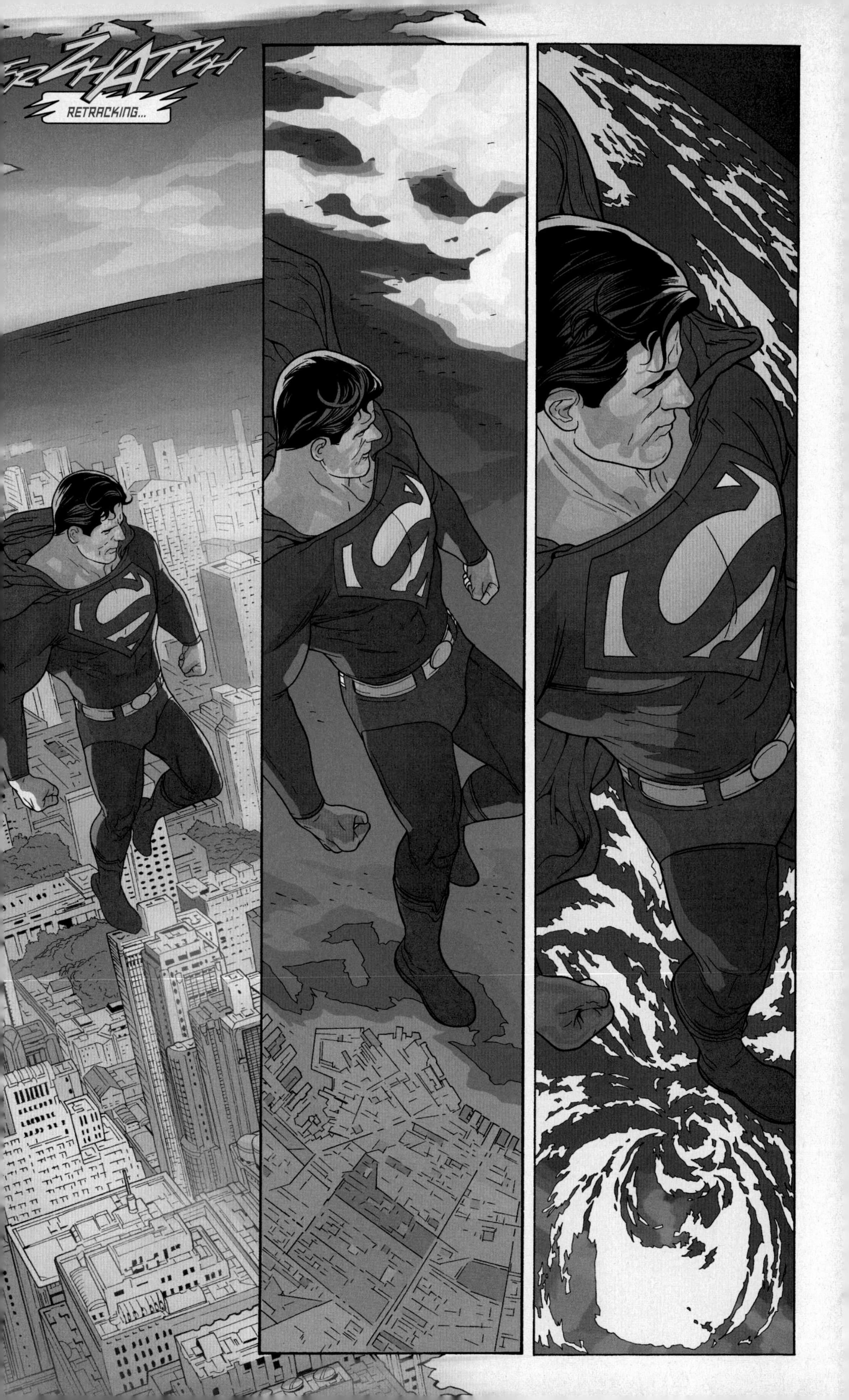

RETRACKING...

OH, *PLEASE.* NOW HE'S JUST *MOPING.*

AND THAT'S SOMETHING *YOU* NEVER DO?

BESIDES, I THINK WHEN YOU DO IT FROM *ORBIT,* IT'S *CALLED* "BROODING."

HE'S LIKE *NO ONE* HE KNOWS. NO ONE HE EVER *EXPECTS* TO KNOW. IT'S ONLY *NATURAL,* FOR A BEING LIKE THAT TO REFLECT FROM TIME TO TIME ...

... ON HIS *ISOLATION,* ON THE *GULF* BETWEEN HIM AND THOSE AROUND HIM...

YOU TALKING ABOUT *HIM,* BRAINY, OR ABOUT...

I'M SKIPPING *AHEAD* NOW.

FRZHATZH *FRZHATZH* *FRZHATZH*

WAIT!

THERE! STOP *THERE!*

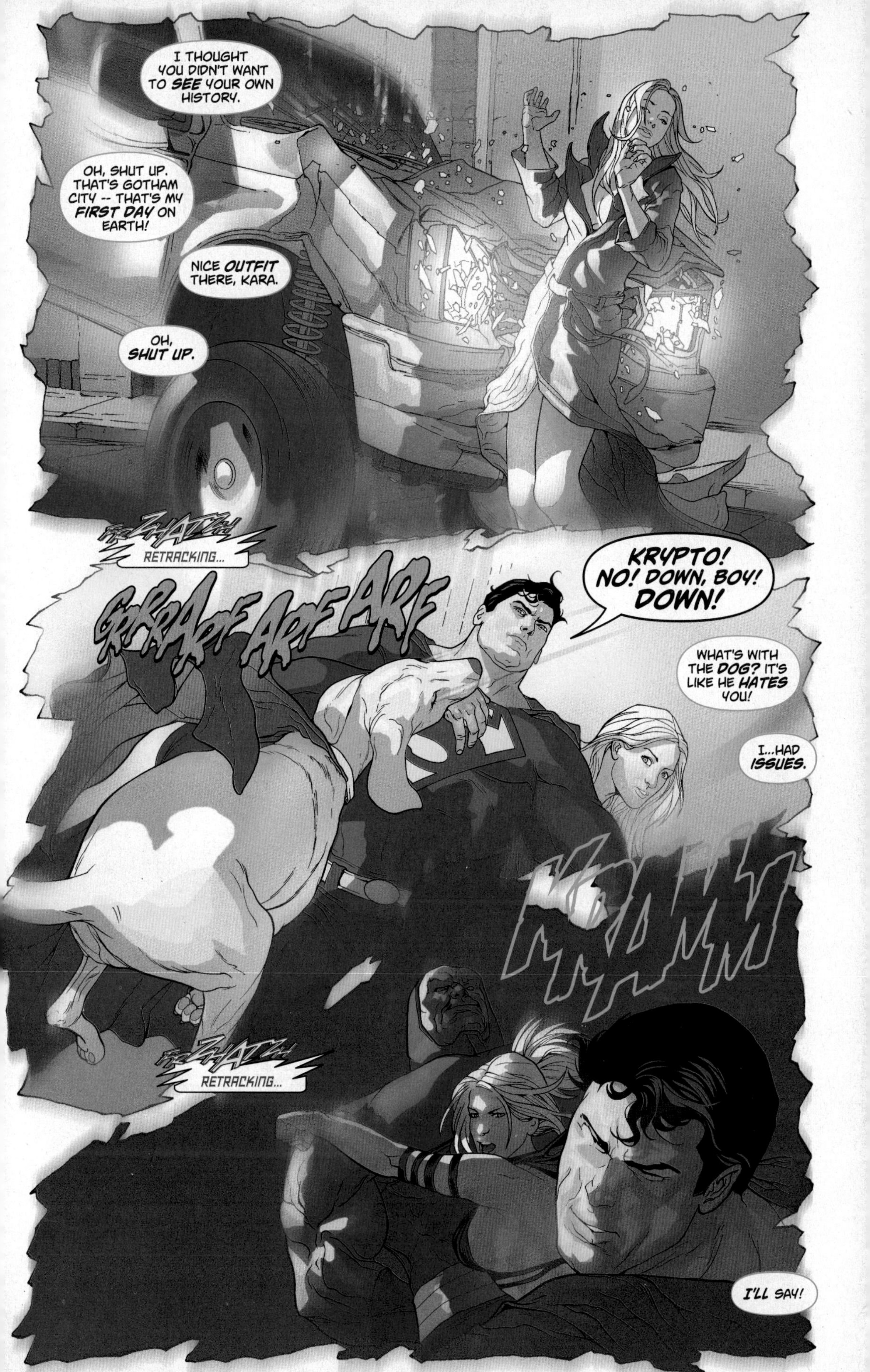
I THOUGHT YOU DIDN'T WANT TO SEE YOUR OWN HISTORY.
OH, SHUT UP. THAT'S GOTHAM CITY -- THAT'S MY FIRST DAY ON EARTH!
NICE OUTFIT THERE, KARA.
OH, SHUT UP.
RETRACKING...
KRYPTO! NO! DOWN, BOY! DOWN!
WHAT'S WITH THE DOG? IT'S LIKE HE HATES YOU!
I...HAD ISSUES.
RETRACKING...
I'LL SAY!

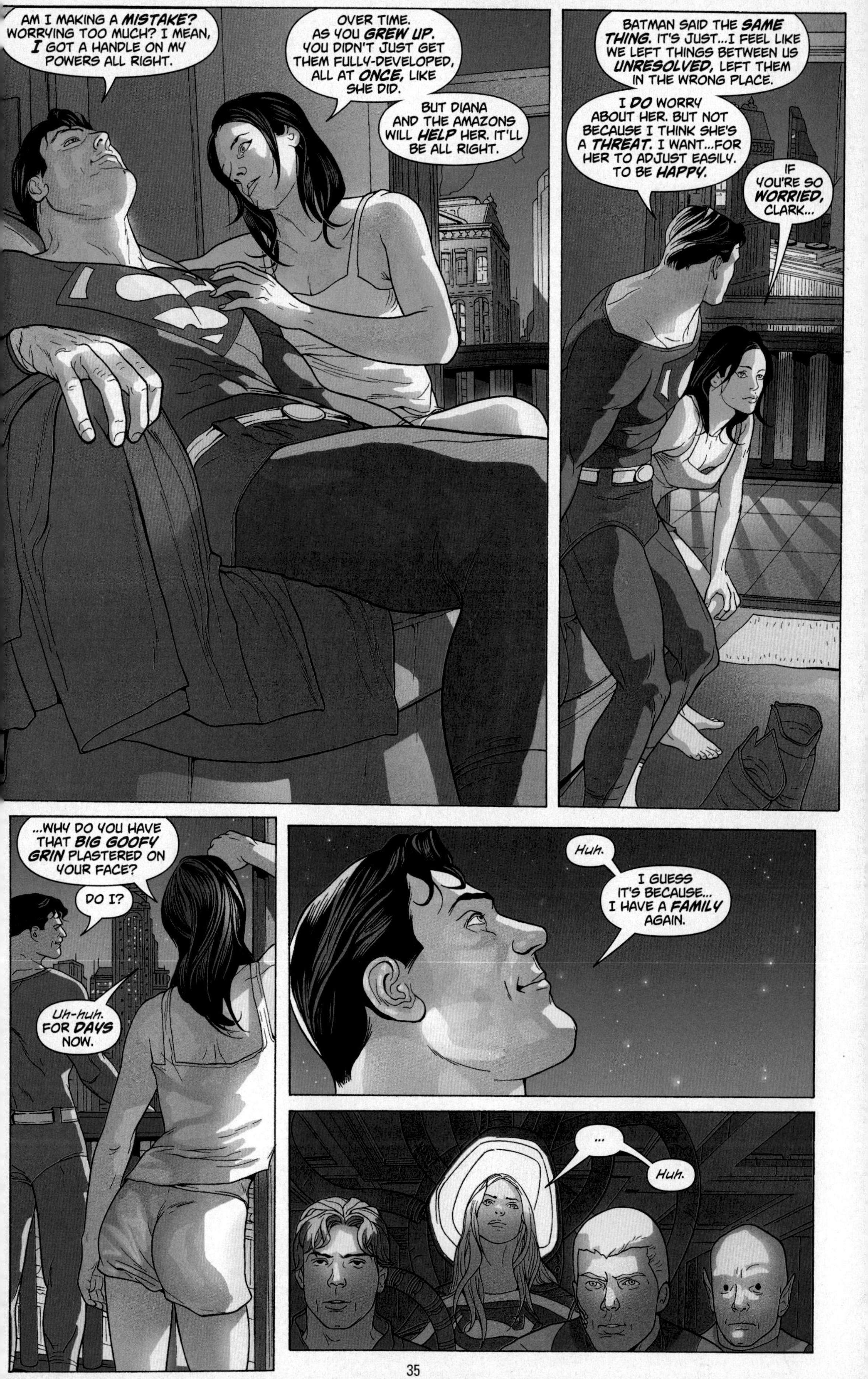
AM I MAKING A MISTAKE? WORRYING TOO MUCH? I MEAN, I GOT A HANDLE ON MY POWERS ALL RIGHT.
OVER TIME. AS YOU GREW UP. YOU DIDN'T JUST GET THEM FULLY-DEVELOPED, ALL AT ONCE, LIKE SHE DID.
BUT DIANA AND THE AMAZONS WILL HELP HER. IT'LL BE ALL RIGHT.
BATMAN SAID THE SAME THING. IT'S JUST...I FEEL LIKE WE LEFT THINGS BETWEEN US UNRESOLVED, LEFT THEM IN THE WRONG PLACE.
I DO WORRY ABOUT HER. BUT NOT BECAUSE I THINK SHE'S A THREAT. I WANT...FOR HER TO ADJUST EASILY. TO BE HAPPY.
IF YOU'RE SO WORRIED, CLARK...
...WHY DO YOU HAVE THAT BIG GOOFY GRIN PLASTERED ON YOUR FACE?
DO I?
Uh-huh. FOR DAYS NOW.
Huh.
I GUESS IT'S BECAUSE... I HAVE A FAMILY AGAIN.
...
Huh.

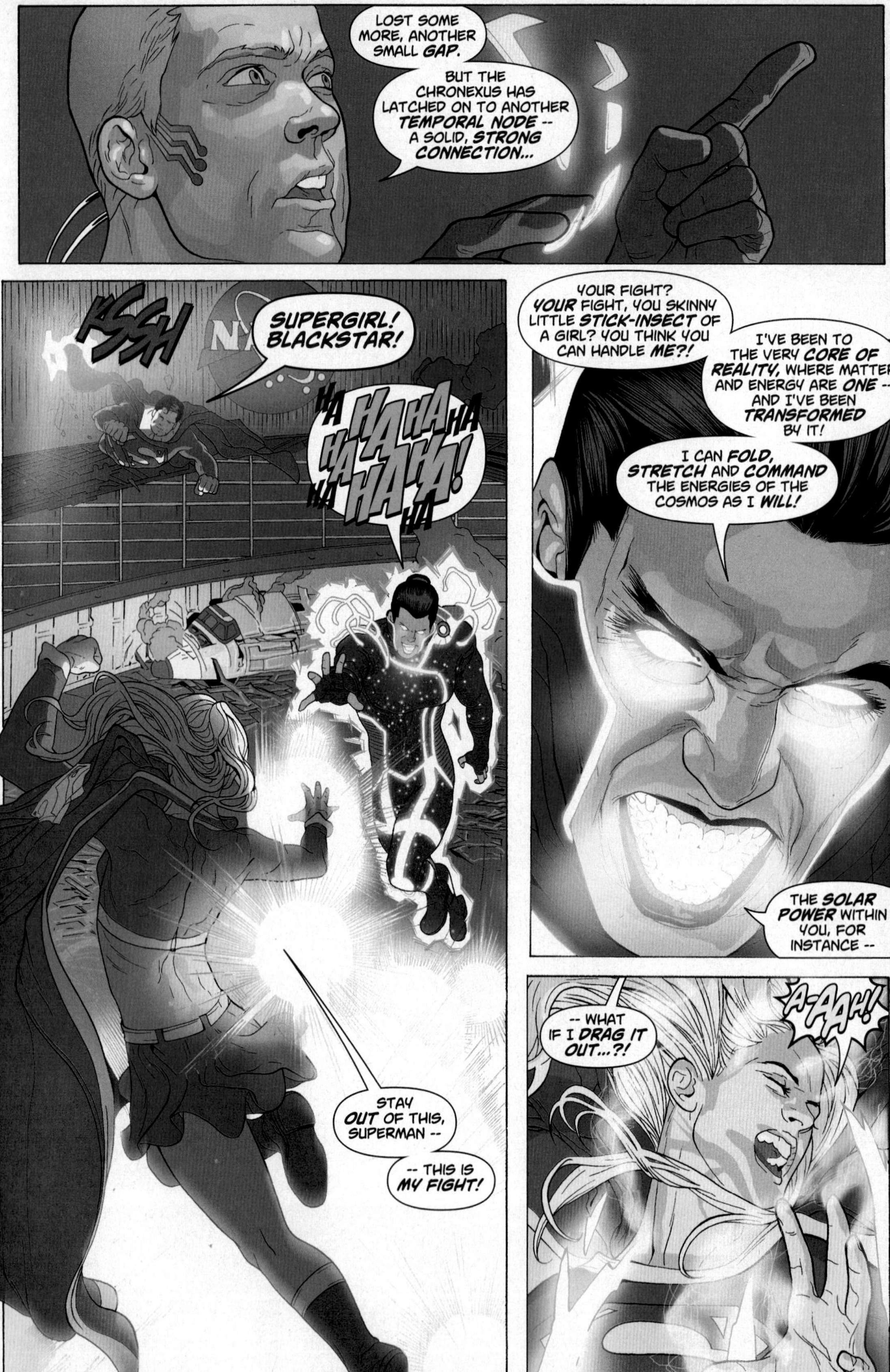
LOST SOME MORE, ANOTHER SMALL GAP.
BUT THE CHRONEXUS HAS LATCHED ON TO ANOTHER TEMPORAL NODE -- A SOLID, STRONG CONNECTION...
KSSH
SUPERGIRL! BLACKSTAR!
HA HA HA HA HA HA HA HA HA HA HA HA!
STAY OUT OF THIS, SUPERMAN --
-- THIS IS MY FIGHT!
YOUR FIGHT? YOUR FIGHT, YOU SKINNY LITTLE STICK-INSECT OF A GIRL? YOU THINK YOU CAN HANDLE ME?!
I'VE BEEN TO THE VERY CORE OF REALITY, WHERE MATTER AND ENERGY ARE ONE -- AND I'VE BEEN TRANSFORMED BY IT!
I CAN FOLD, STRETCH AND COMMAND THE ENERGIES OF THE COSMOS AS I WILL!
THE SOLAR POWER WITHIN YOU, FOR INSTANCE --
-- WHAT IF I DRAG IT OUT...?!
A-AAH!

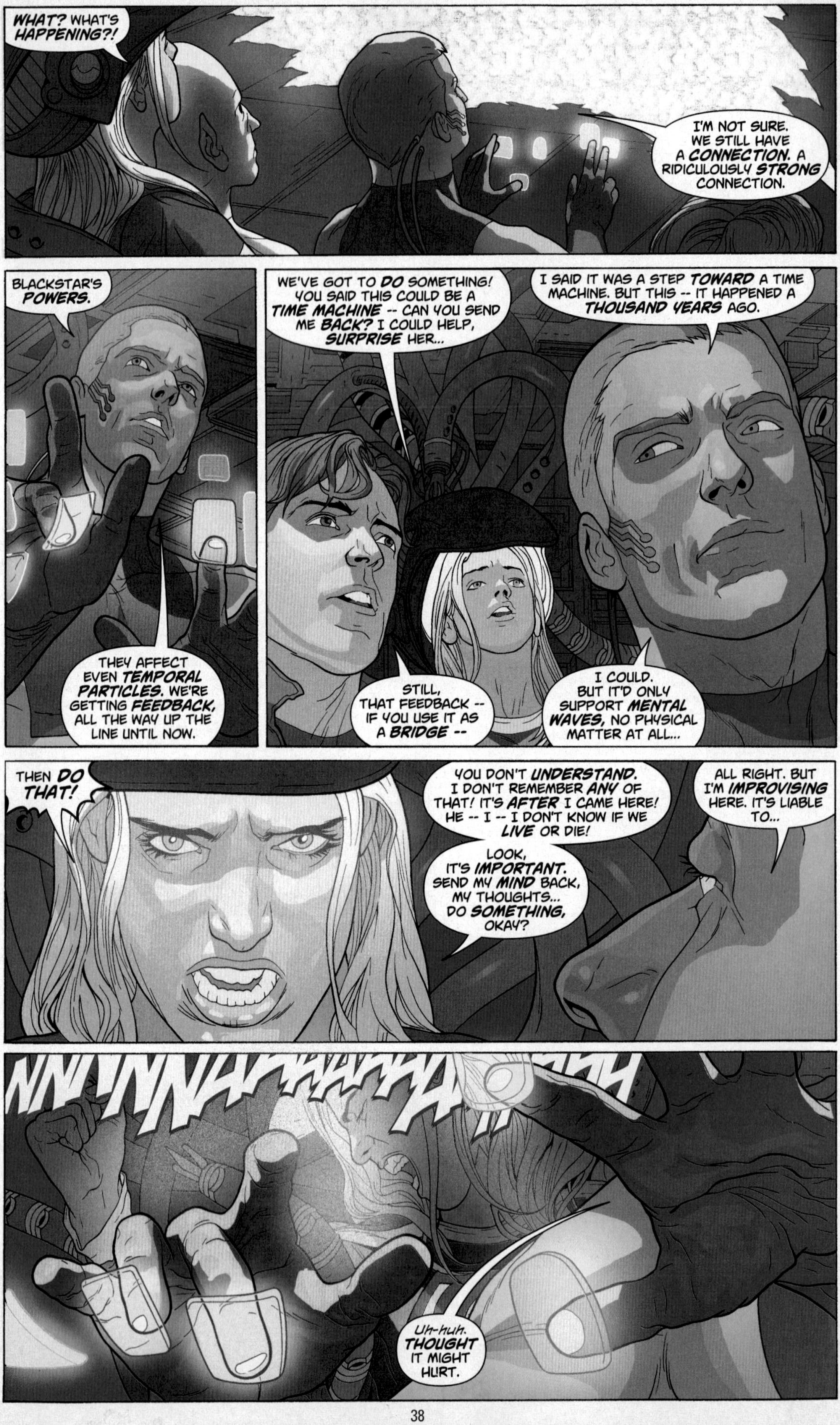

WHAT? WHAT'S HAPPENING?!
I'M NOT SURE. WE STILL HAVE A CONNECTION. A RIDICULOUSLY STRONG CONNECTION.
BLACKSTAR'S POWERS.
THEY AFFECT EVEN TEMPORAL PARTICLES. WE'RE GETTING FEEDBACK, ALL THE WAY UP THE LINE UNTIL NOW.
WE'VE GOT TO DO SOMETHING! YOU SAID THIS COULD BE A TIME MACHINE -- CAN YOU SEND ME BACK? I COULD HELP, SURPRISE HER...
I SAID IT WAS A STEP TOWARD A TIME MACHINE. BUT THIS -- IT HAPPENED A THOUSAND YEARS AGO.
STILL, THAT FEEDBACK -- IF YOU USE IT AS A BRIDGE --
I COULD. BUT IT'D ONLY SUPPORT MENTAL WAVES, NO PHYSICAL MATTER AT ALL...
THEN DO THAT!
YOU DON'T UNDERSTAND. I DON'T REMEMBER ANY OF THAT! IT'S AFTER I CAME HERE! HE -- I -- I DON'T KNOW IF WE LIVE OR DIE!
LOOK, IT'S IMPORTANT. SEND MY MIND BACK, MY THOUGHTS... DO SOMETHING, OKAY?
ALL RIGHT. BUT I'M IMPROVISING HERE. IT'S LIABLE TO...
NNNNNAAAAAAAAAAAAAAA
Uh-huh. THOUGHT IT MIGHT HURT.

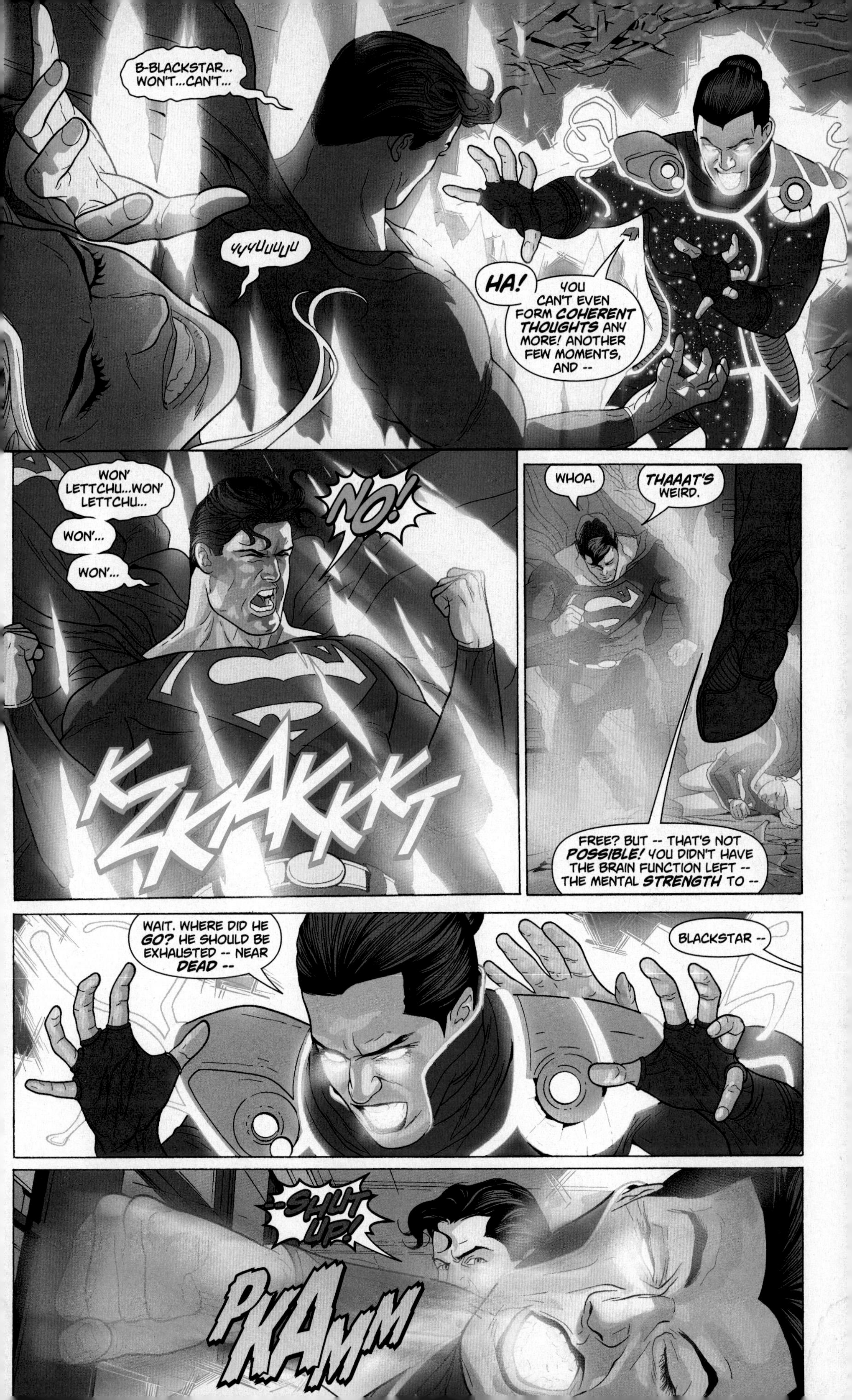
B-BLACKSTAR... WON'T...CAN'T...
YYYUUUUU
HA!
YOU CAN'T EVEN FORM COHERENT THOUGHTS ANY MORE! ANOTHER FEW MOMENTS, AND --
WON' LETTCHU...WON' LETTCHU...
WON'...
WON'...
NO!
KZZKAKKKT
WHOA.
THAAAT'S WEIRD.
FREE? BUT -- THAT'S NOT POSSIBLE! YOU DIDN'T HAVE THE BRAIN FUNCTION LEFT -- THE MENTAL STRENGTH TO --
WAIT. WHERE DID HE GO? HE SHOULD BE EXHAUSTED -- NEAR DEAD --
BLACKSTAR --
--SHUT UP!
PKAMM

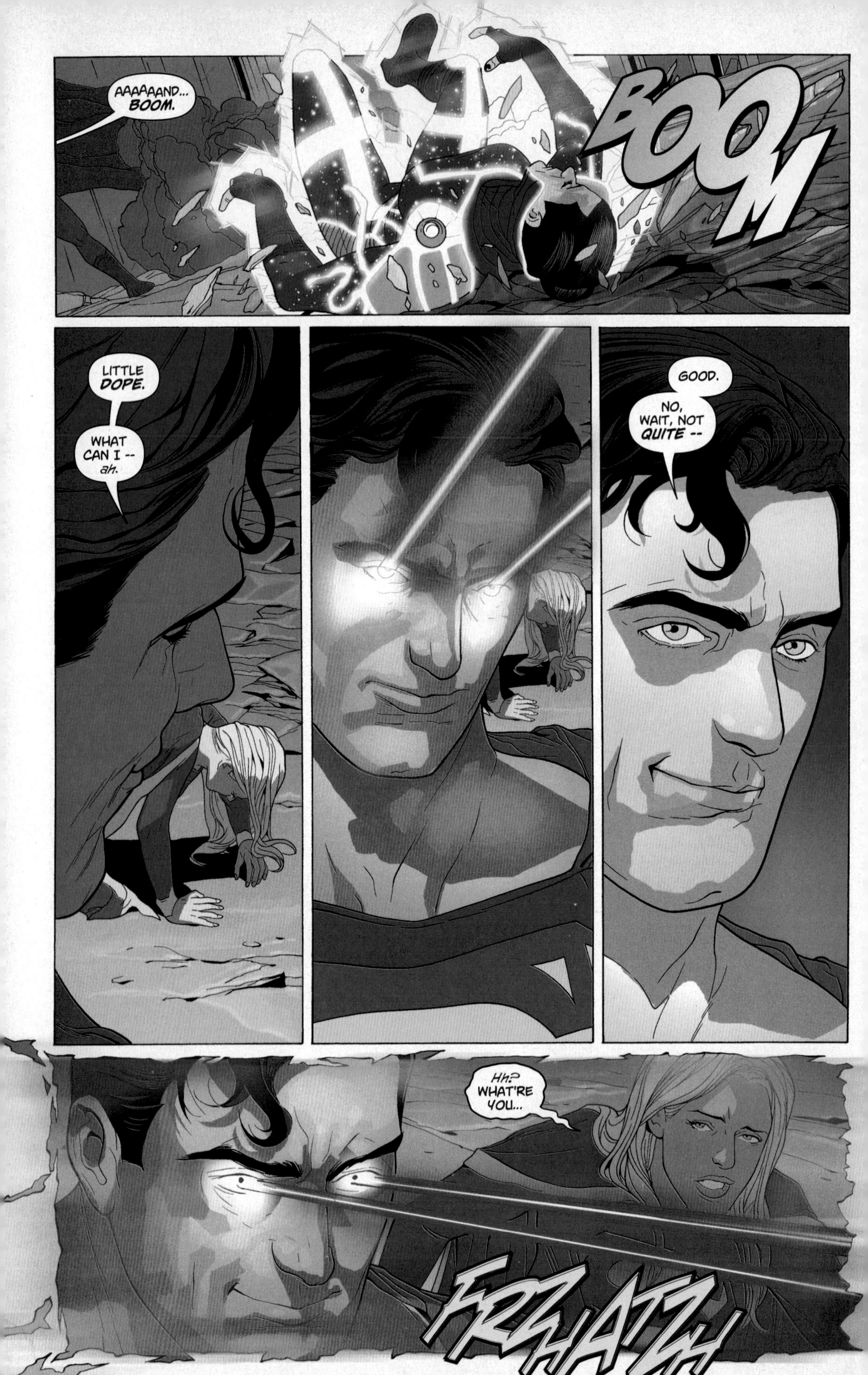
AAAAAAND... BOOM.
BOOM
LITTLE DOPE.
WHAT CAN I -- ah.
GOOD.
NO, WAIT, NOT QUITE --
Hh? WHAT'RE YOU...
FRZHATZH

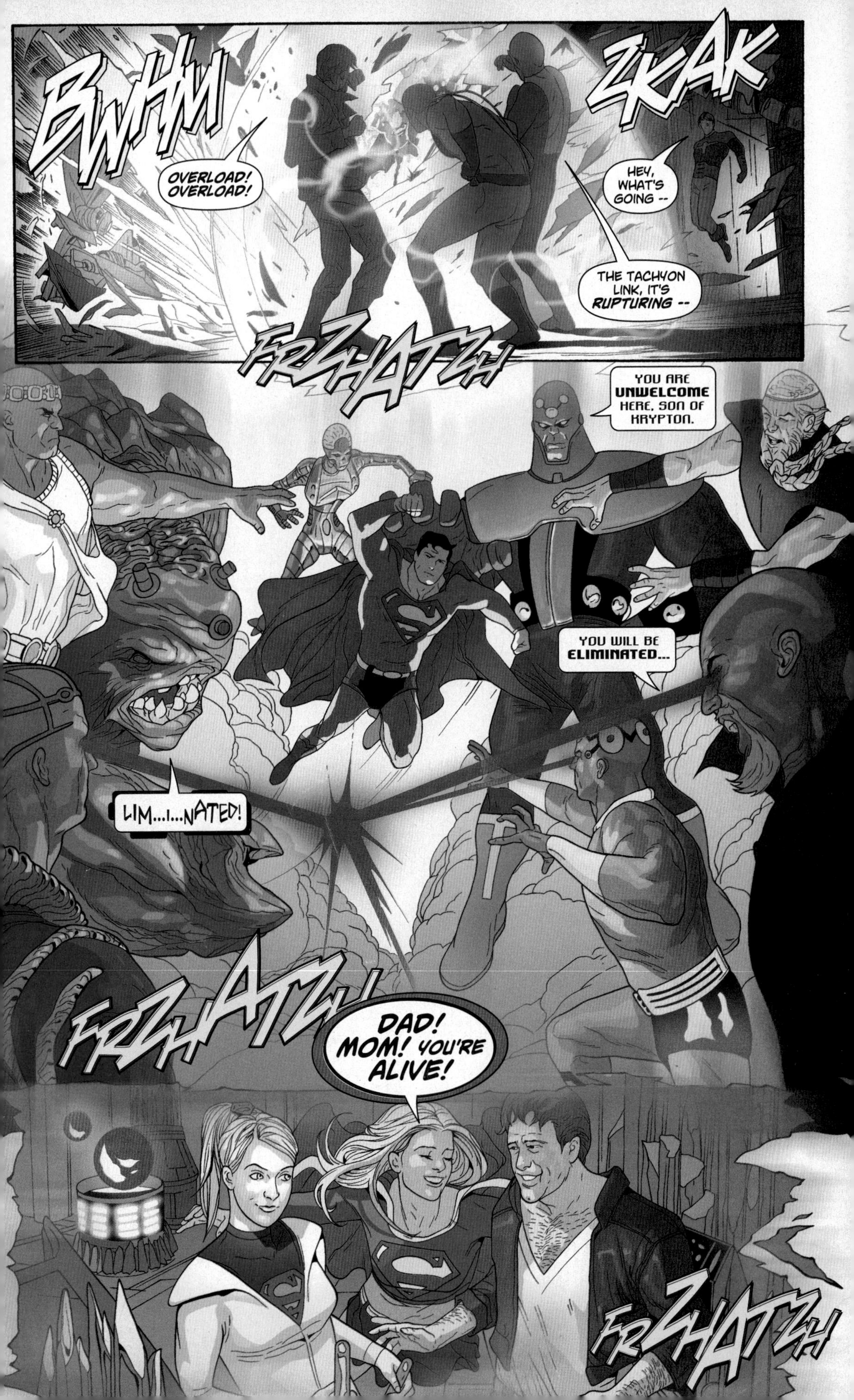
BWHM
ZKAK
OVERLOAD! OVERLOAD!
HEY, WHAT'S GOING --
THE TACHYON LINK, IT'S RUPTURING --
FRZHATZH
YOU ARE UNWELCOME HERE, SON OF KRYPTON.
YOU WILL BE ELIMINATED...
LIM...I...NATED!
FRZHATZH
DAD! MOM! YOU'RE ALIVE!
FRZHATZH

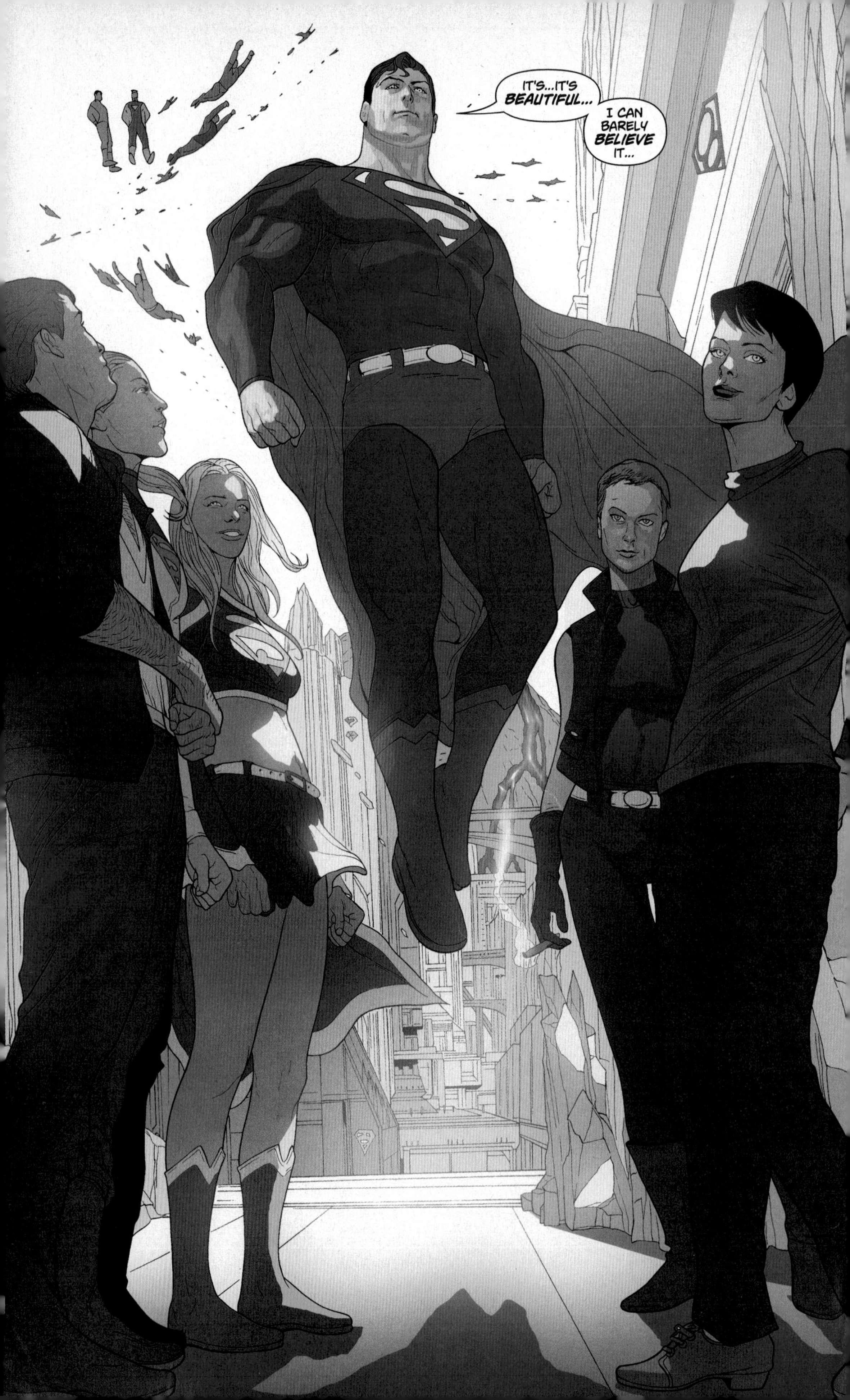
IT'S...IT'S BEAUTIFUL...
I CAN BARELY BELIEVE IT...

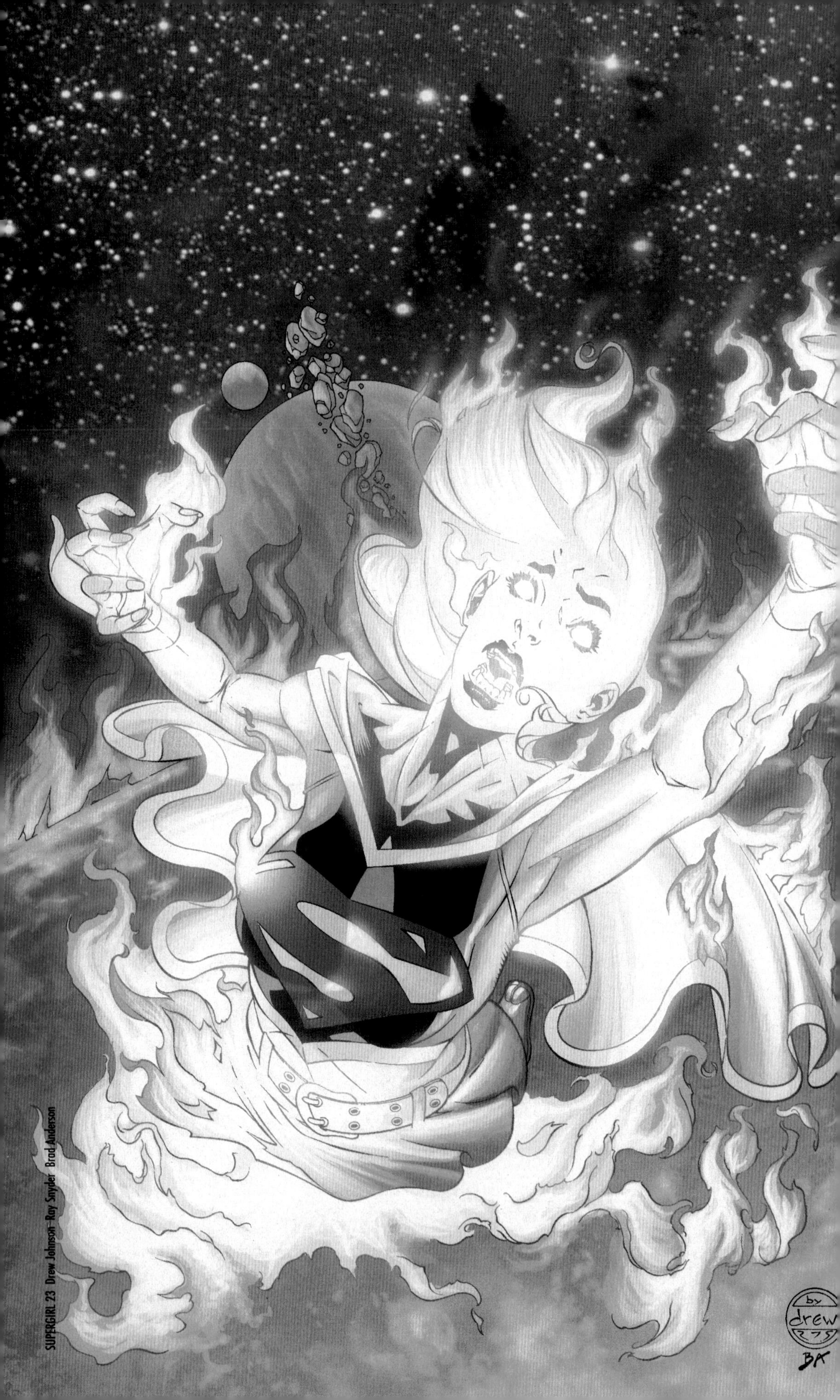
SUPERGIRL 23 Drew Johnson–Ray Snyder Brad Anderson
by drew
BA

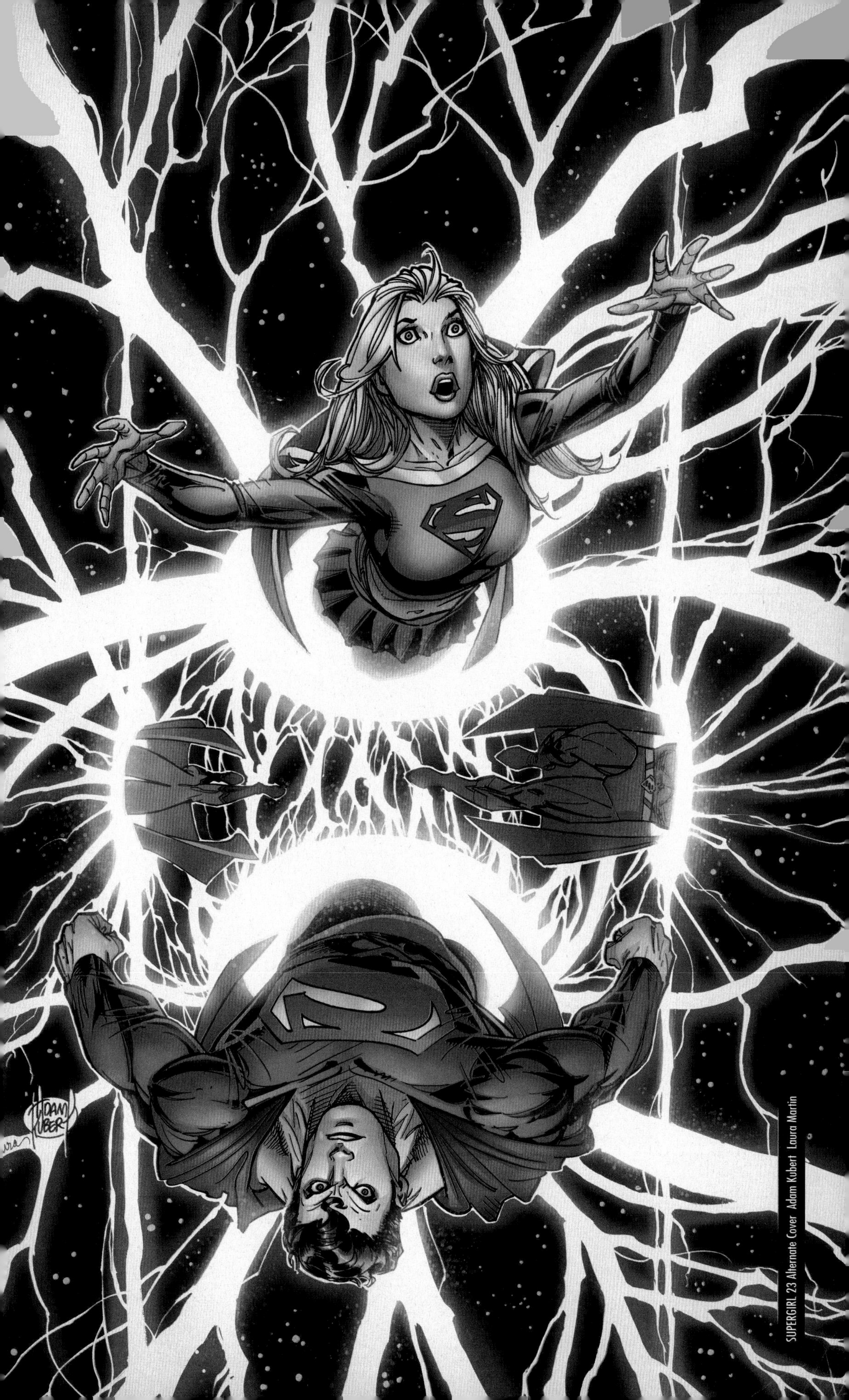

SUPERGIRL 23 Alternate Cover Adam Kubert Laura Martin

TESSERACT

KELLEY PUCKETT   WRITER
DREW JOHNSON   PENCILS
RAY SNYDER   INKS

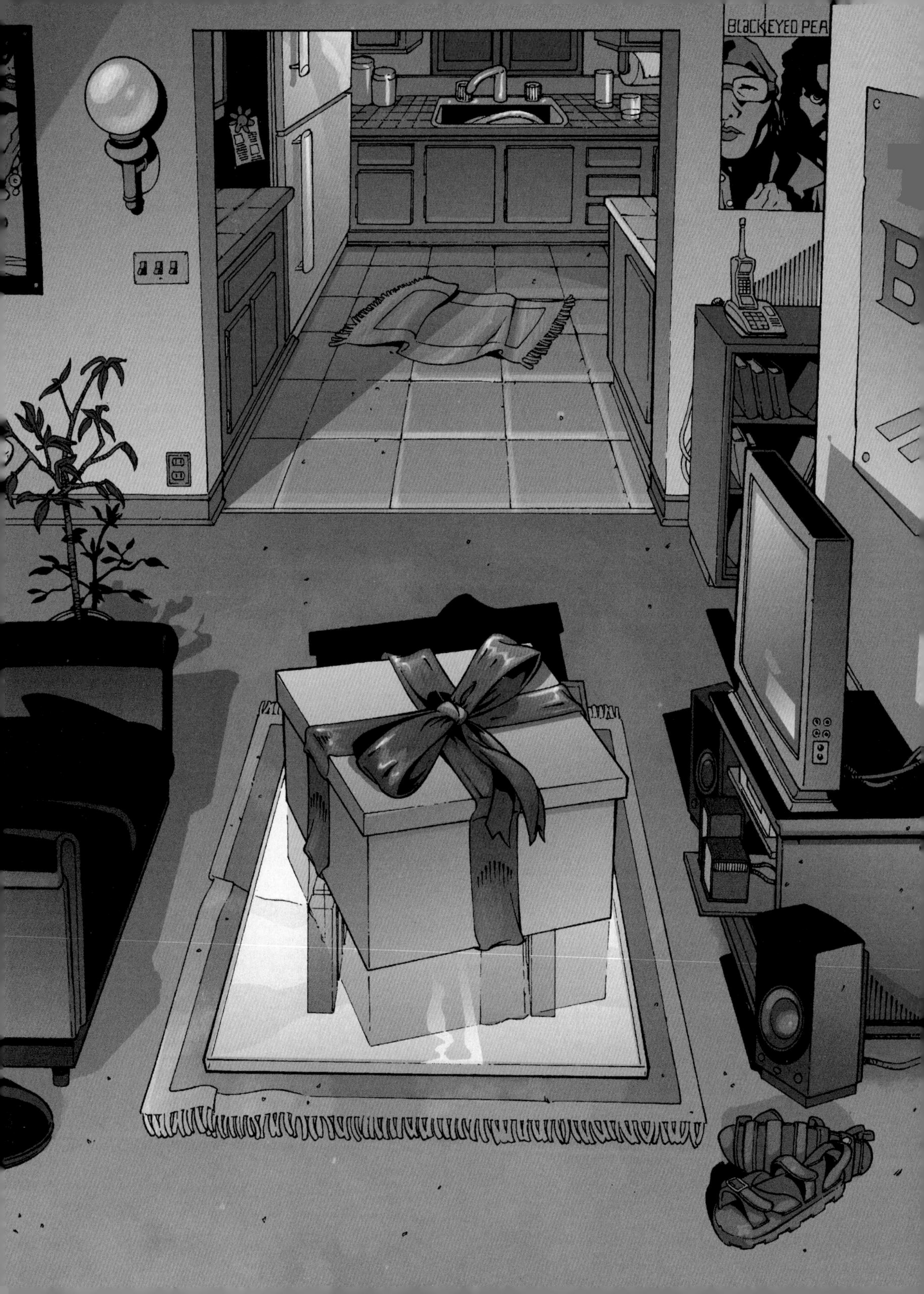
BLACKEYED PEA

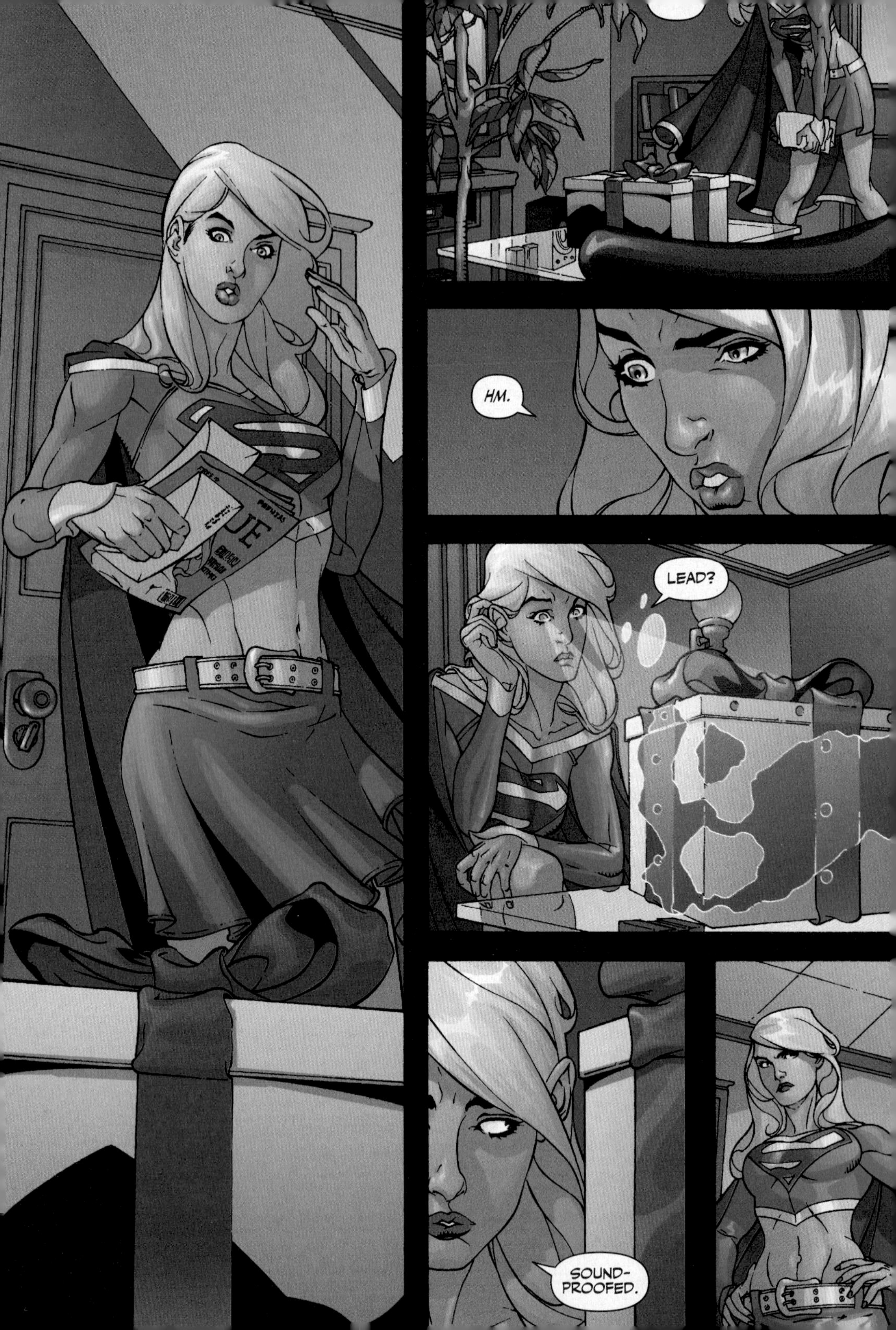
HM.
LEAD?
SOUND-
PROOFED.

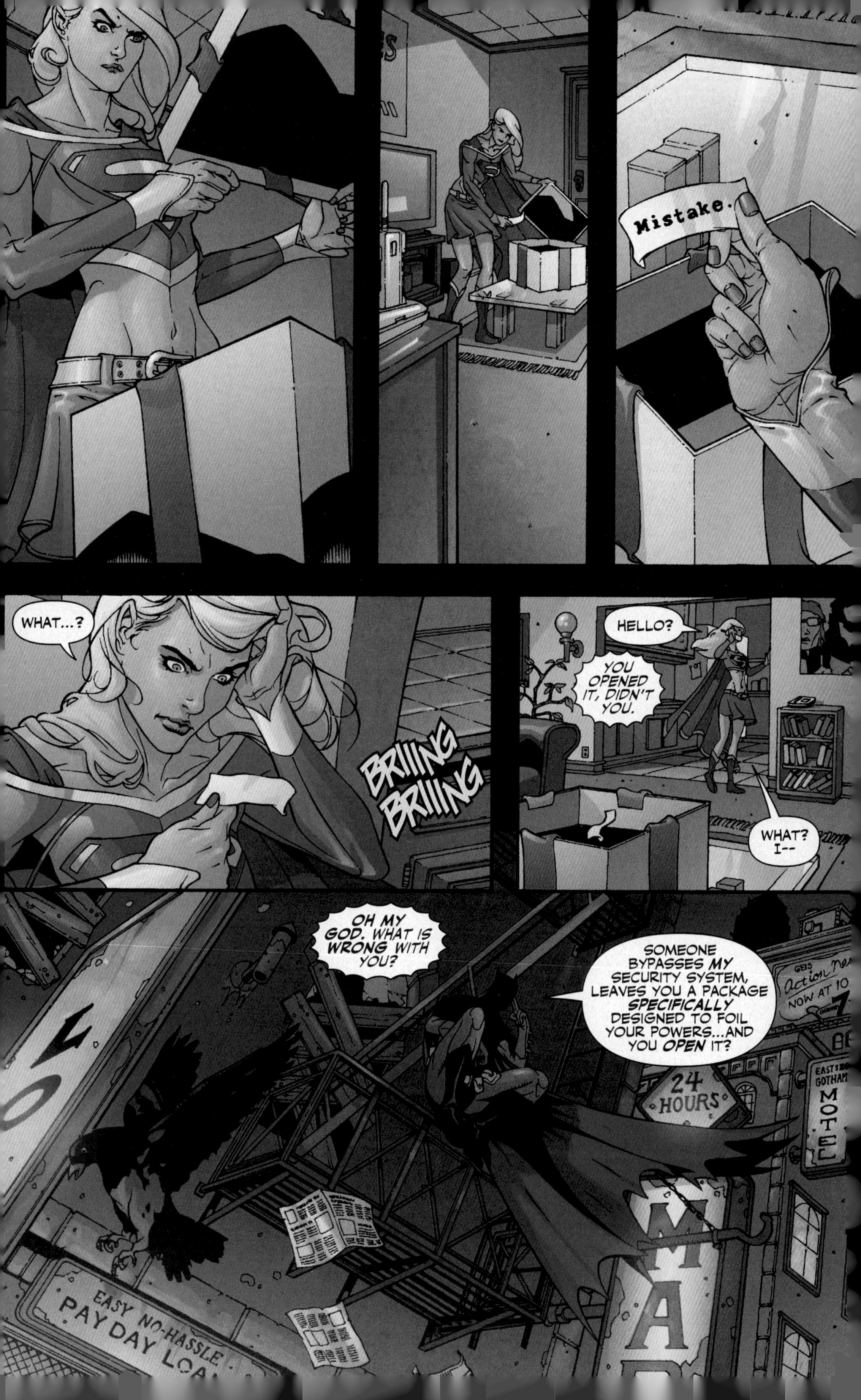
Mistake.
WHAT...?
BRIIING BRIIING
HELLO?
YOU OPENED IT, DIDN'T YOU.
WHAT? I--
OH MY GOD. WHAT IS WRONG WITH YOU?
SOMEONE BYPASSES MY SECURITY SYSTEM, LEAVES YOU A PACKAGE SPECIFICALLY DESIGNED TO FOIL YOUR POWERS...AND YOU OPEN IT?
24 HOURS
MOTEL
EASY NO-HASSLE PAY DAY LOA

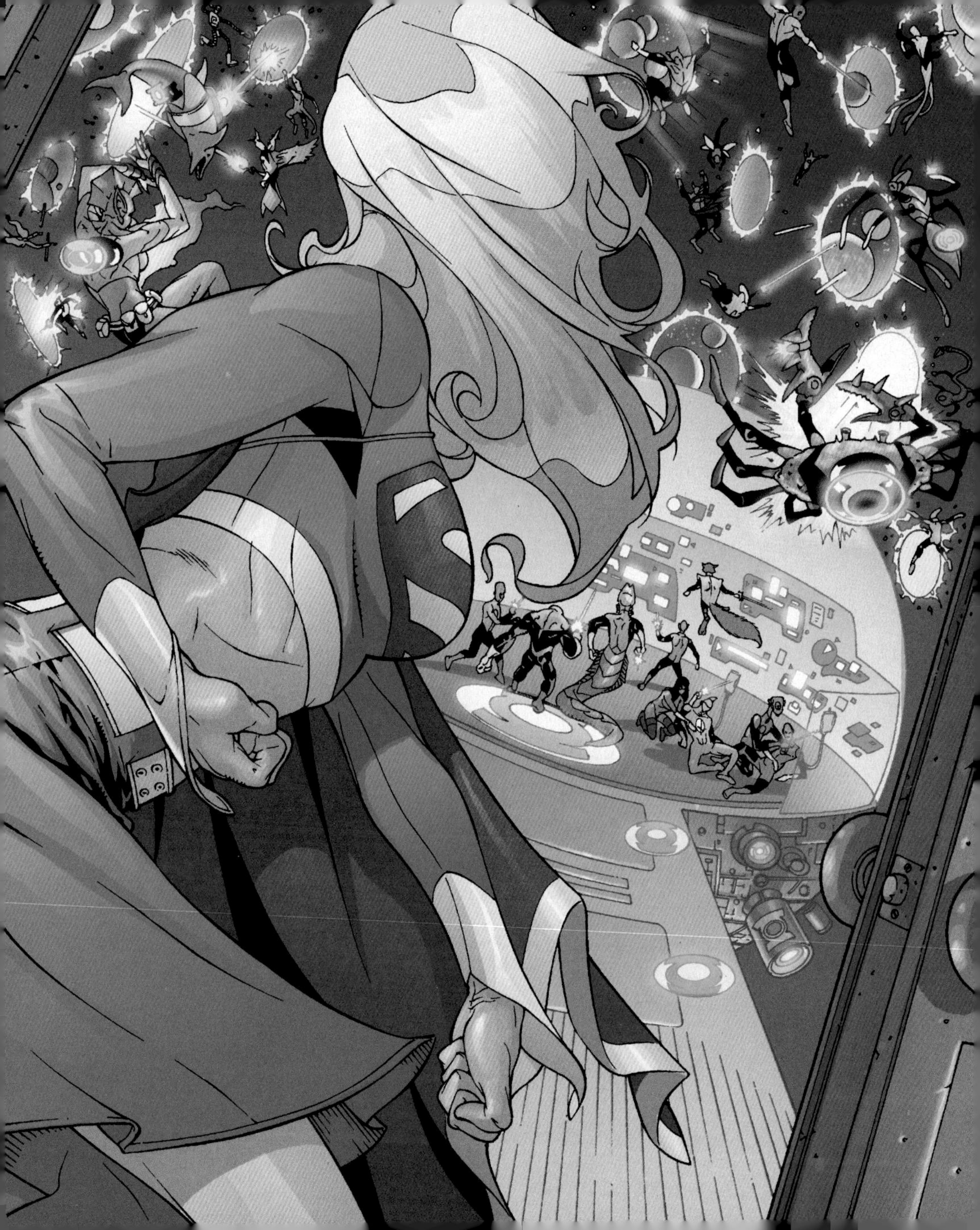

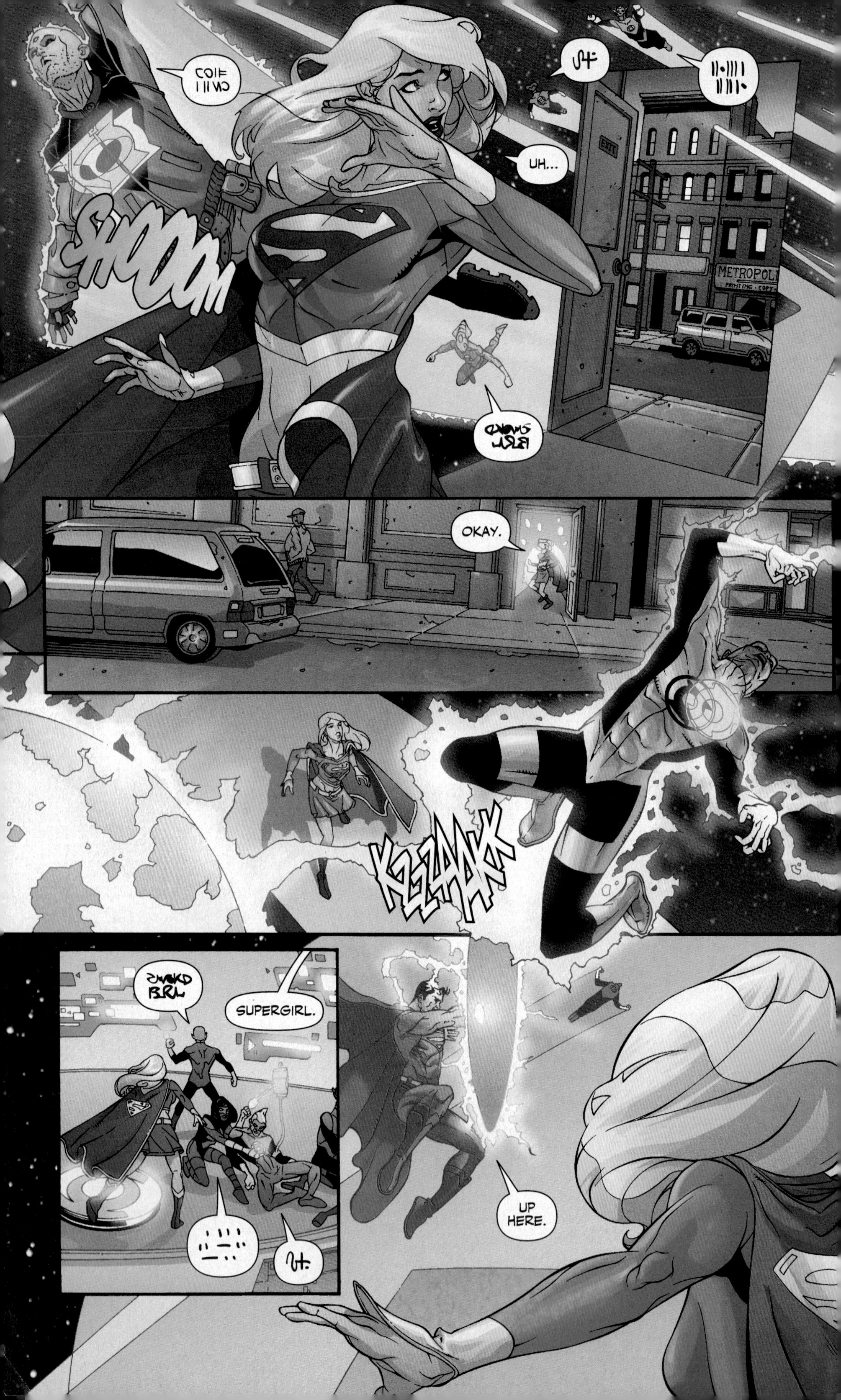

UH...
SHOOOM
EXIT
METROPOLI
PRINTING · COPY
OKAY.
SUPERGIRL.
UP HERE.

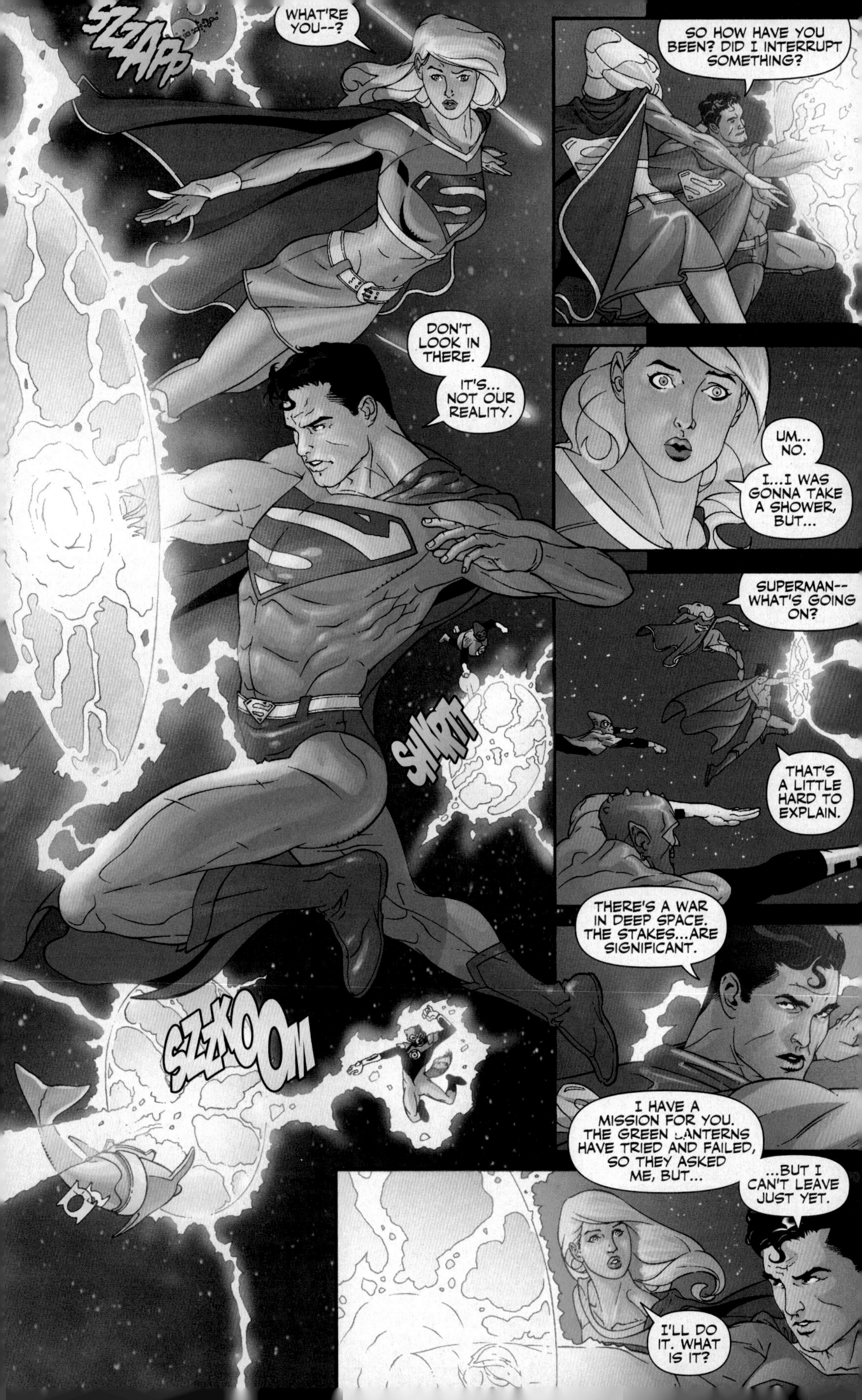
SZZAPP
WHAT'RE YOU--?
SO HOW HAVE YOU BEEN? DID I INTERRUPT SOMETHING?
DON'T LOOK IN THERE.
IT'S... NOT OUR REALITY.
UM... NO.
I...I WAS GONNA TAKE A SHOWER, BUT...
SHRTT
SUPERMAN--WHAT'S GOING ON?
THAT'S A LITTLE HARD TO EXPLAIN.
THERE'S A WAR IN DEEP SPACE. THE STAKES...ARE SIGNIFICANT.
SZZKOOM
I HAVE A MISSION FOR YOU. THE GREEN LANTERNS HAVE TRIED AND FAILED, SO THEY ASKED ME, BUT...
...BUT I CAN'T LEAVE JUST YET.
I'LL DO IT. WHAT IS IT?

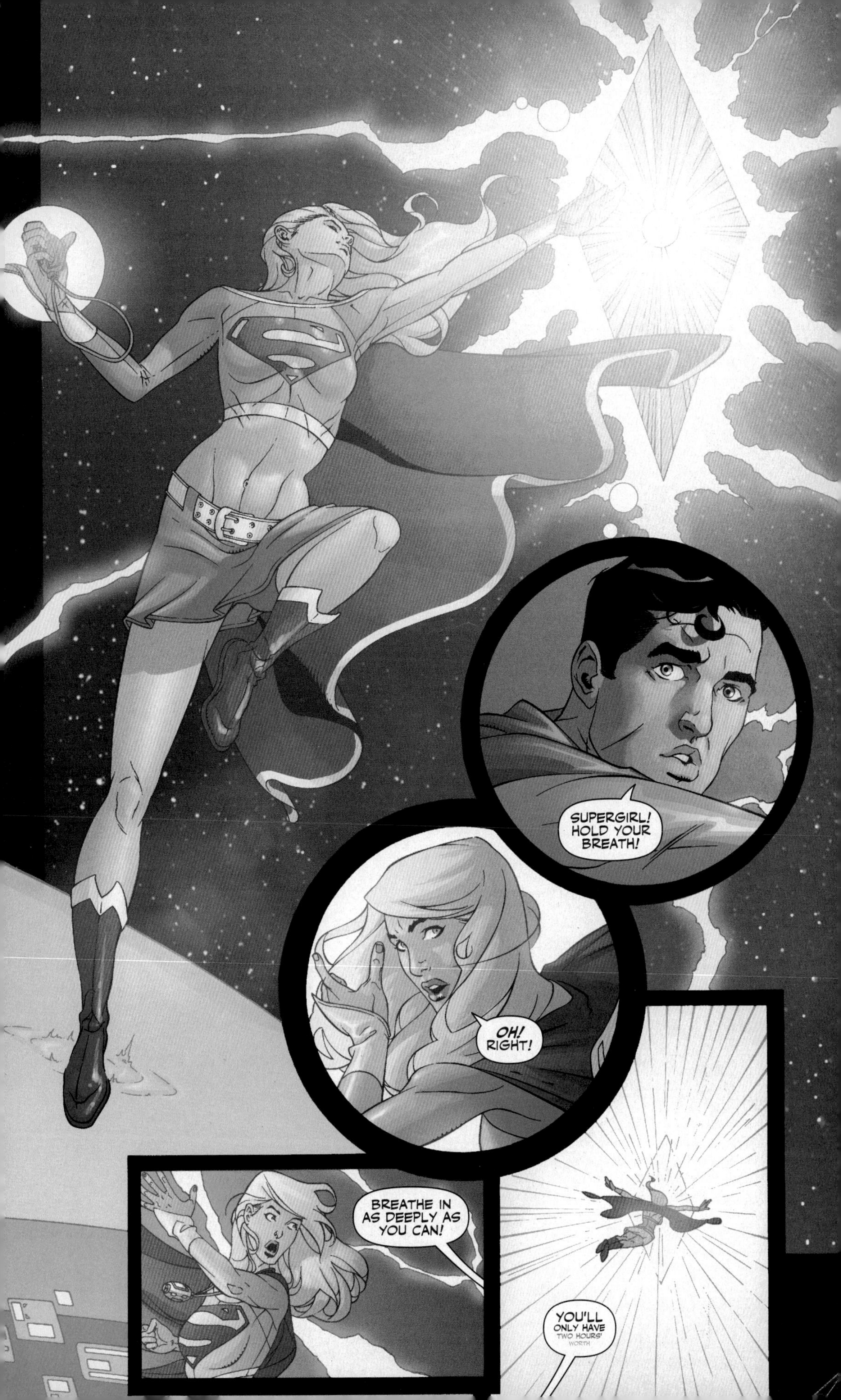
SUPERGIRL! HOLD YOUR BREATH!
OH! RIGHT!
BREATHE IN AS DEEPLY AS YOU CAN!
YOU'LL ONLY HAVE TWO HOURS' WORTH

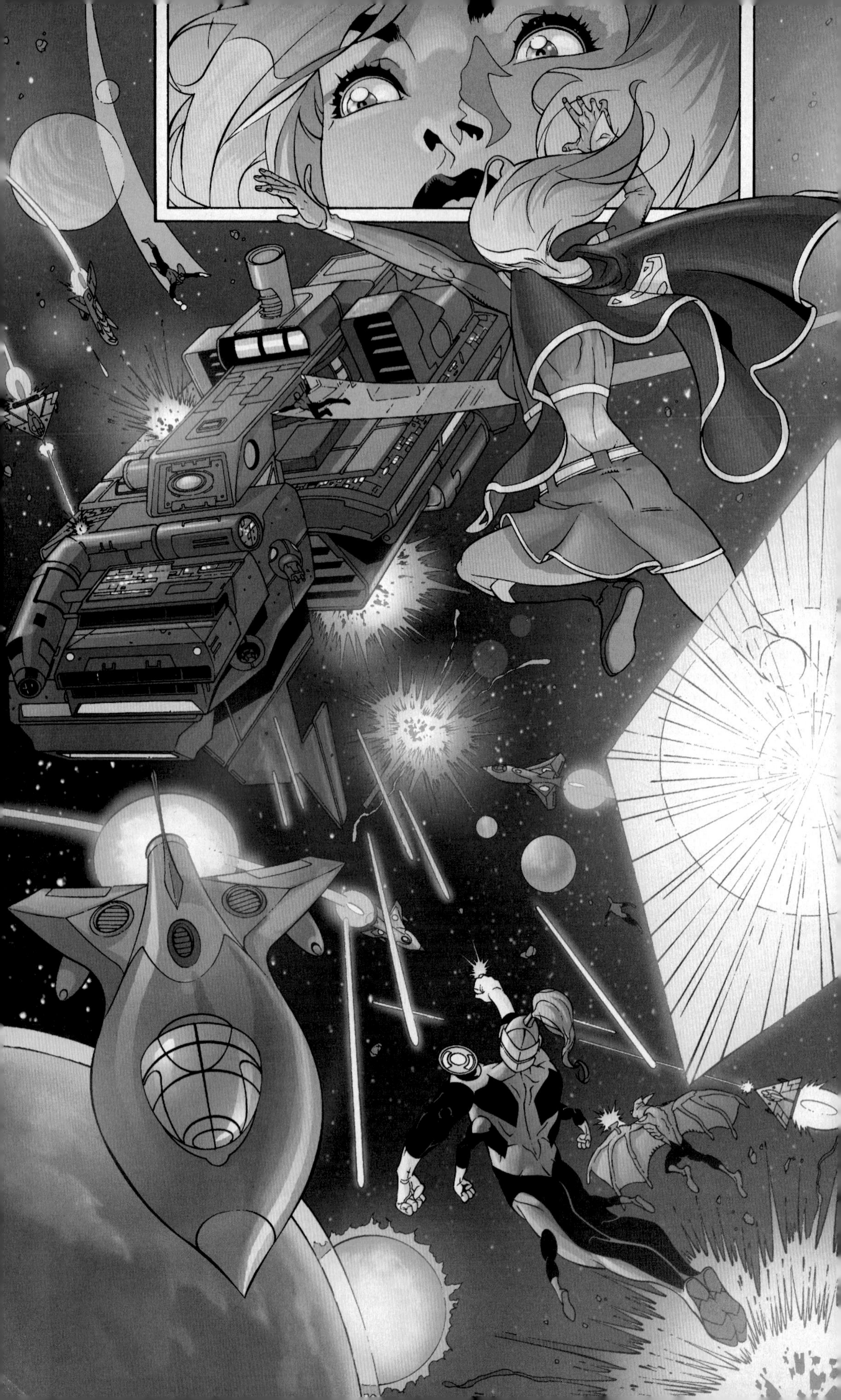

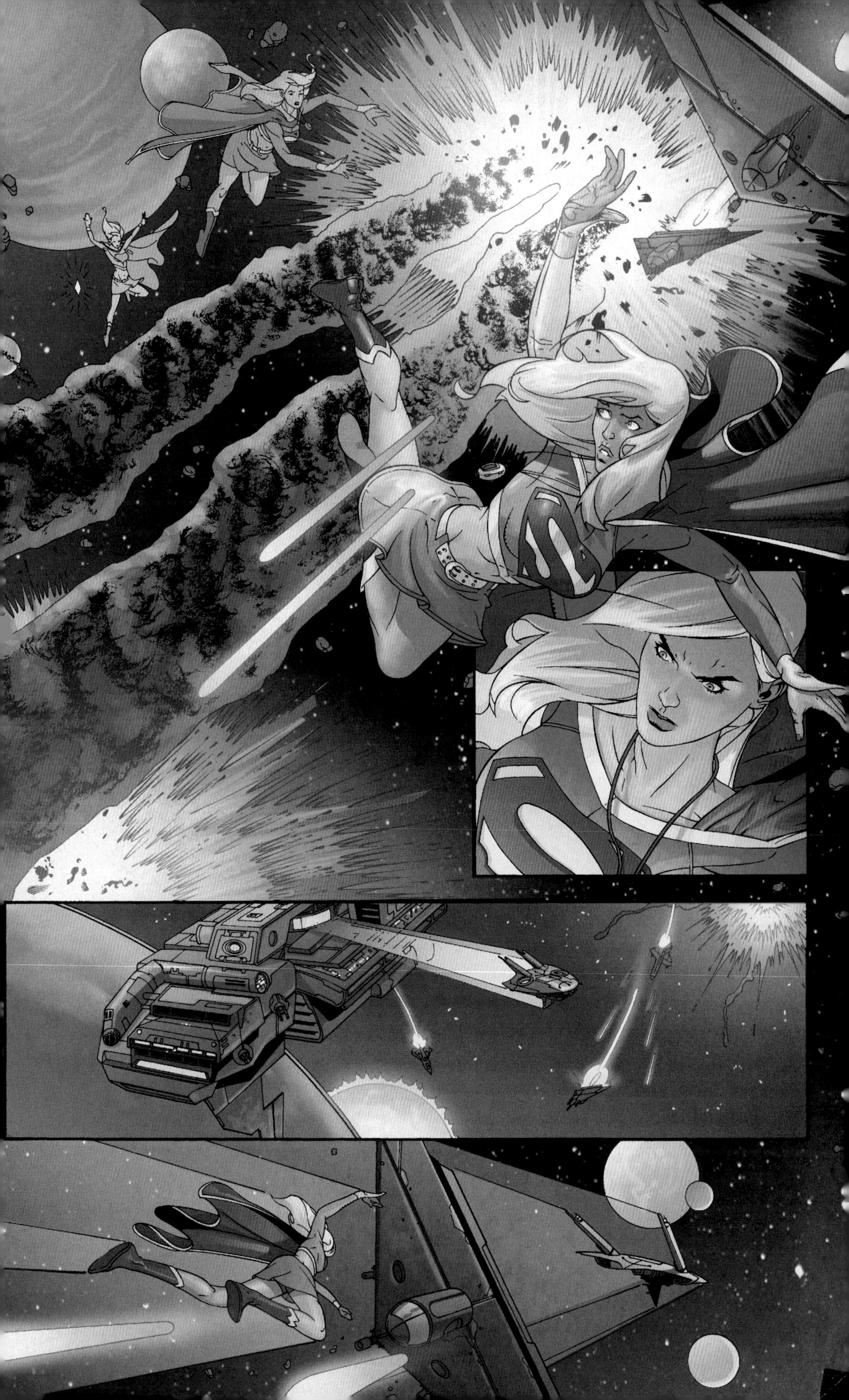

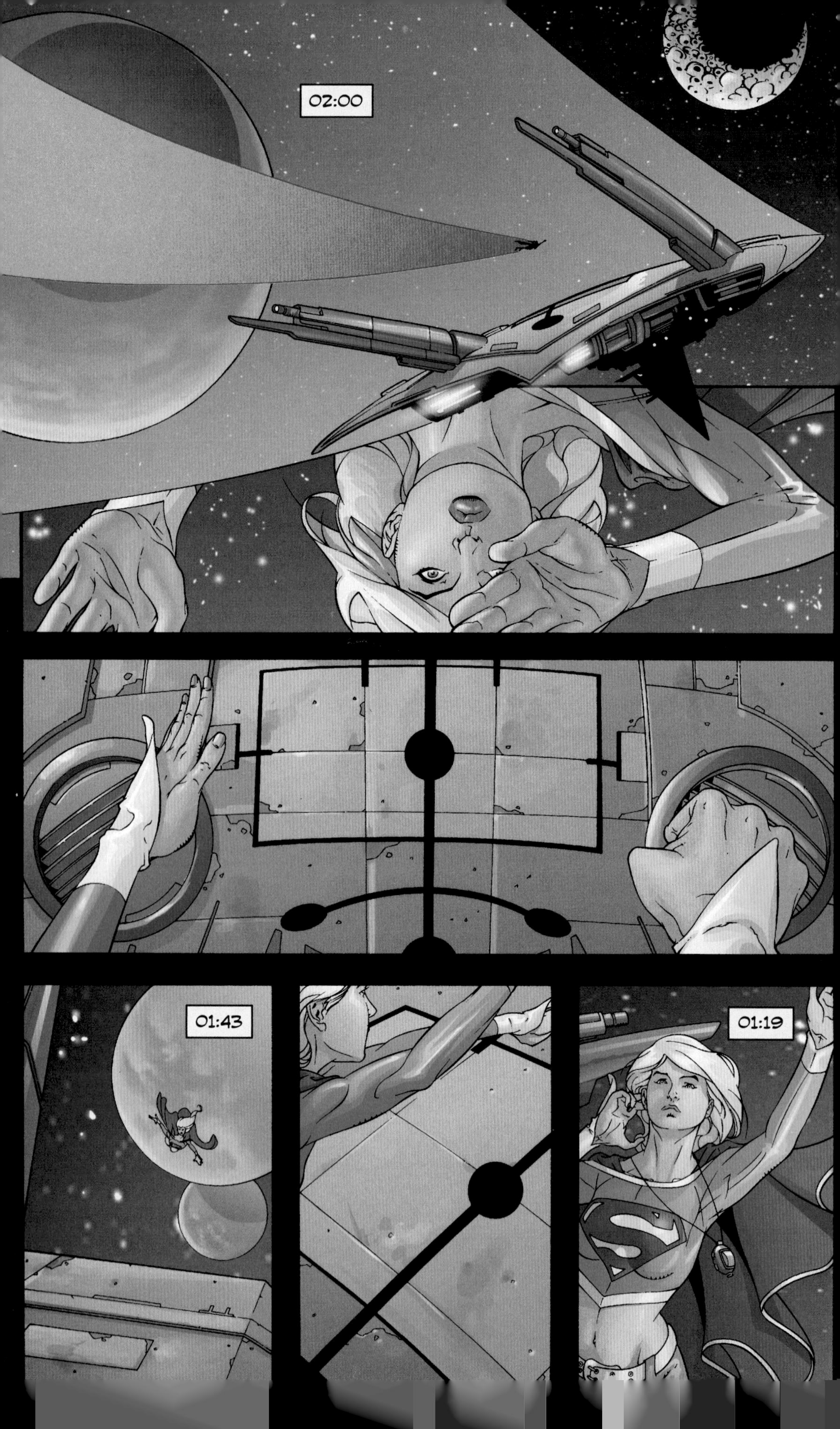
02:00
01:43
01:19

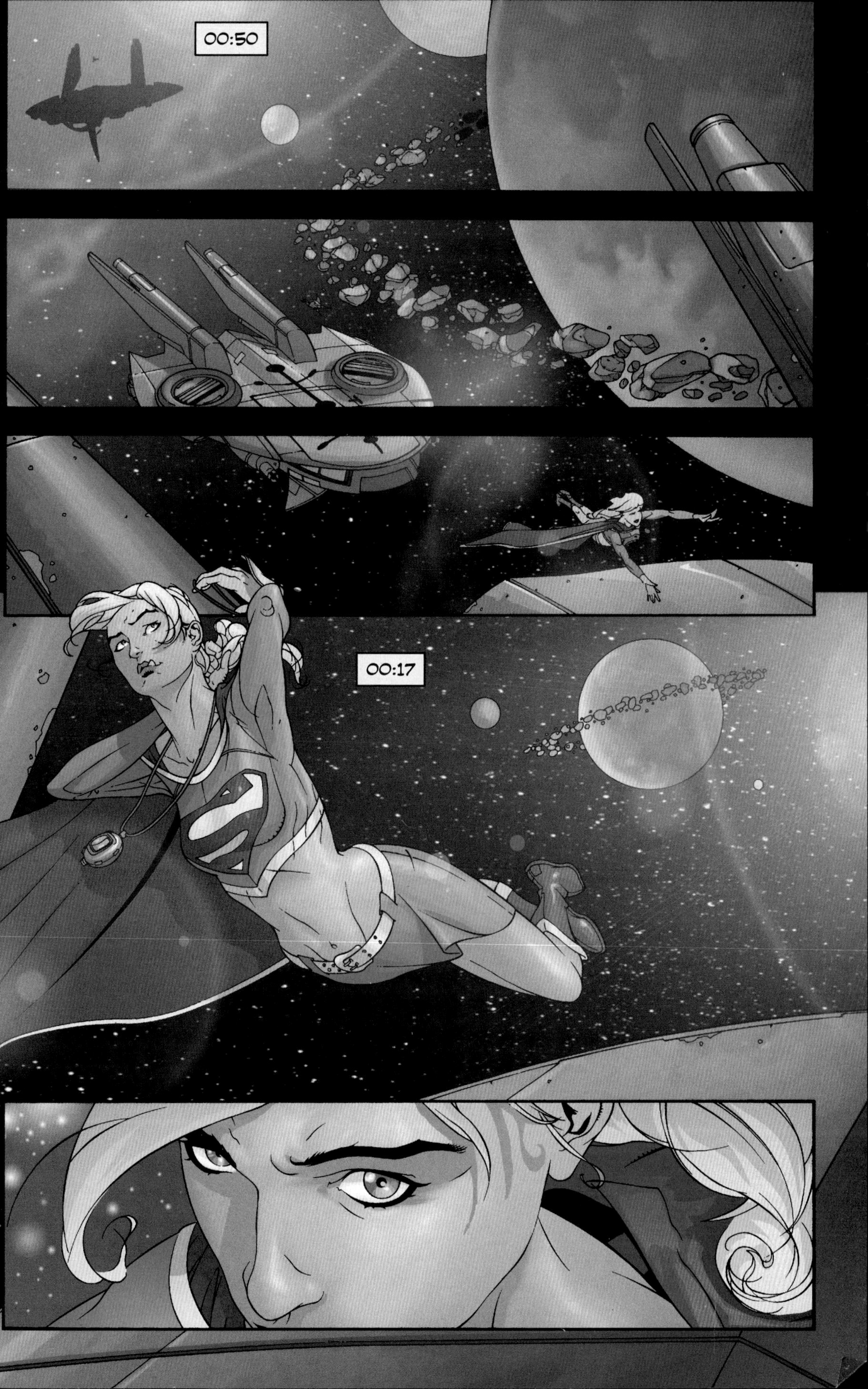
00:50
00:17

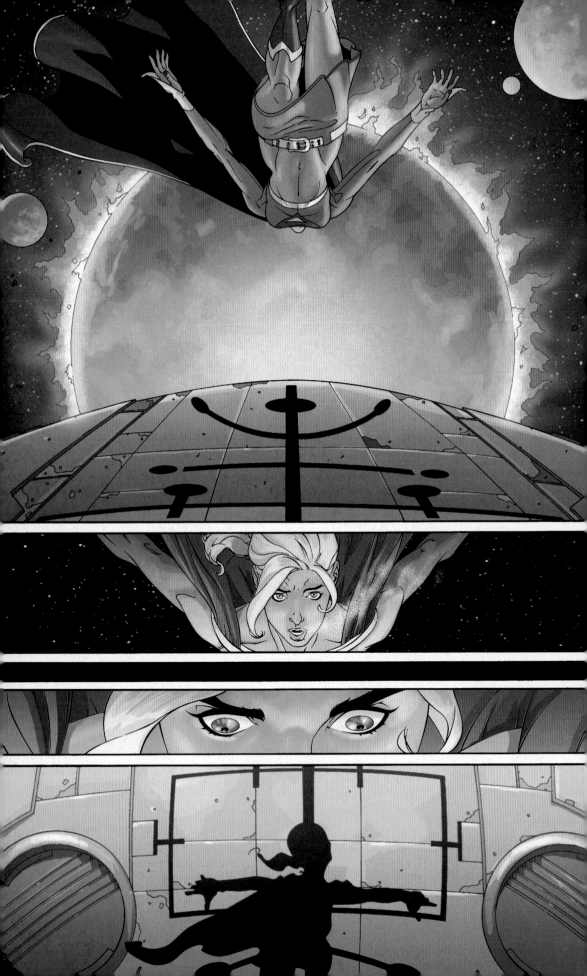

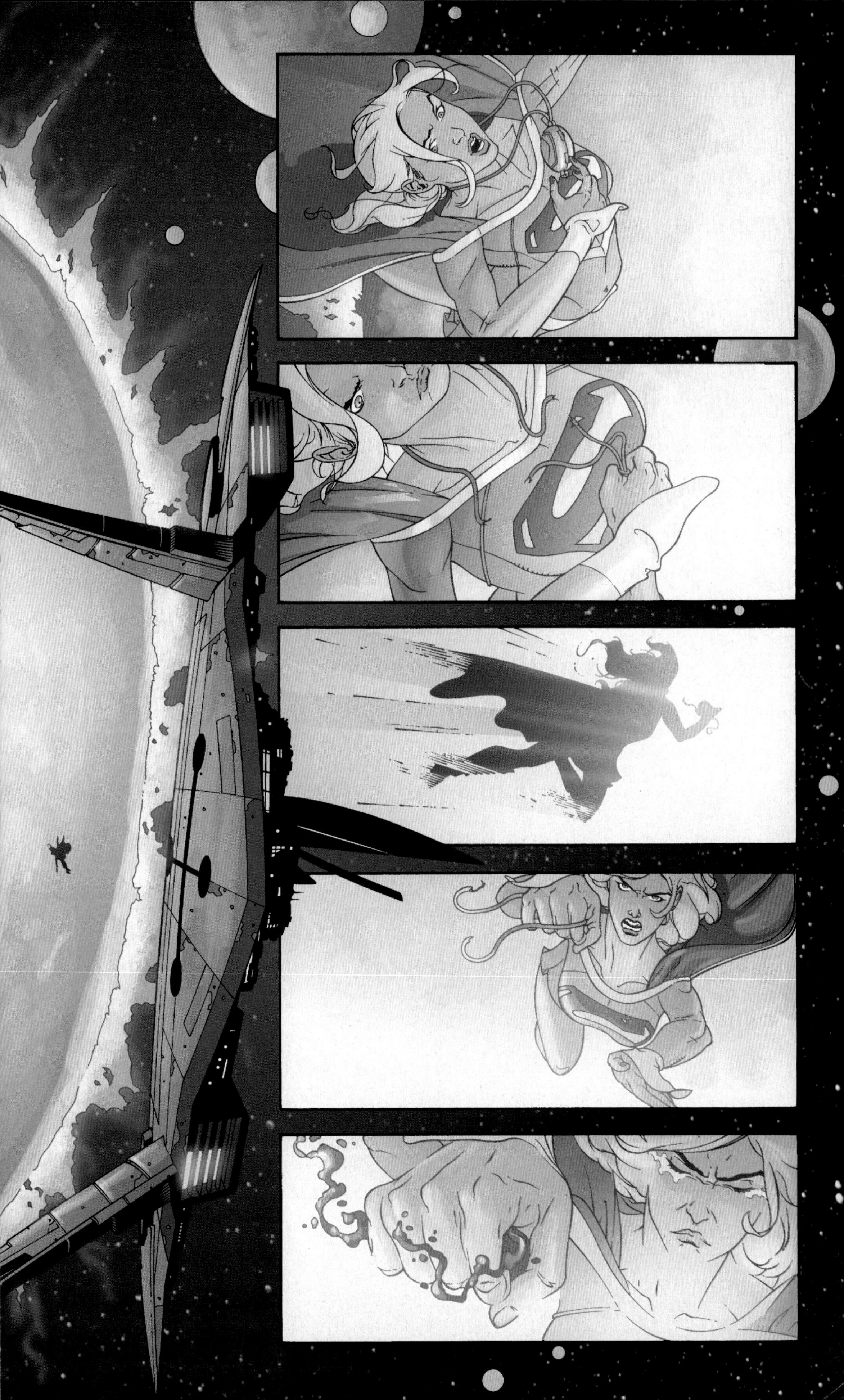

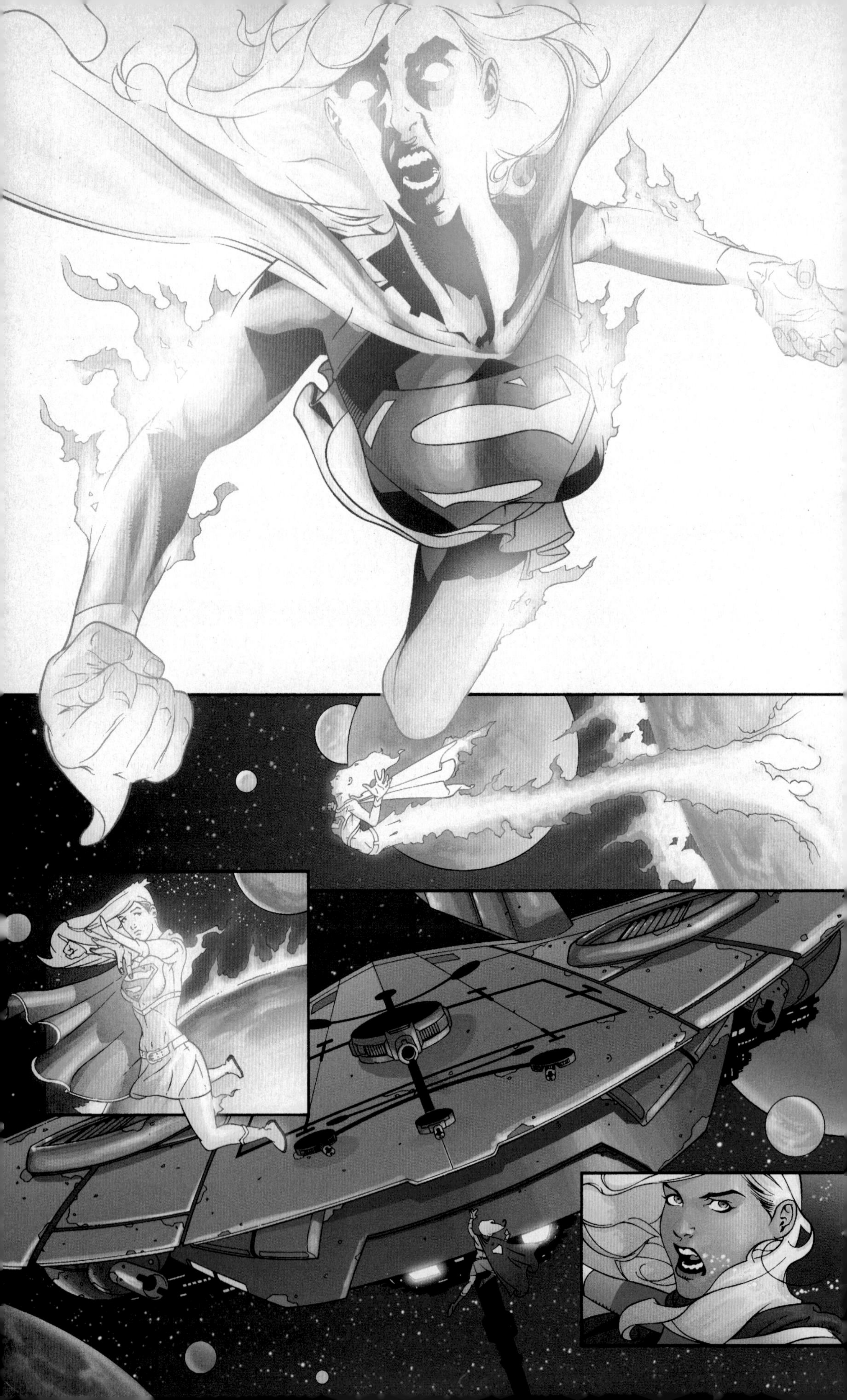

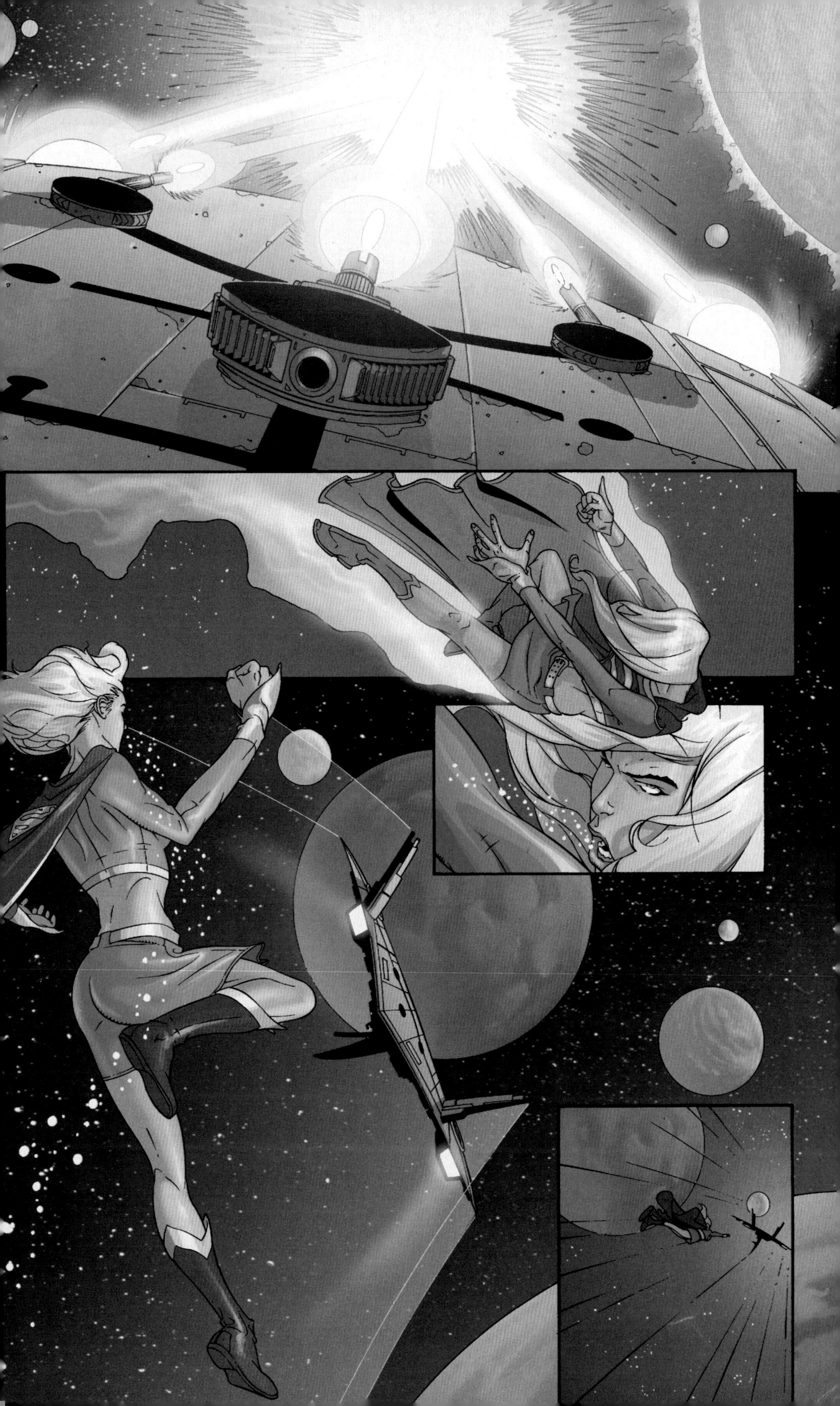

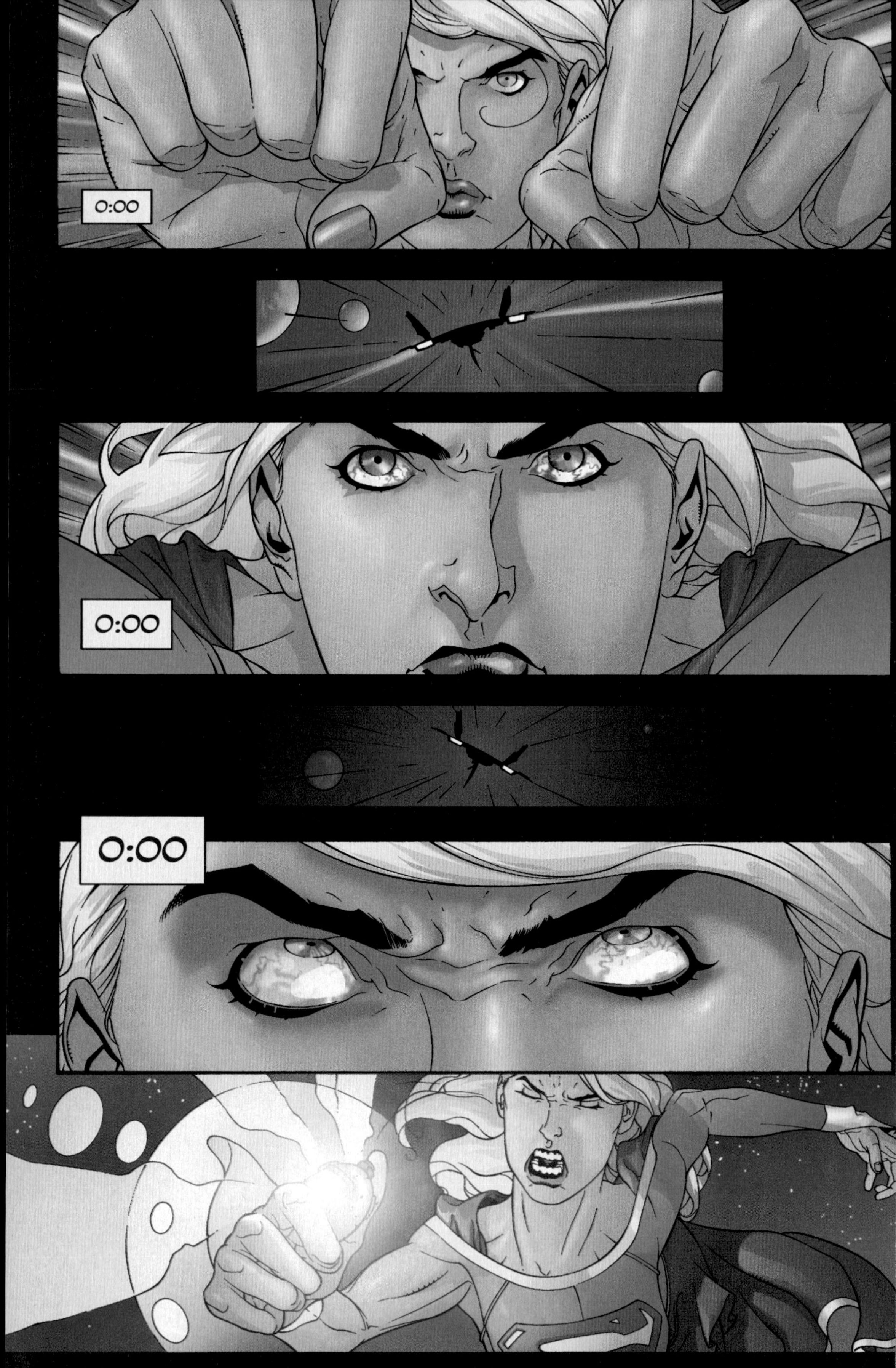
0:00
0:00
0:00

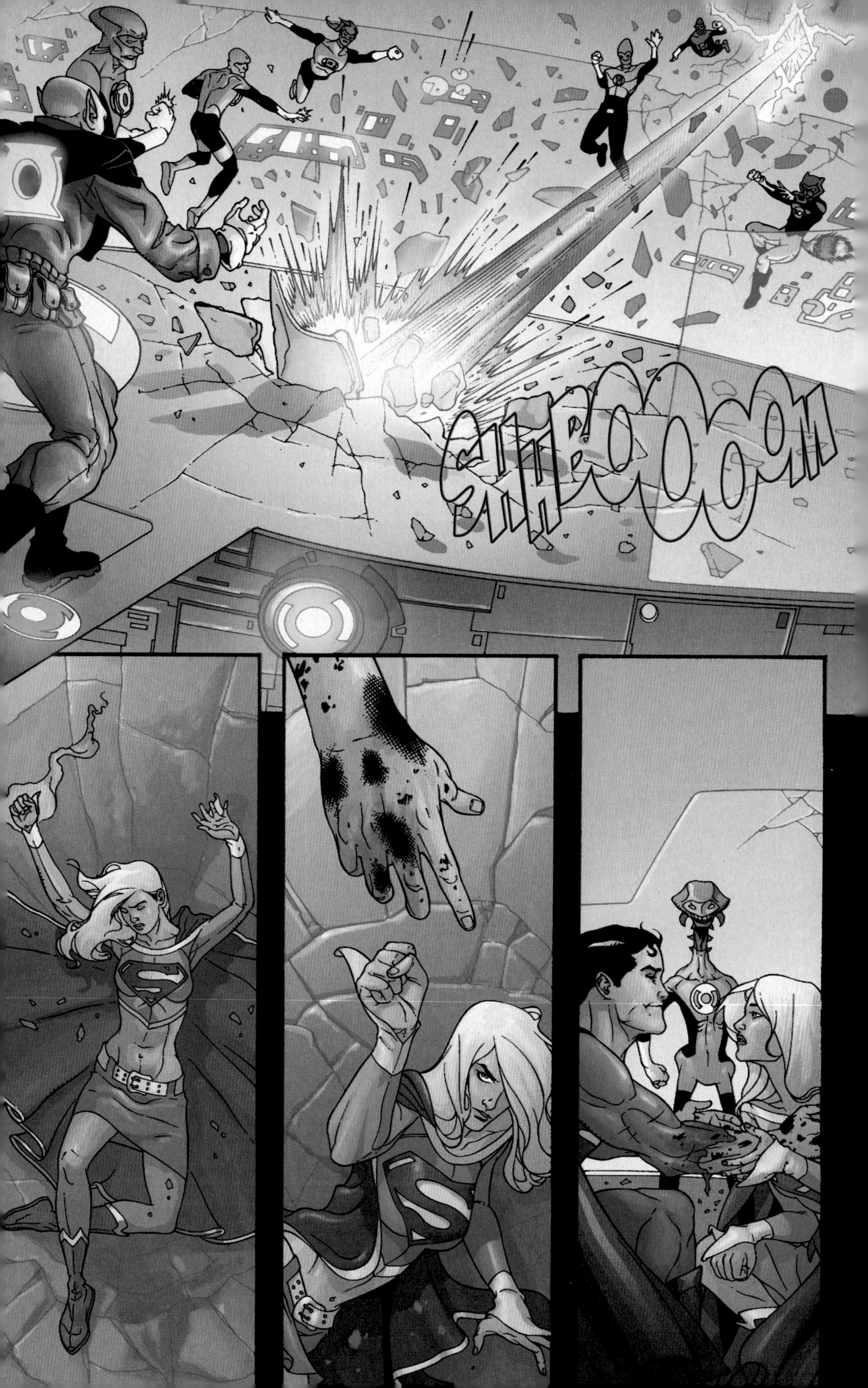
SHROOOOM

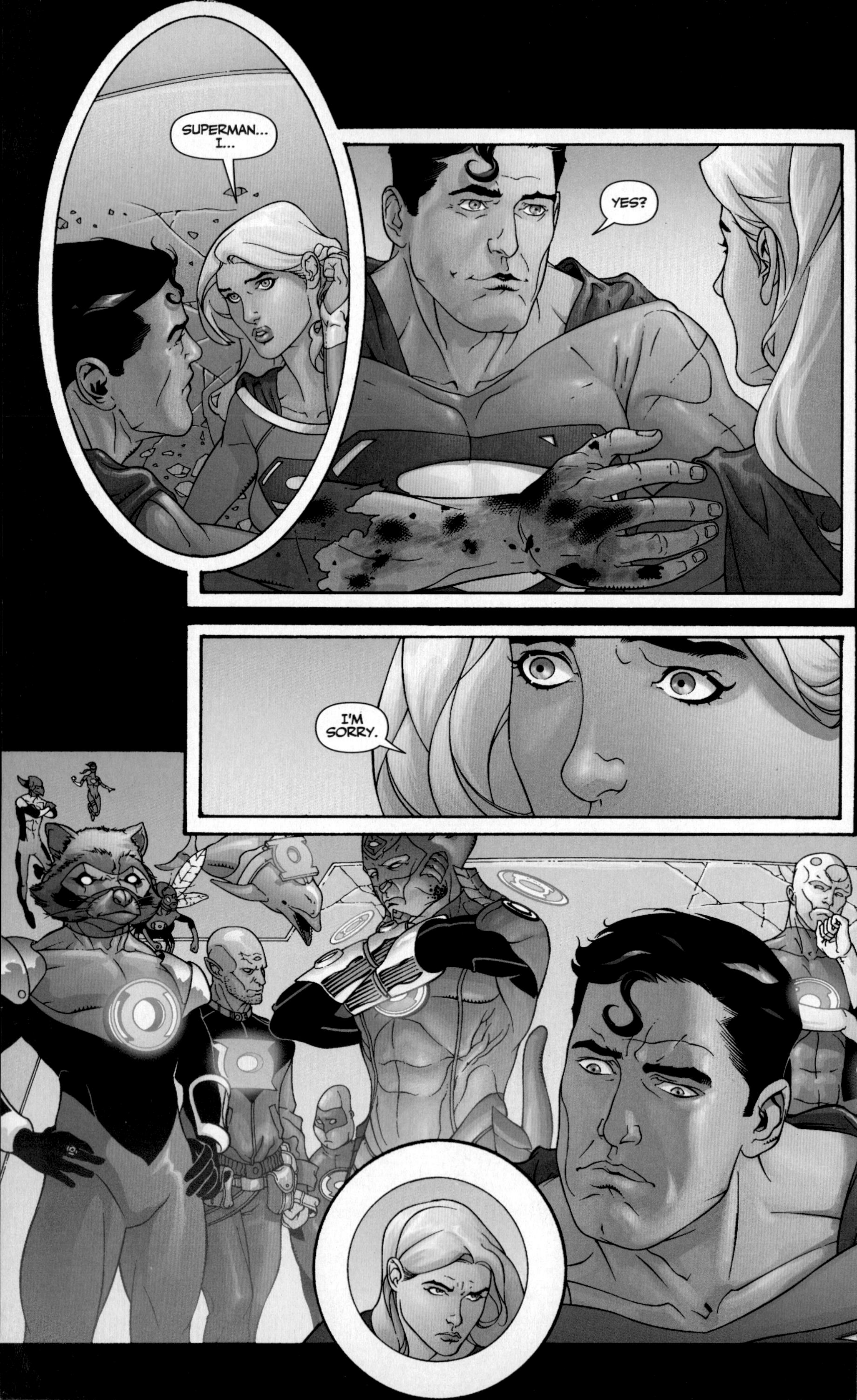
SUPERMAN...
I...
YES?
I'M SORRY.

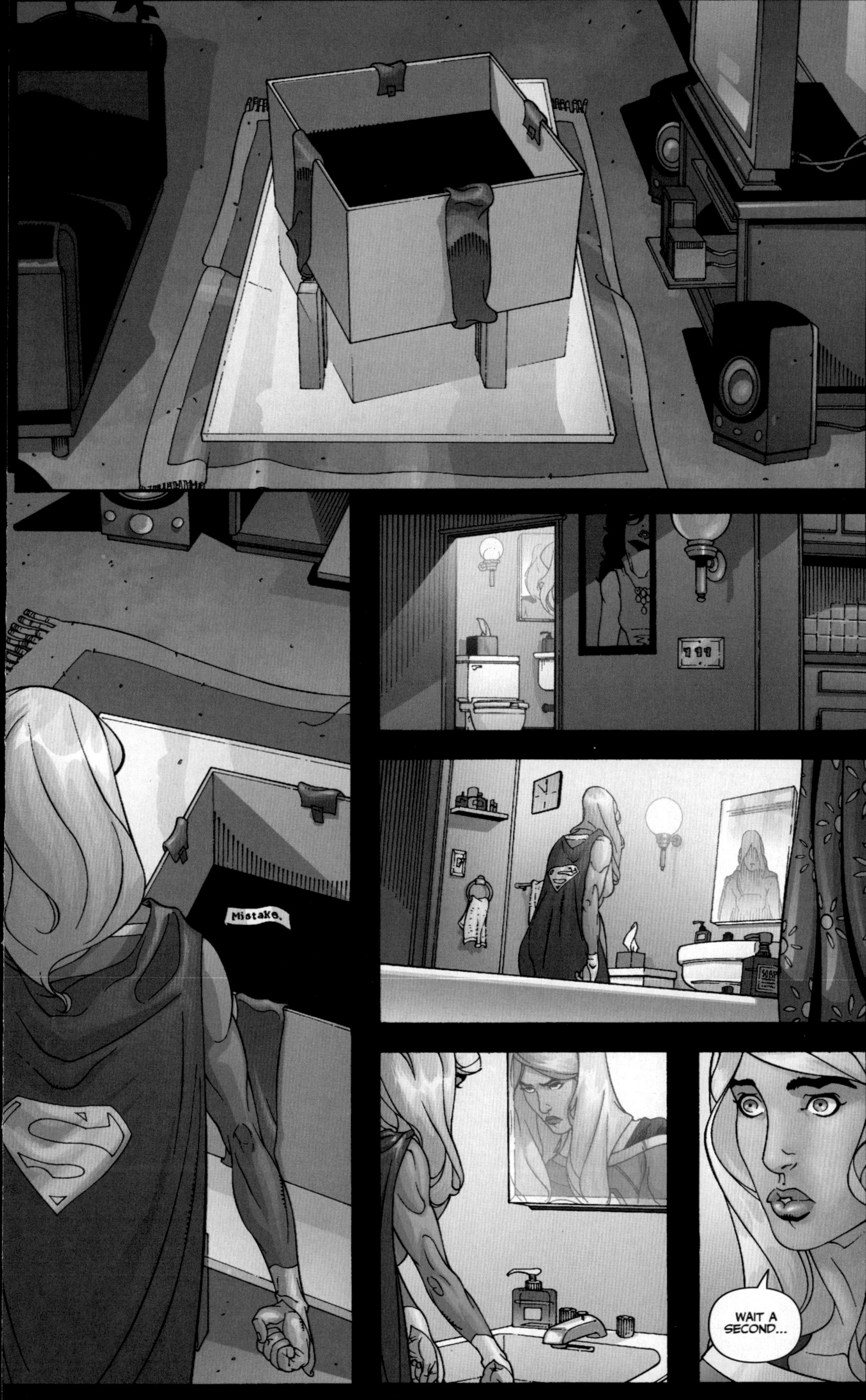
Mistake.
WAIT A SECOND...

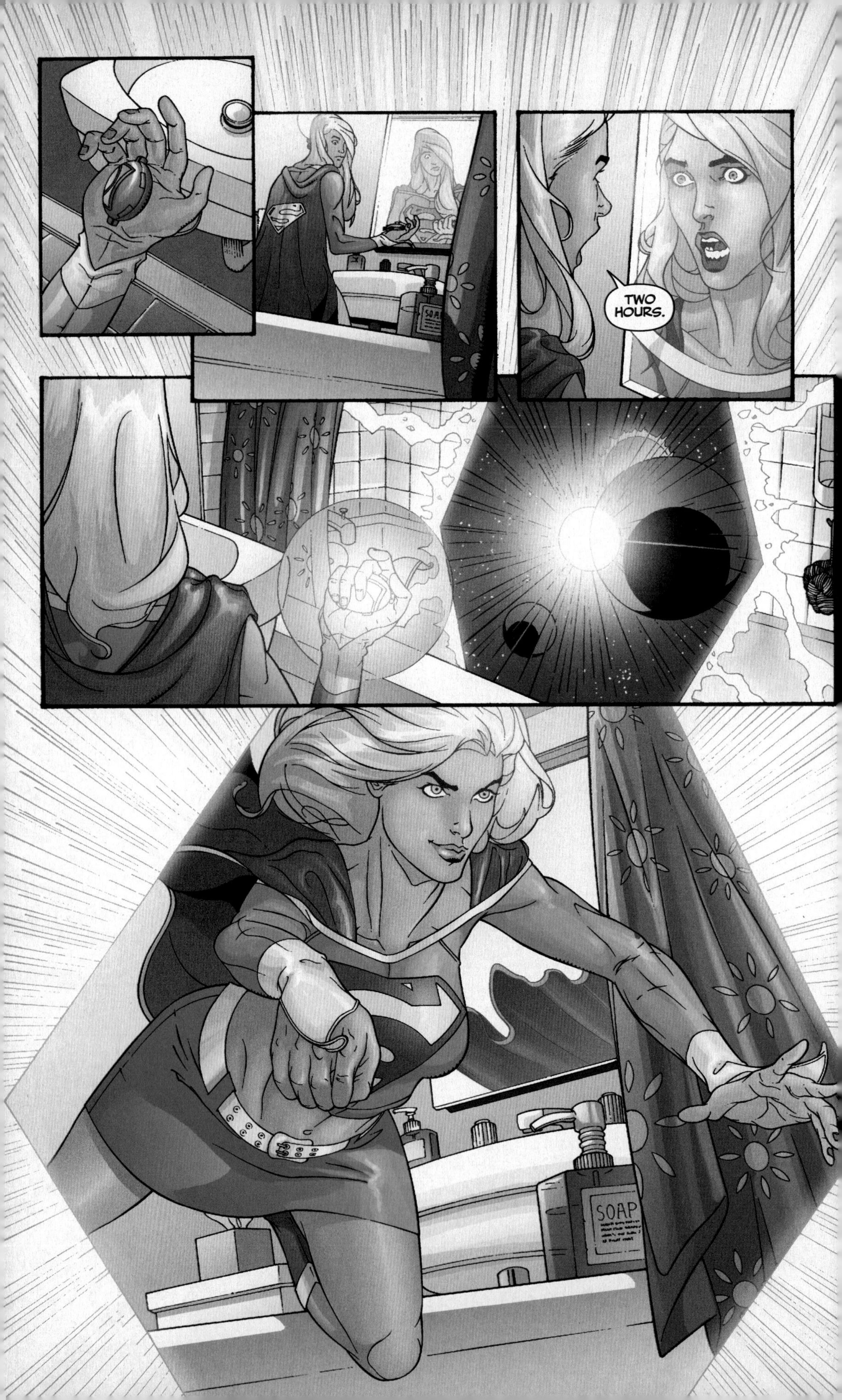
SOAP
TWO HOURS.
SOAP

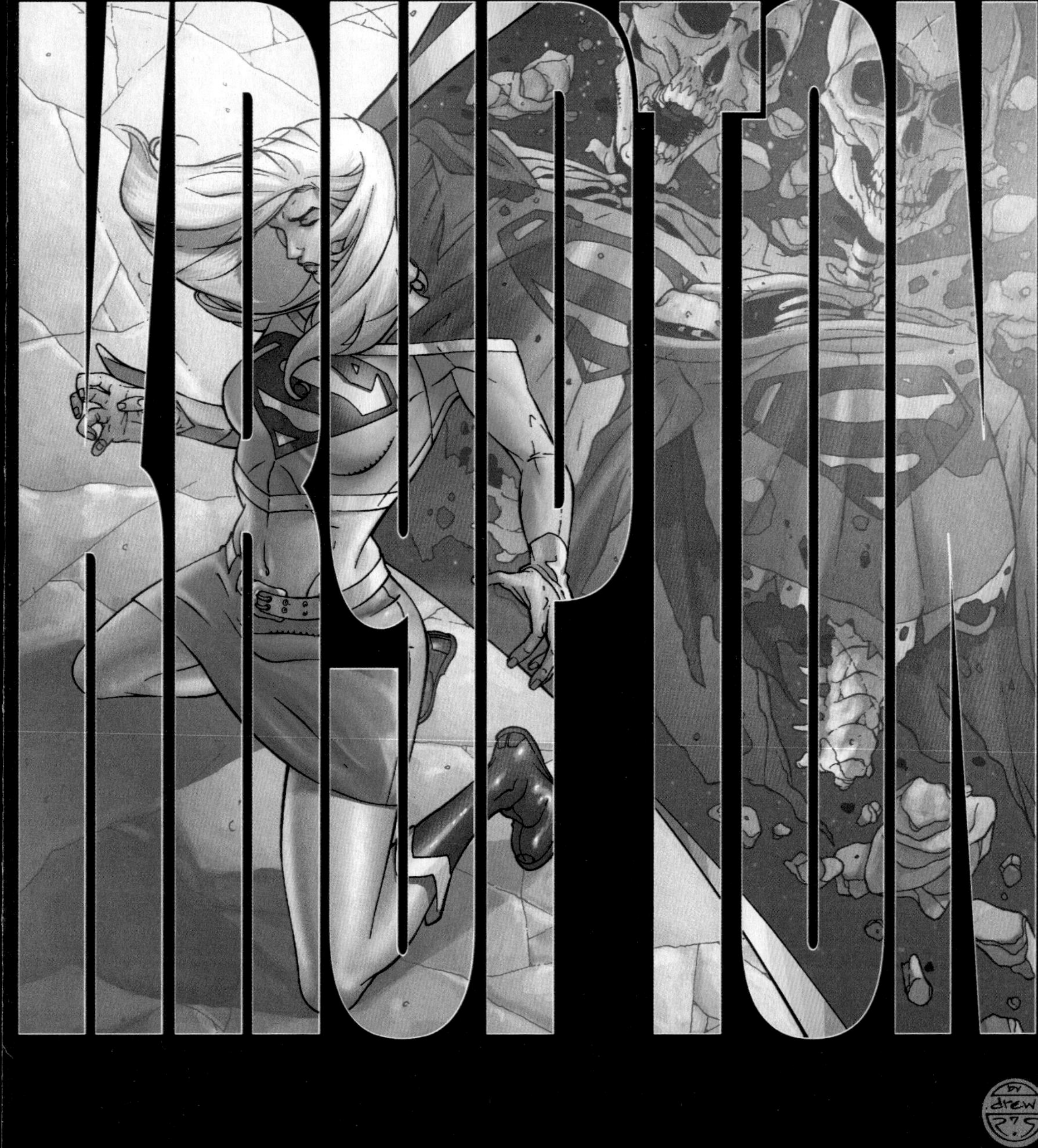

STAR CHILD

KELLEY PUCKETT WRITER
DREW JOHNSON LEE FERGUSON PENCILS
RAY SNYDER INKS

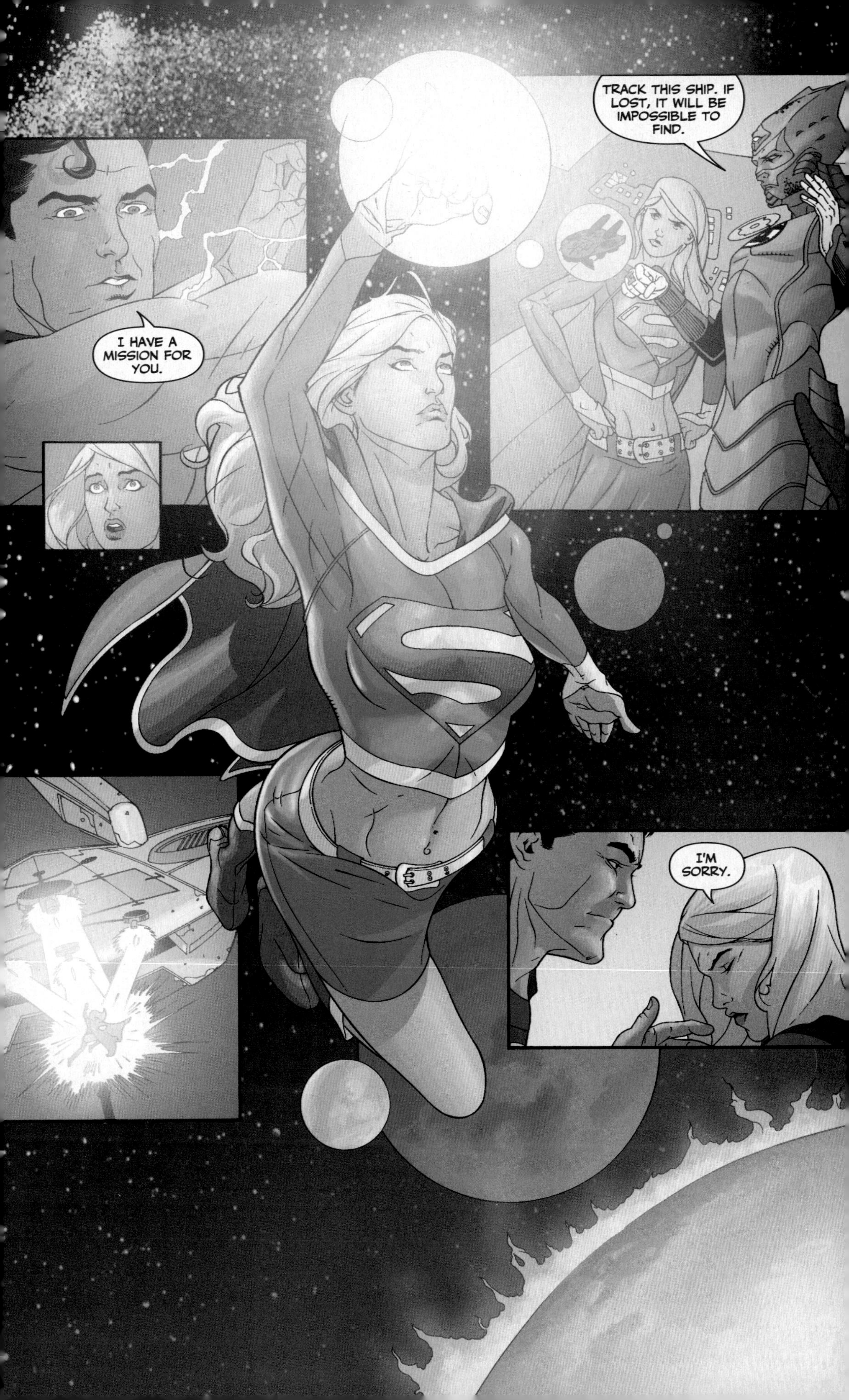
I HAVE A MISSION FOR YOU.
TRACK THIS SHIP. IF LOST, IT WILL BE IMPOSSIBLE TO FIND.
I'M SORRY.

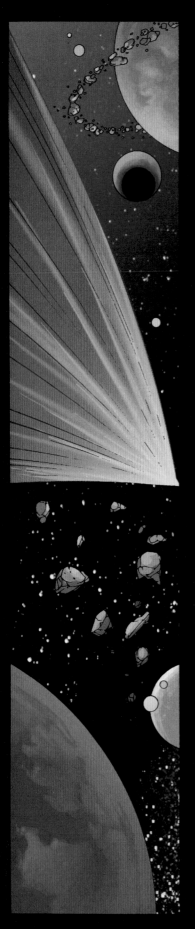

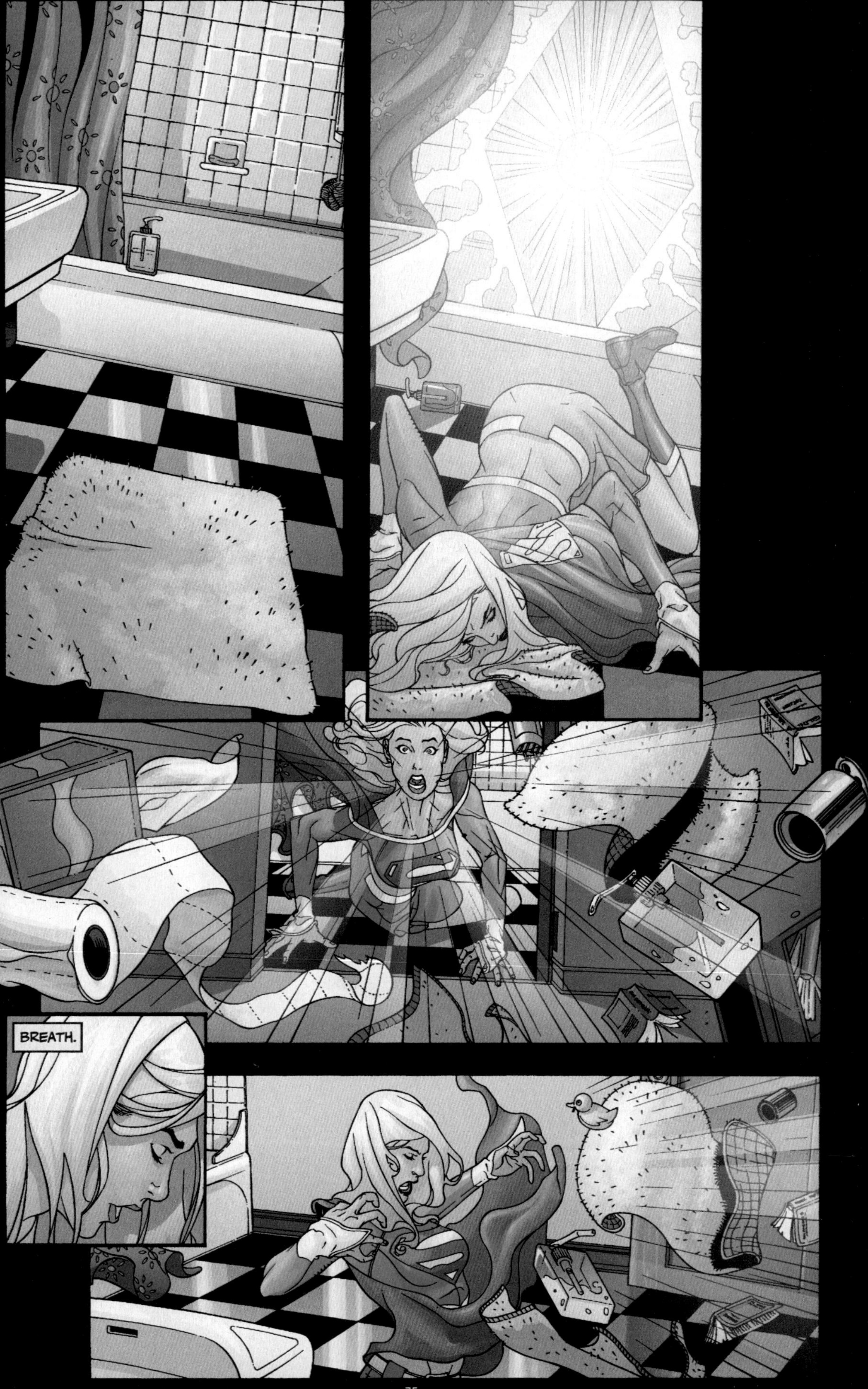
BREATH.

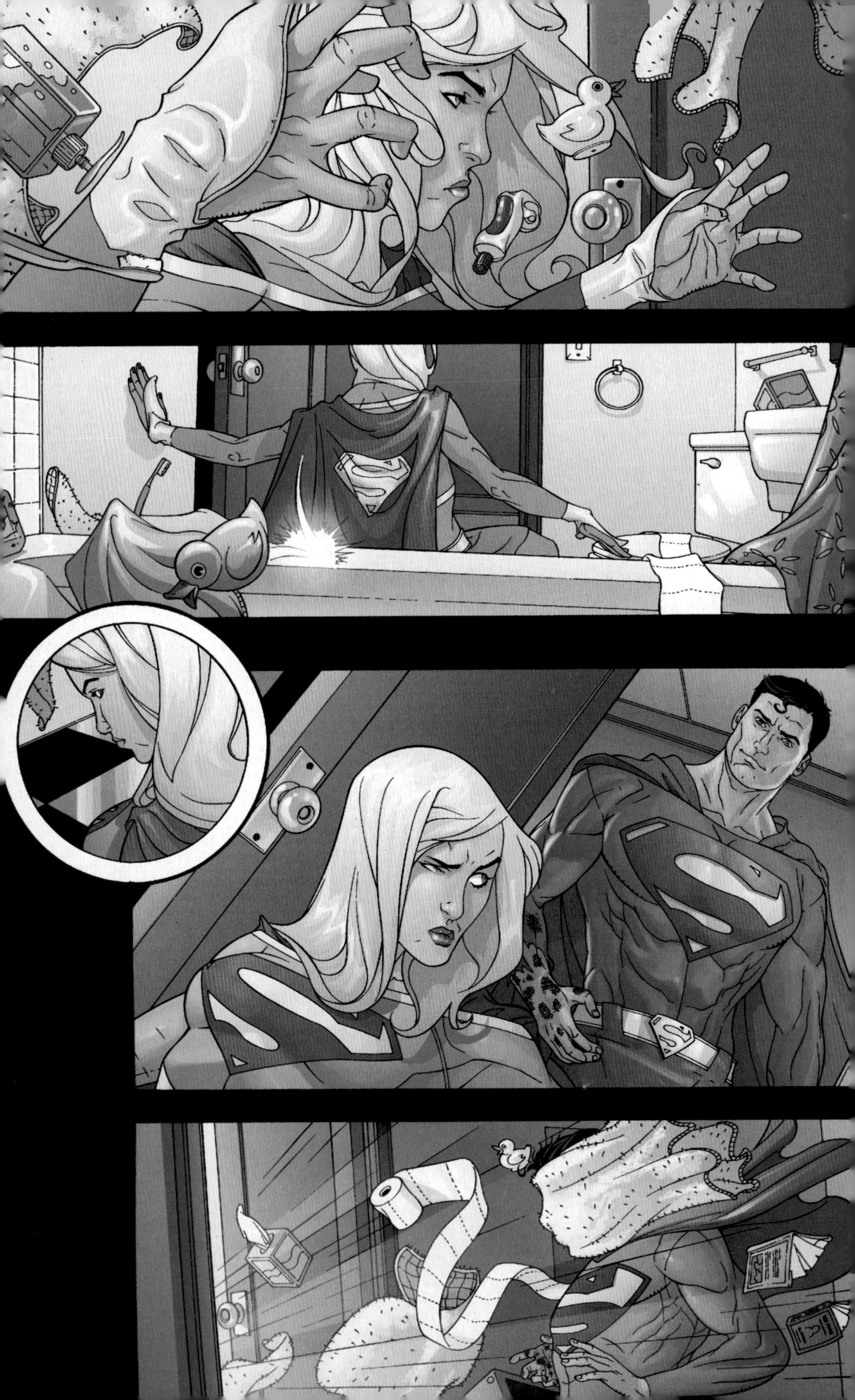

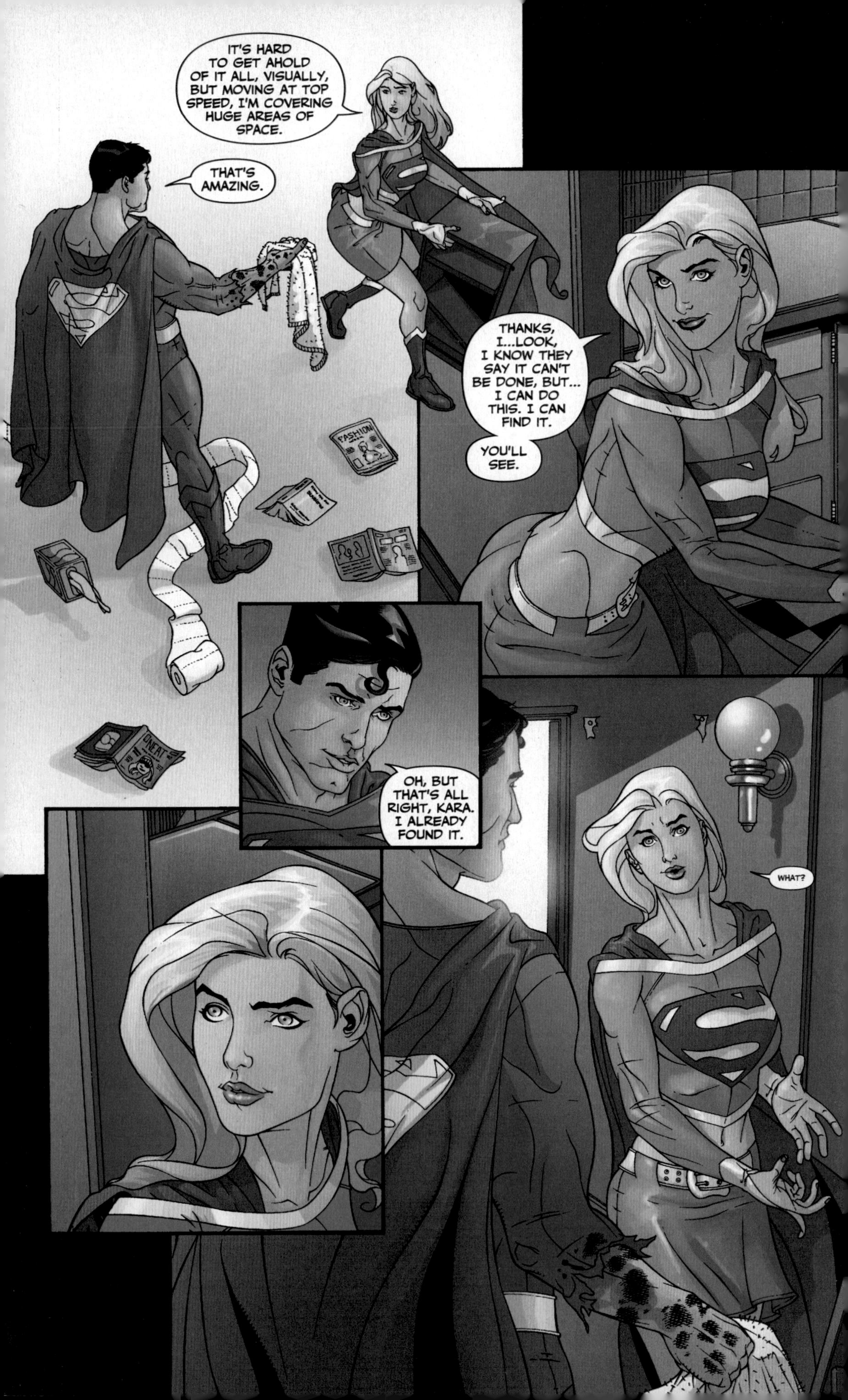
IT'S HARD TO GET AHOLD OF IT ALL, VISUALLY, BUT MOVING AT TOP SPEED, I'M COVERING HUGE AREAS OF SPACE.
THAT'S AMAZING.
THANKS, I...LOOK, I KNOW THEY SAY IT CAN'T BE DONE, BUT... I CAN DO THIS. I CAN FIND IT.
YOU'LL SEE.
OH, BUT THAT'S ALL RIGHT, KARA. I ALREADY FOUND IT.
WHAT?

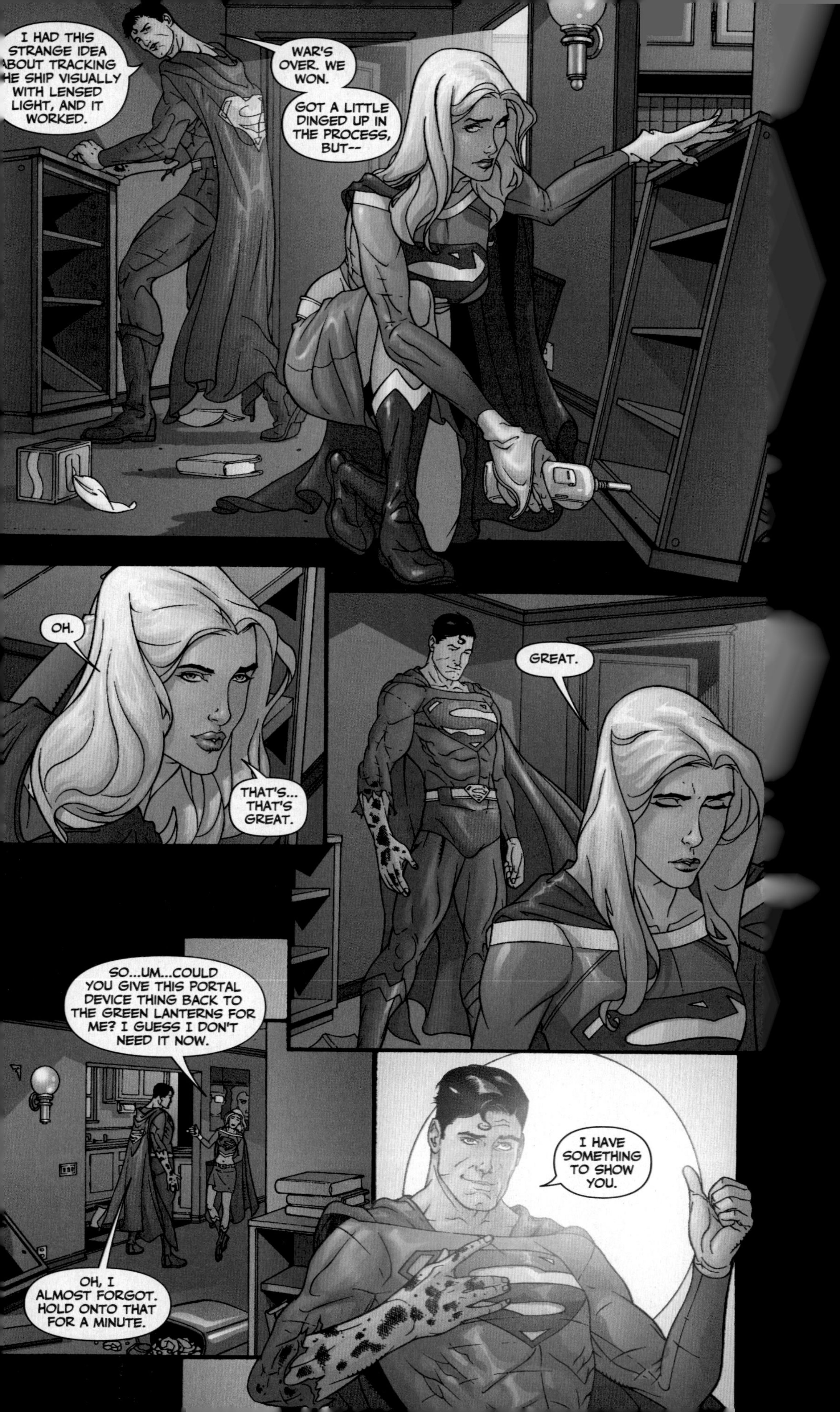

I HAD THIS STRANGE IDEA ABOUT TRACKING THE SHIP VISUALLY WITH LENSED LIGHT, AND IT WORKED.
WAR'S OVER. WE WON.
GOT A LITTLE DINGED UP IN THE PROCESS, BUT--
OH.
THAT'S... THAT'S GREAT.
GREAT.
SO...UM...COULD YOU GIVE THIS PORTAL DEVICE THING BACK TO THE GREEN LANTERNS FOR ME? I GUESS I DON'T NEED IT NOW.
OH, I ALMOST FORGOT. HOLD ONTO THAT FOR A MINUTE.
I HAVE SOMETHING TO SHOW YOU.

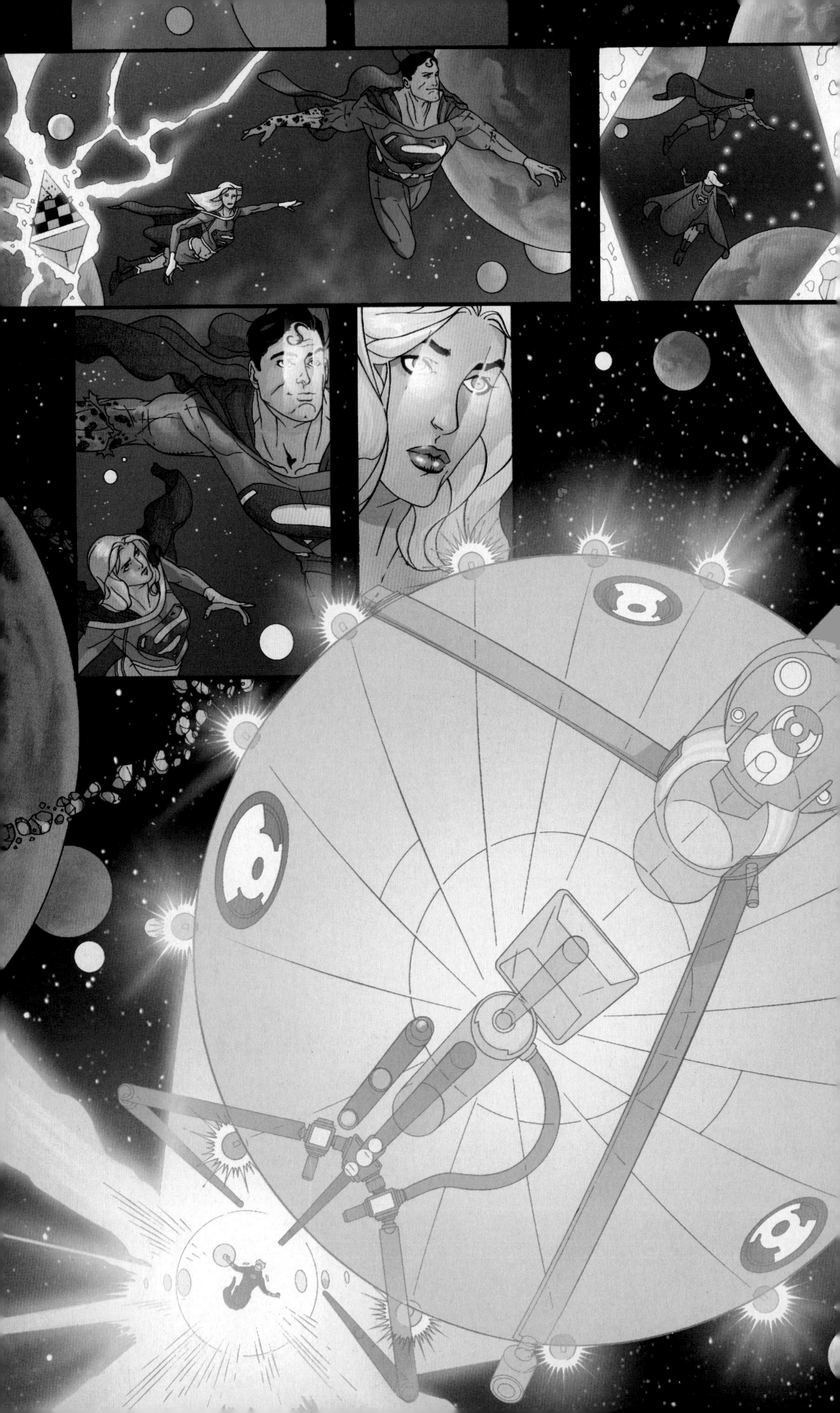

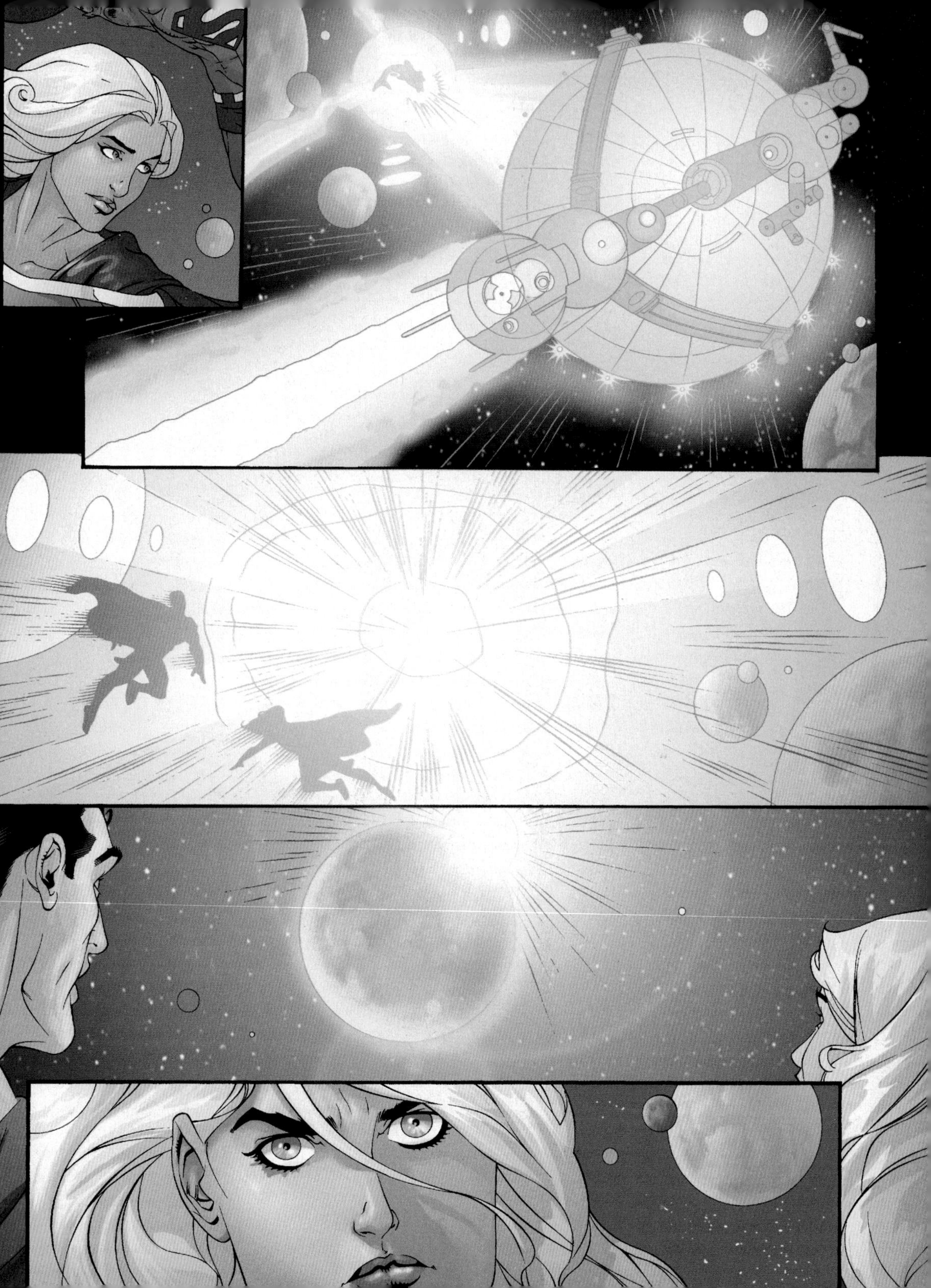

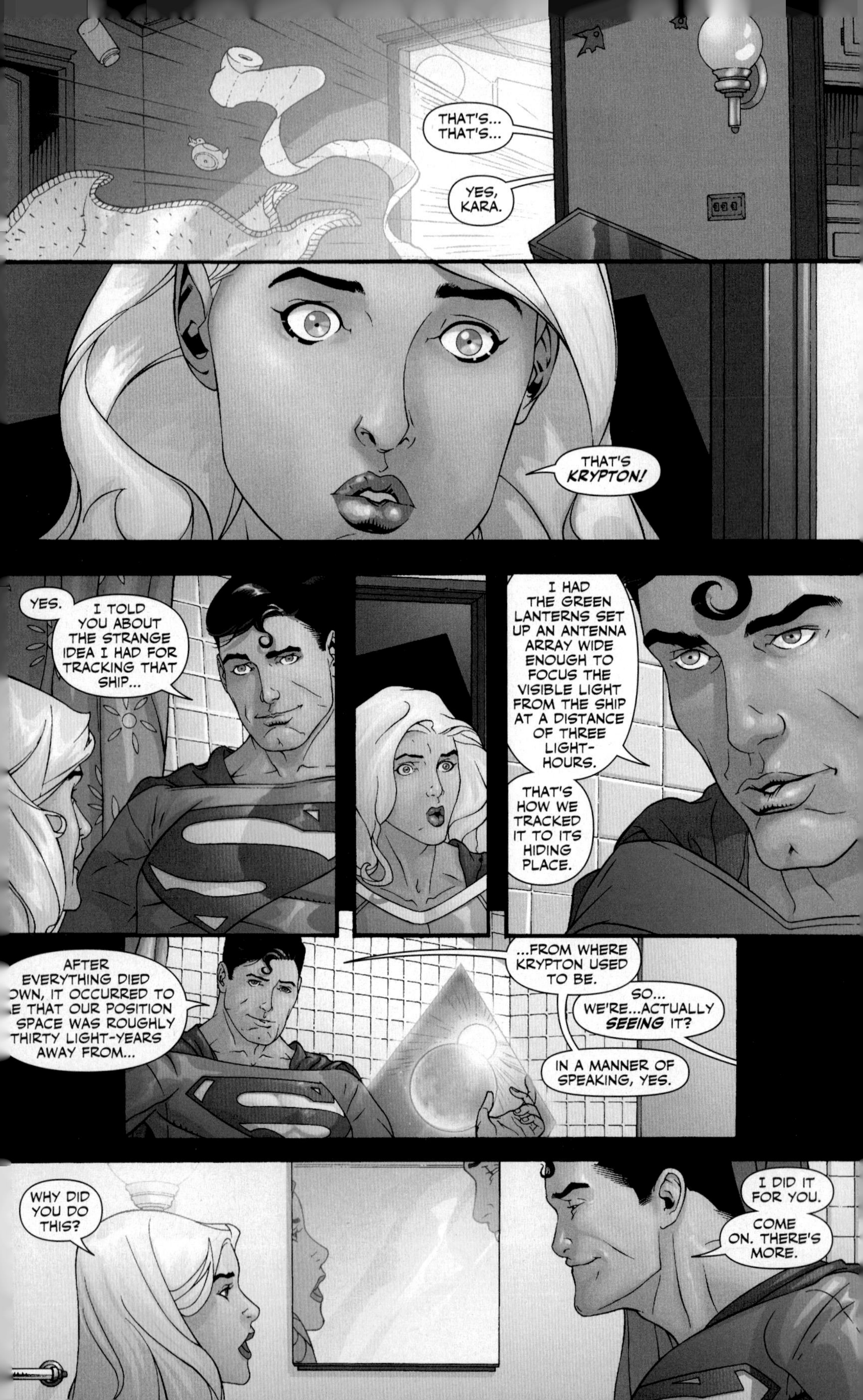
THAT'S... THAT'S...
YES, KARA.
THAT'S KRYPTON!
YES.
I TOLD YOU ABOUT THE STRANGE IDEA I HAD FOR TRACKING THAT SHIP...
I HAD THE GREEN LANTERNS SET UP AN ANTENNA ARRAY WIDE ENOUGH TO FOCUS THE VISIBLE LIGHT FROM THE SHIP AT A DISTANCE OF THREE LIGHT-HOURS.
THAT'S HOW WE TRACKED IT TO ITS HIDING PLACE.
AFTER EVERYTHING DIED OWN, IT OCCURRED TO E THAT OUR POSITION SPACE WAS ROUGHLY THIRTY LIGHT-YEARS AWAY FROM...
...FROM WHERE KRYPTON USED TO BE.
SO... WE'RE...ACTUALLY SEEING IT?
IN A MANNER OF SPEAKING, YES.
WHY DID YOU DO THIS?
I DID IT FOR YOU.
COME ON. THERE'S MORE.

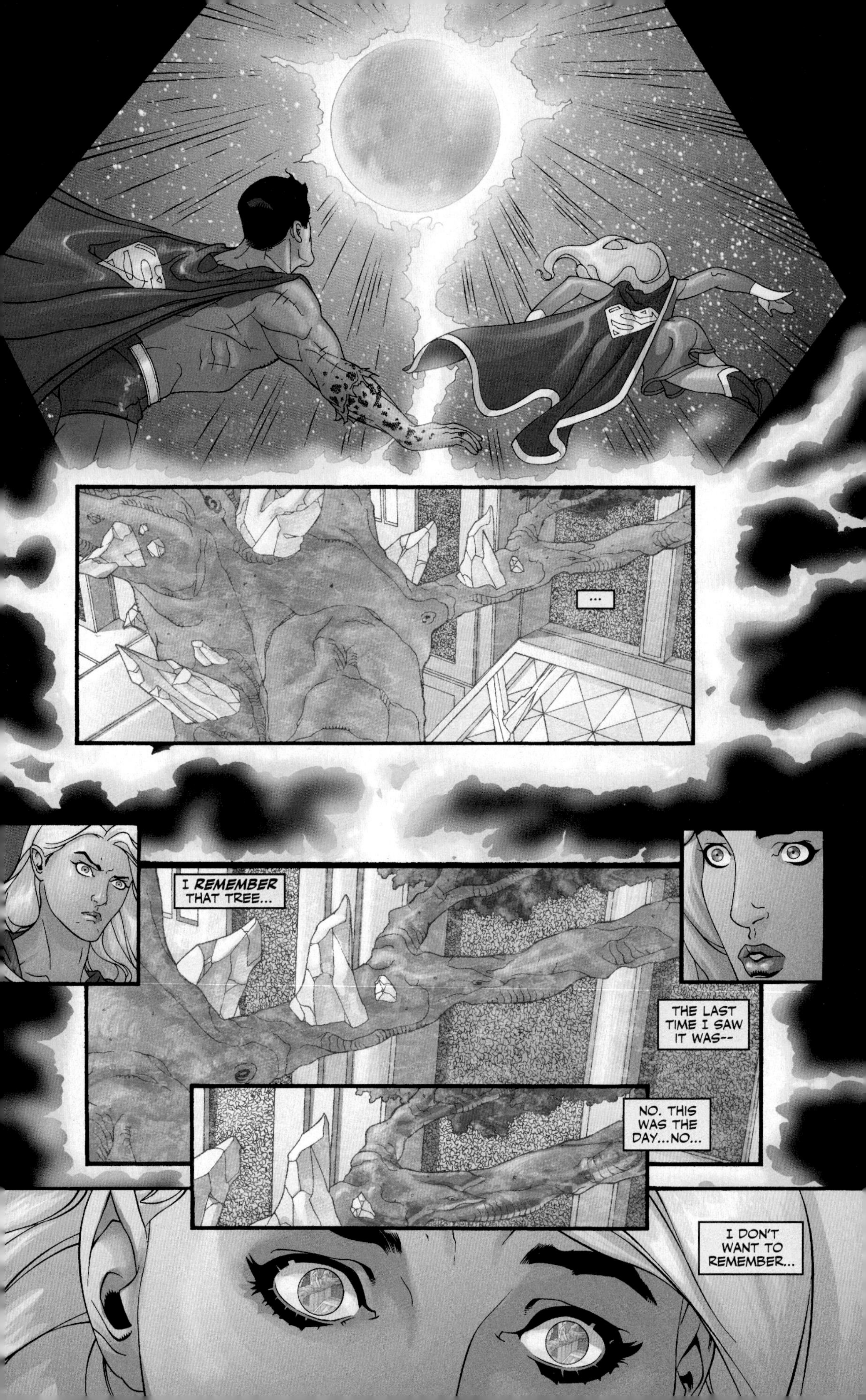
...
I REMEMBER THAT TREE...
THE LAST TIME I SAW IT WAS--
NO. THIS WAS THE DAY...NO...
I DON'T WANT TO REMEMBER...

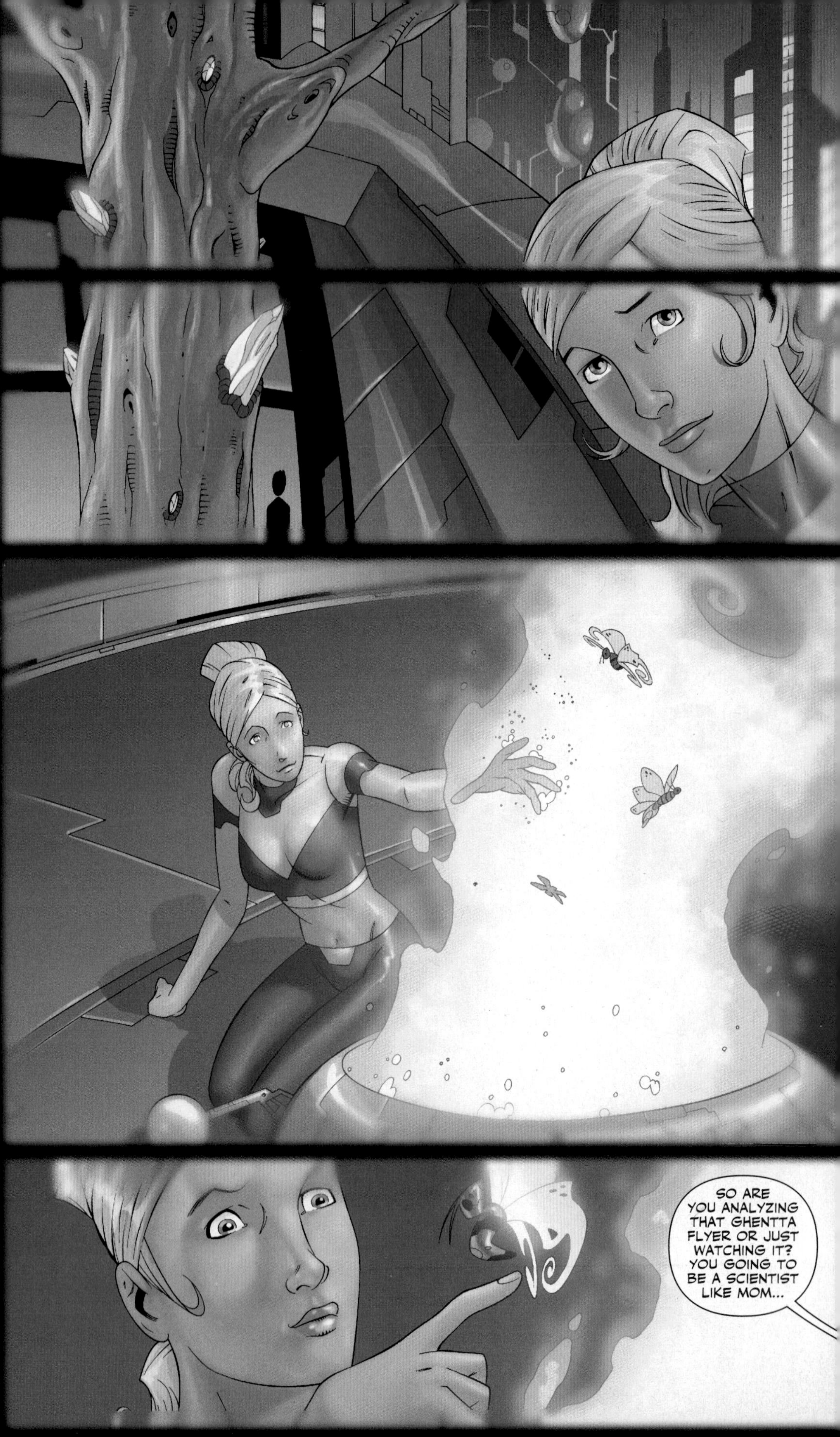
SO ARE YOU ANALYZING THAT GHENTTA FLYER OR JUST WATCHING IT? YOU GOING TO BE A SCIENTIST LIKE MOM...

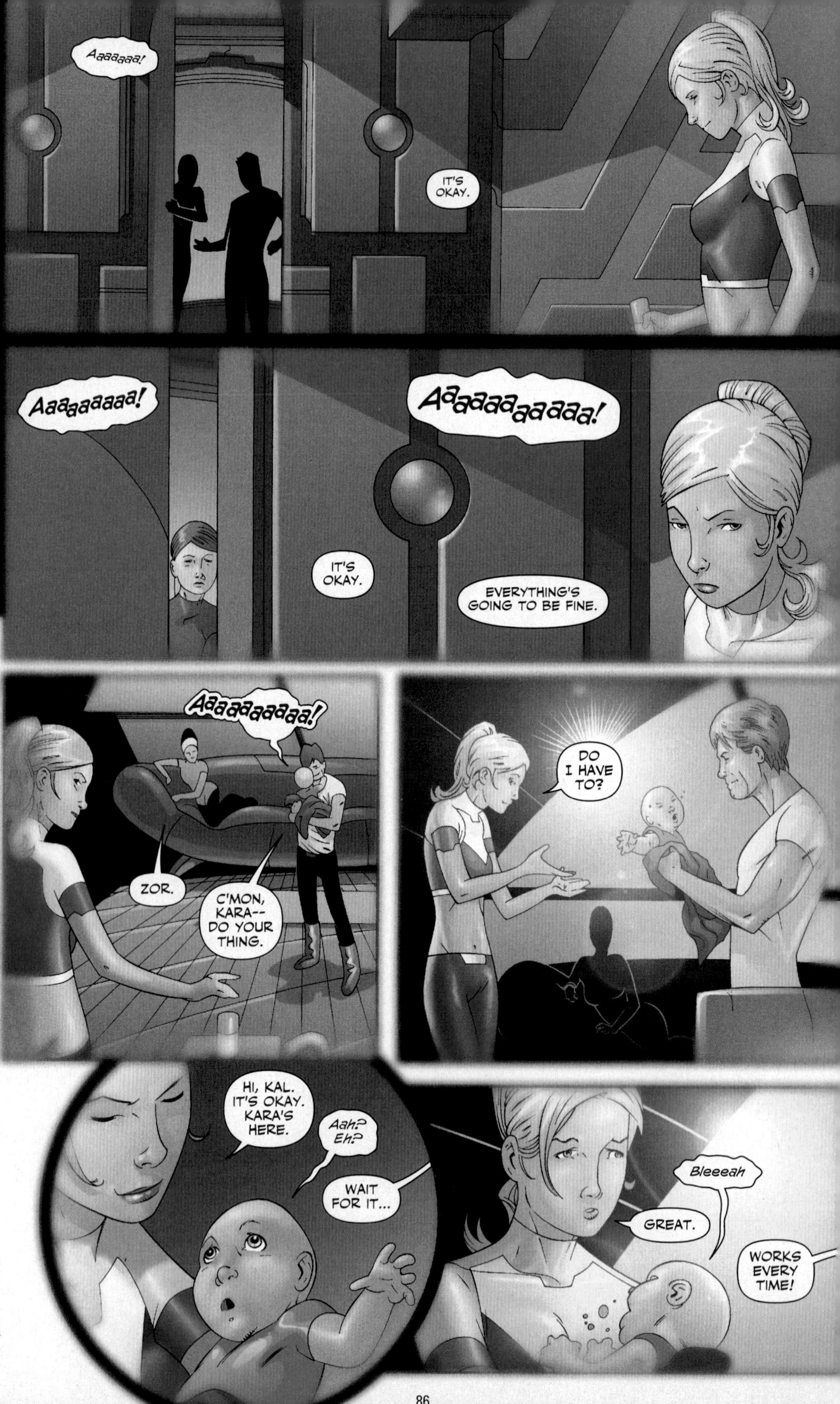

Aaaaaaa!
IT'S OKAY.
Aaaaaaaaa!
Aaaaaaaaaaaa!
IT'S OKAY.
EVERYTHING'S GOING TO BE FINE.
Aaaaaaaaaaa!
ZOR.
C'MON, KARA-- DO YOUR THING.
DO I HAVE TO?
HI, KAL. IT'S OKAY. KARA'S HERE.
Aah? Eh?
WAIT FOR IT...
Bleeeah
GREAT.
WORKS EVERY TIME!

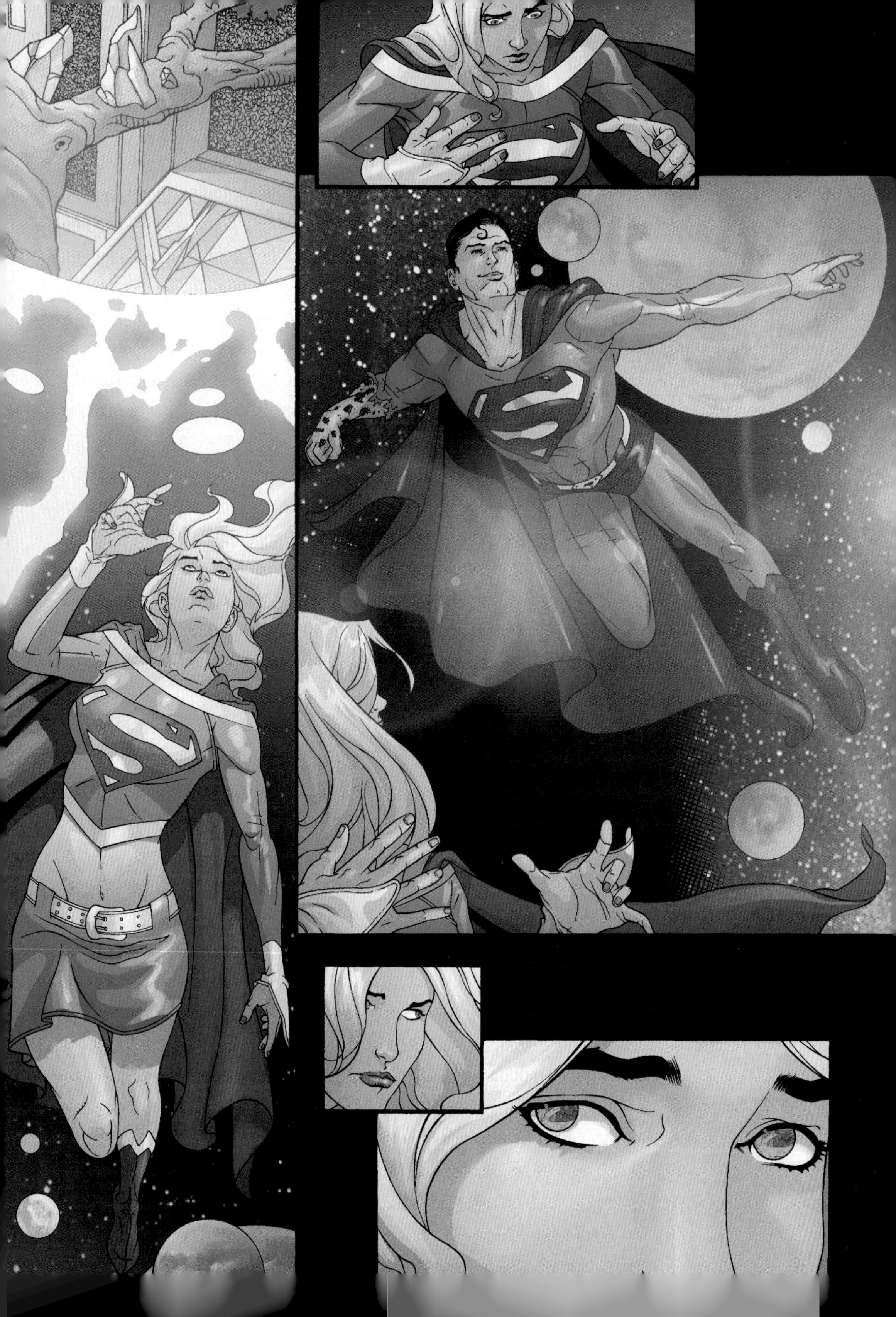

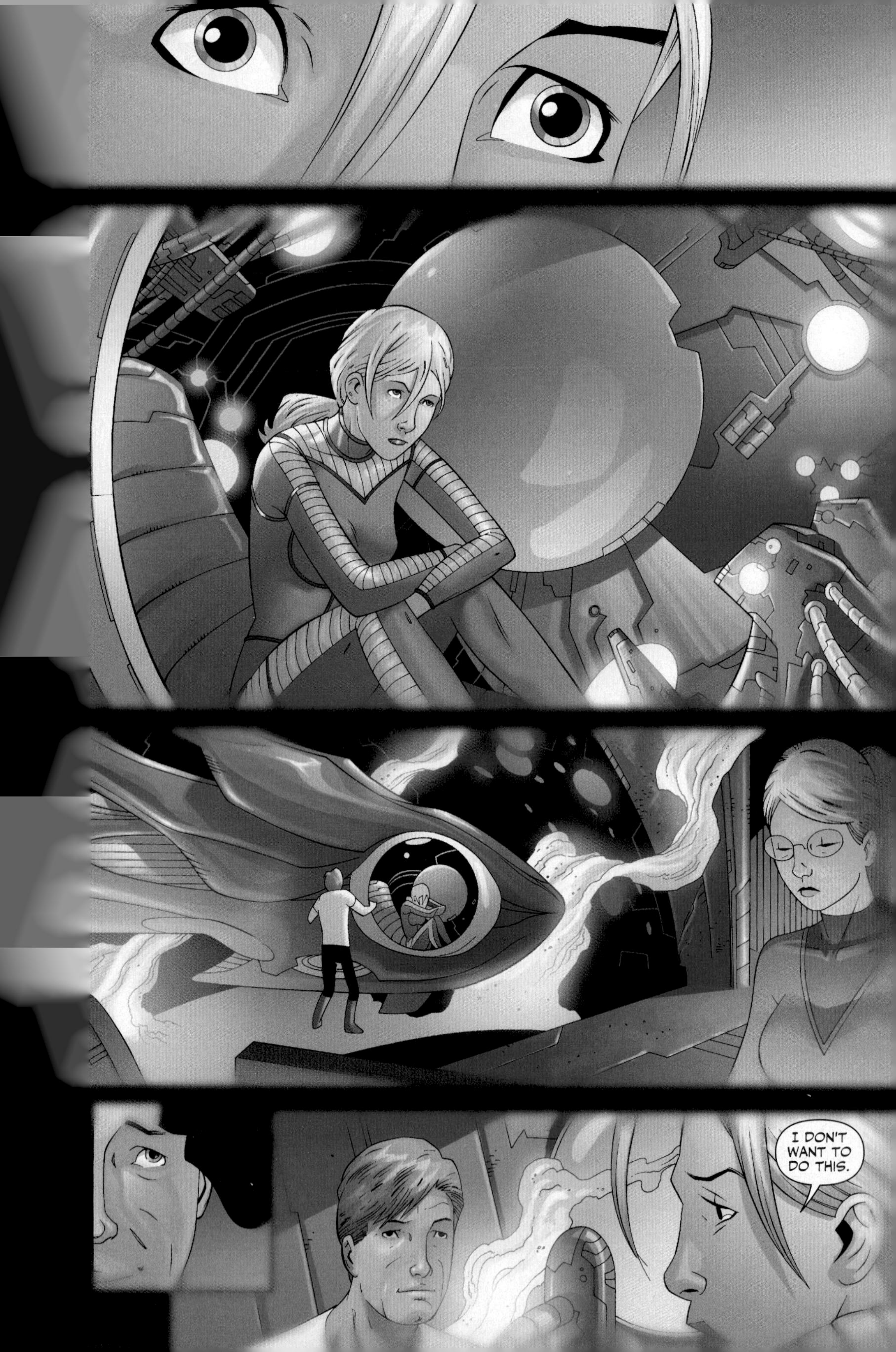
I DON'T WANT TO DO THIS.

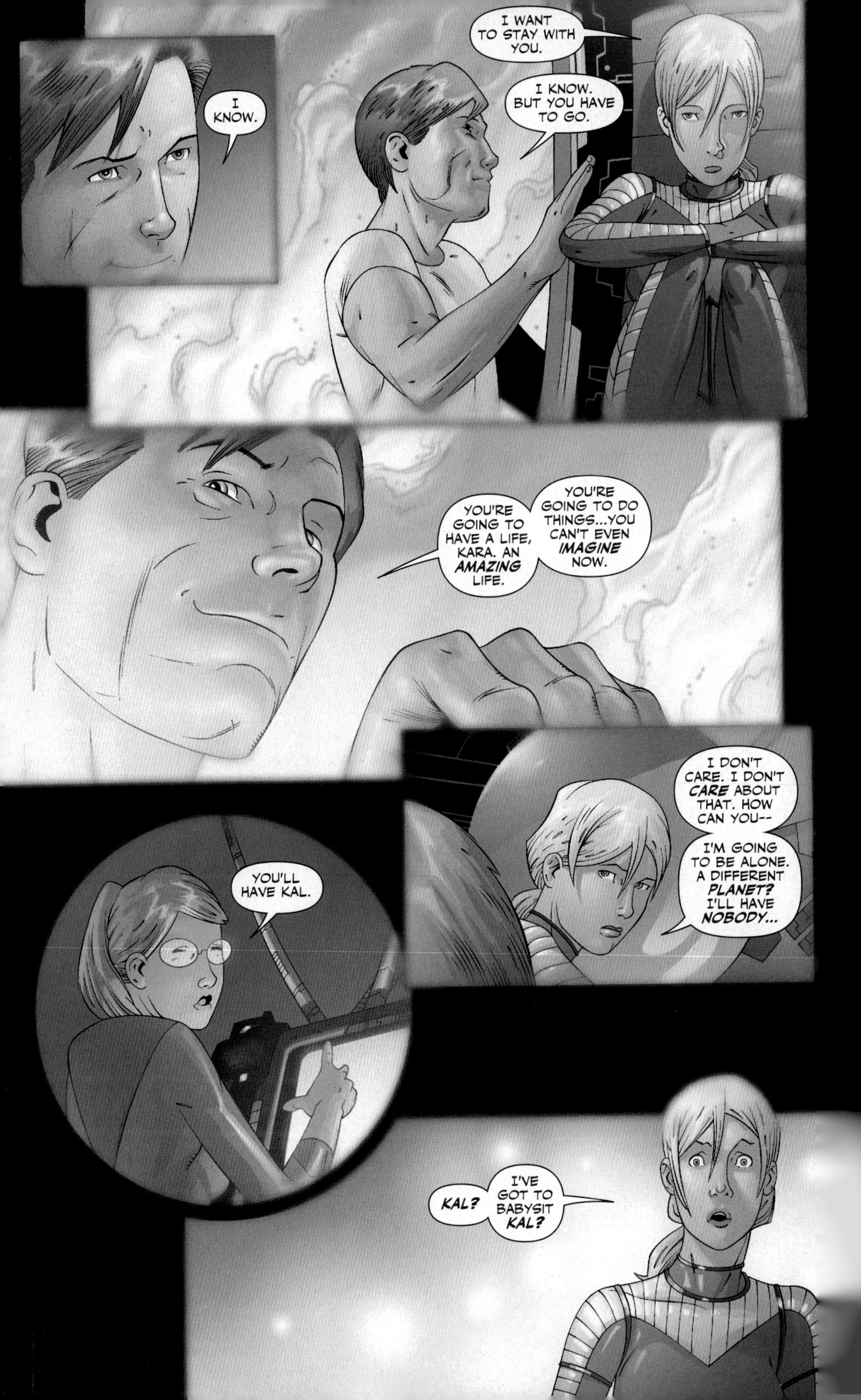
I WANT TO STAY WITH YOU.
I KNOW. BUT YOU HAVE TO GO.
I KNOW.
YOU'RE GOING TO HAVE A LIFE, KARA. AN AMAZING LIFE.
YOU'RE GOING TO DO THINGS...YOU CAN'T EVEN IMAGINE NOW.
I DON'T CARE. I DON'T CARE ABOUT THAT. HOW CAN YOU--
I'M GOING TO BE ALONE. A DIFFERENT PLANET? I'LL HAVE NOBODY...
YOU'LL HAVE KAL.
KAL?
I'VE GOT TO BABYSIT KAL?

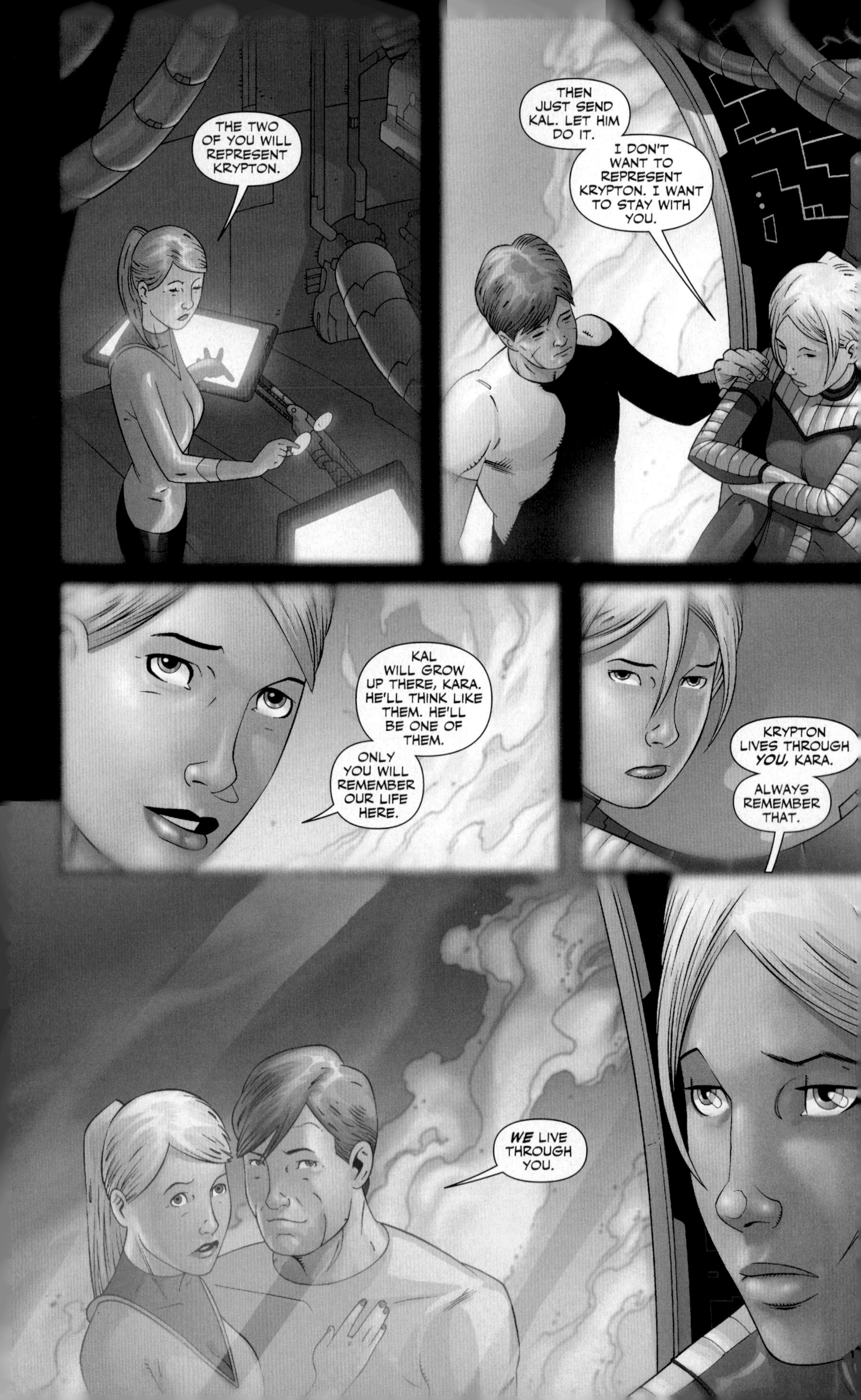
THE TWO OF YOU WILL REPRESENT KRYPTON.
THEN JUST SEND KAL. LET HIM DO IT.
I DON'T WANT TO REPRESENT KRYPTON. I WANT TO STAY WITH YOU.
KAL WILL GROW UP THERE, KARA. HE'LL THINK LIKE THEM. HE'LL BE ONE OF THEM.
ONLY YOU WILL REMEMBER OUR LIFE HERE.
KRYPTON LIVES THROUGH *YOU,* KARA.
ALWAYS REMEMBER THAT.
WE LIVE THROUGH YOU.

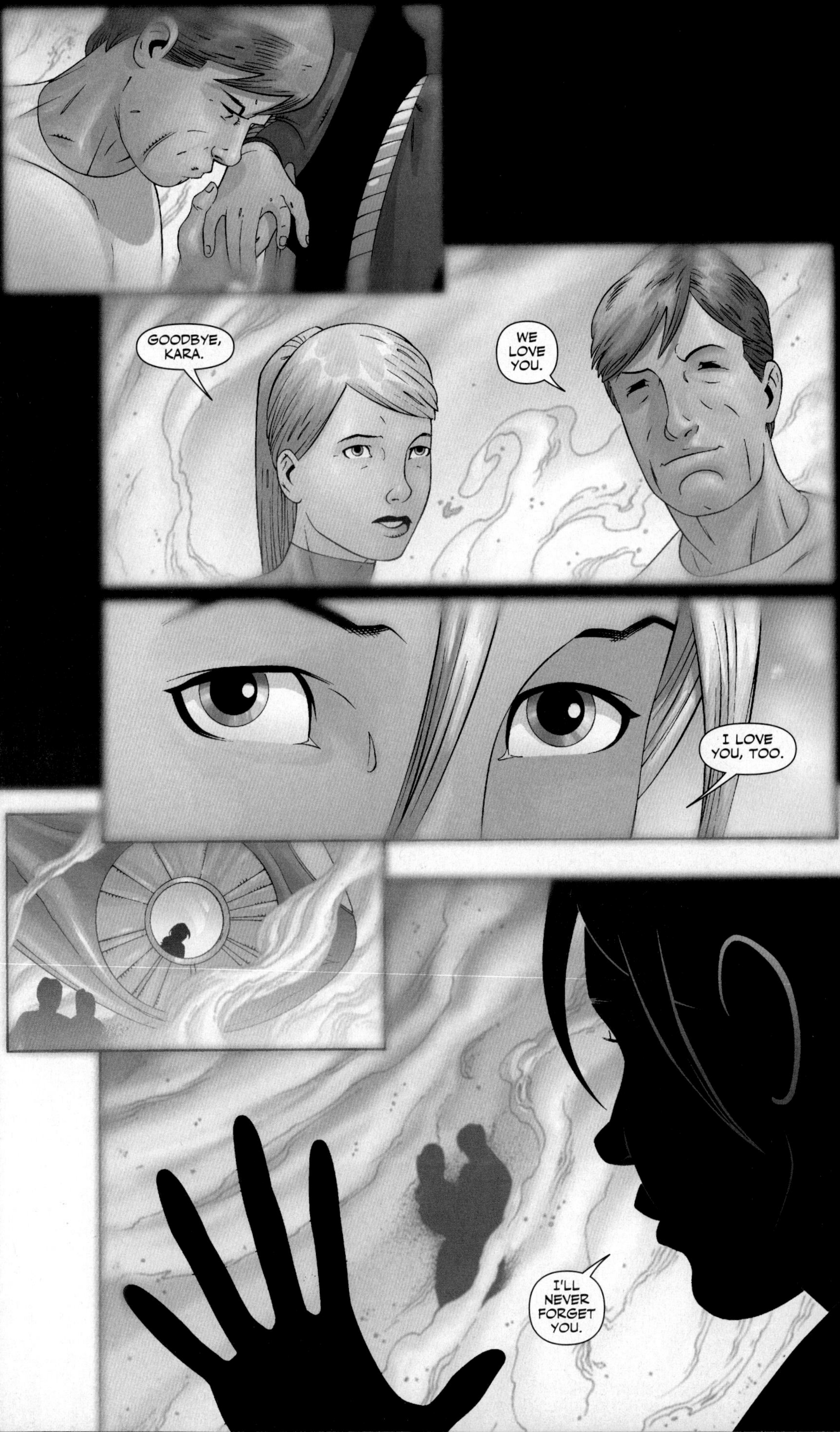
GOODBYE, KARA.
WE LOVE YOU.
I LOVE YOU, TOO.
I'LL NEVER FORGET YOU.

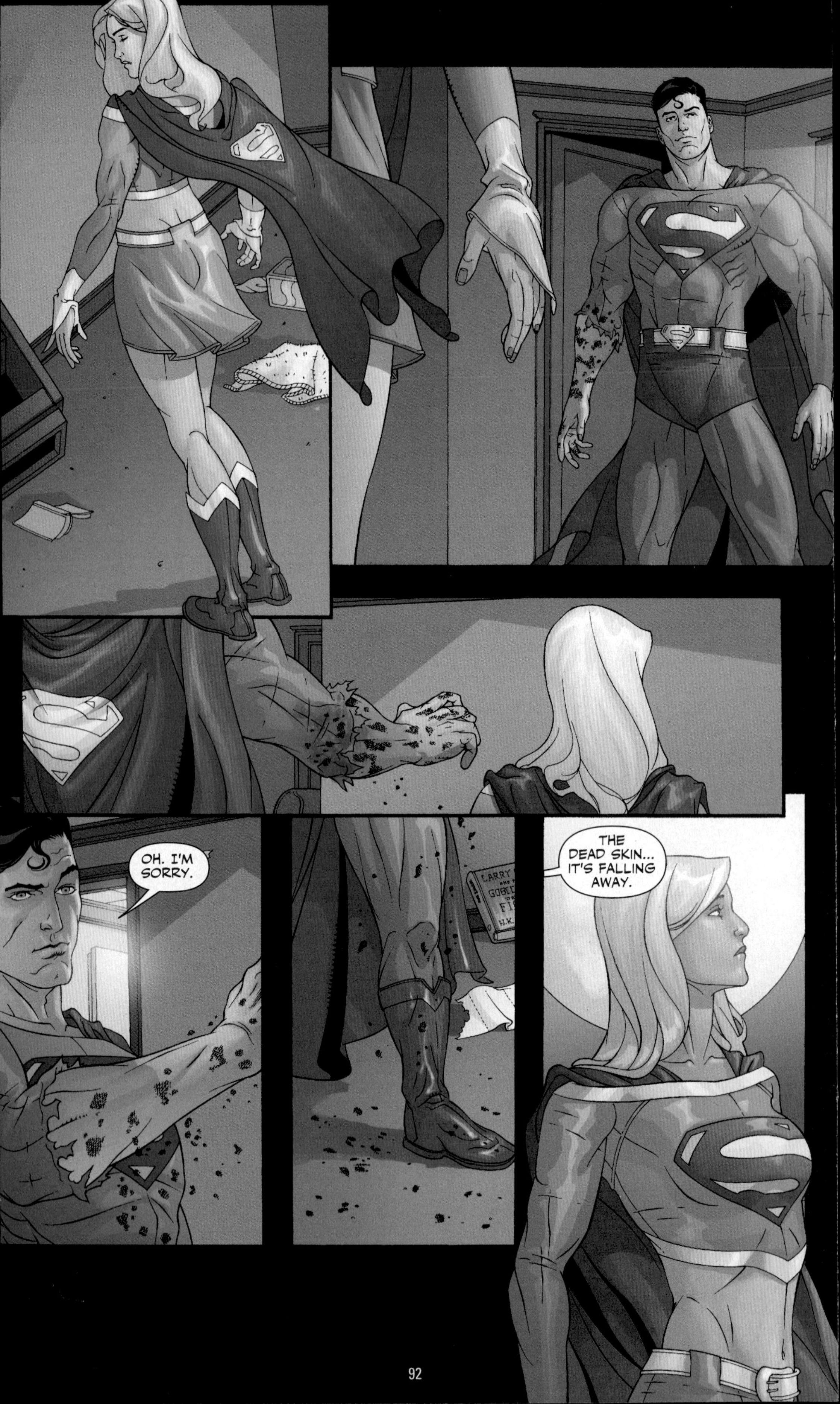
OH. I'M SORRY.
THE DEAD SKIN... IT'S FALLING AWAY.

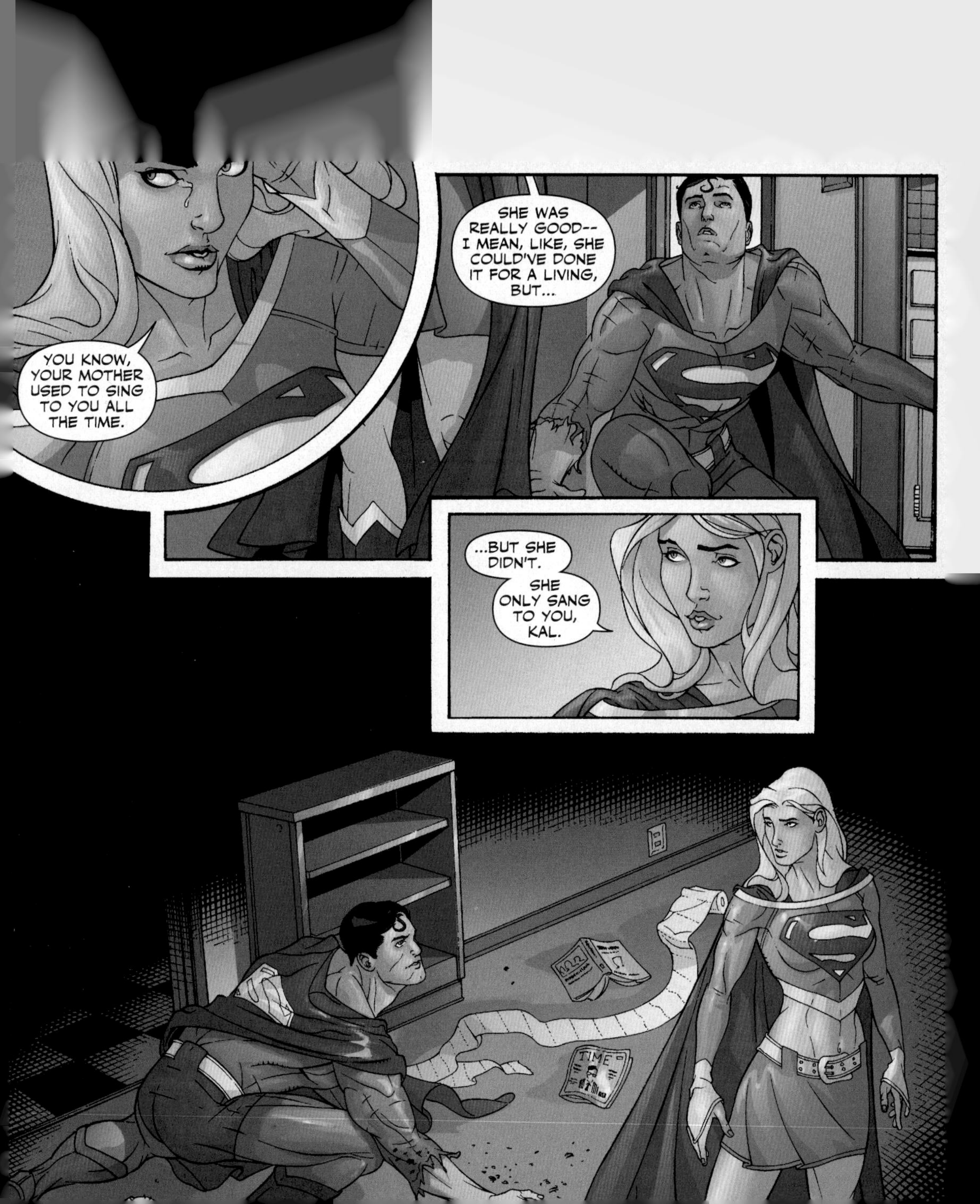
YOU KNOW, YOUR MOTHER USED TO SING TO YOU ALL THE TIME.
SHE WAS REALLY GOOD-- I MEAN, LIKE, SHE COULD'VE DONE IT FOR A LIVING, BUT...
...BUT SHE DIDN'T.
SHE ONLY SANG TO YOU, KAL.
TIME

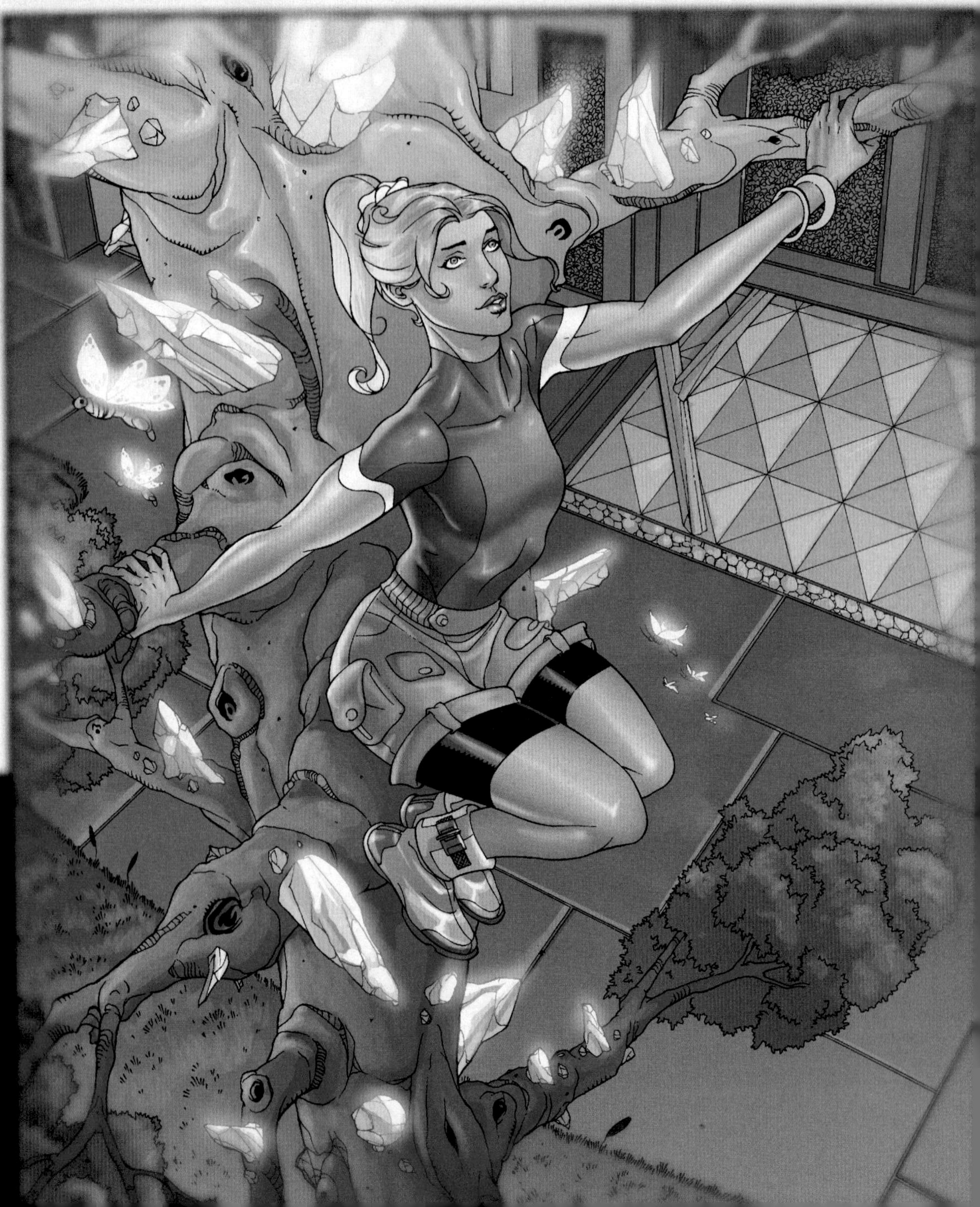

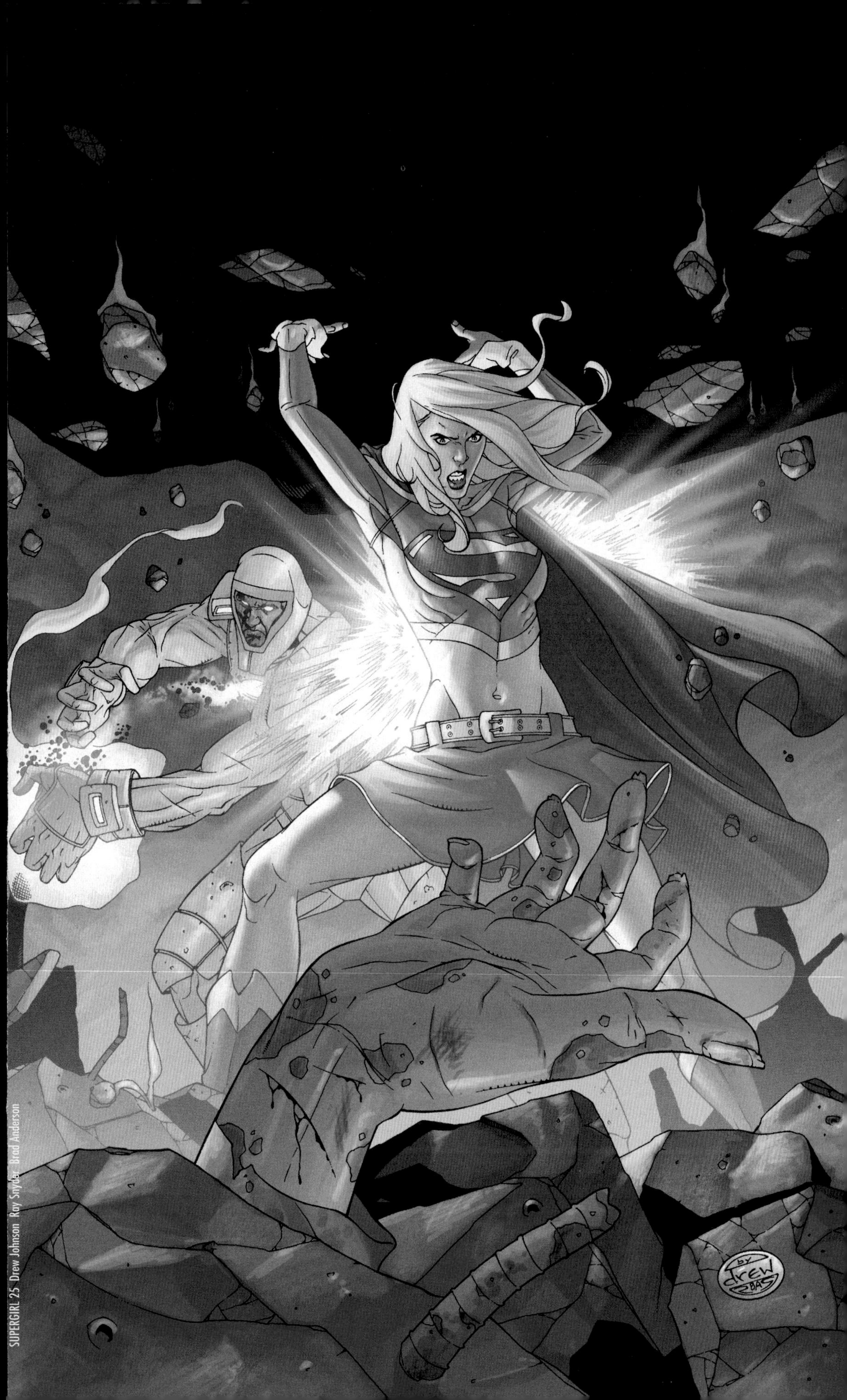

SUPERGIRL 25 Drew Johnson Ray Snyder Brad Anderson

BOOM

KELLEY PUCKETT WRITER
DREW JOHNSON LEE FERGUSON PENCILS
RAY SNYDER INKS

YOU ALWAYS STOOD BY ME, NO MATTER WHAT, KARA. FRIENDS FOREVER!
MY CEILING CRUSHED MY SKULL WHILE I SLEPT.
YOU WANTED TO KISS ME THAT TIME BY THE SPIRE. I WANTED TO KISS YOU, TOO.
I MADE IT THROUGH THE QUAKES AND WAS FLASH-ROASTED BY A STEAM GEYSER.
WE LOVE YOU, DEAR. WE ALWAYS WILL.
WE WERE VAPORIZED INSTANTLY.

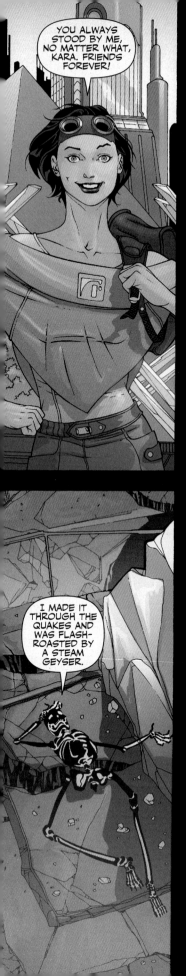

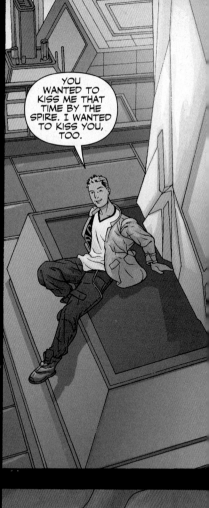

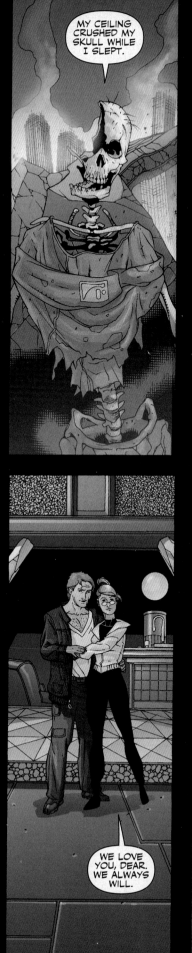

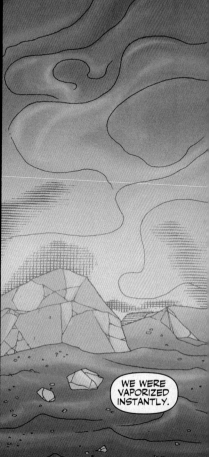

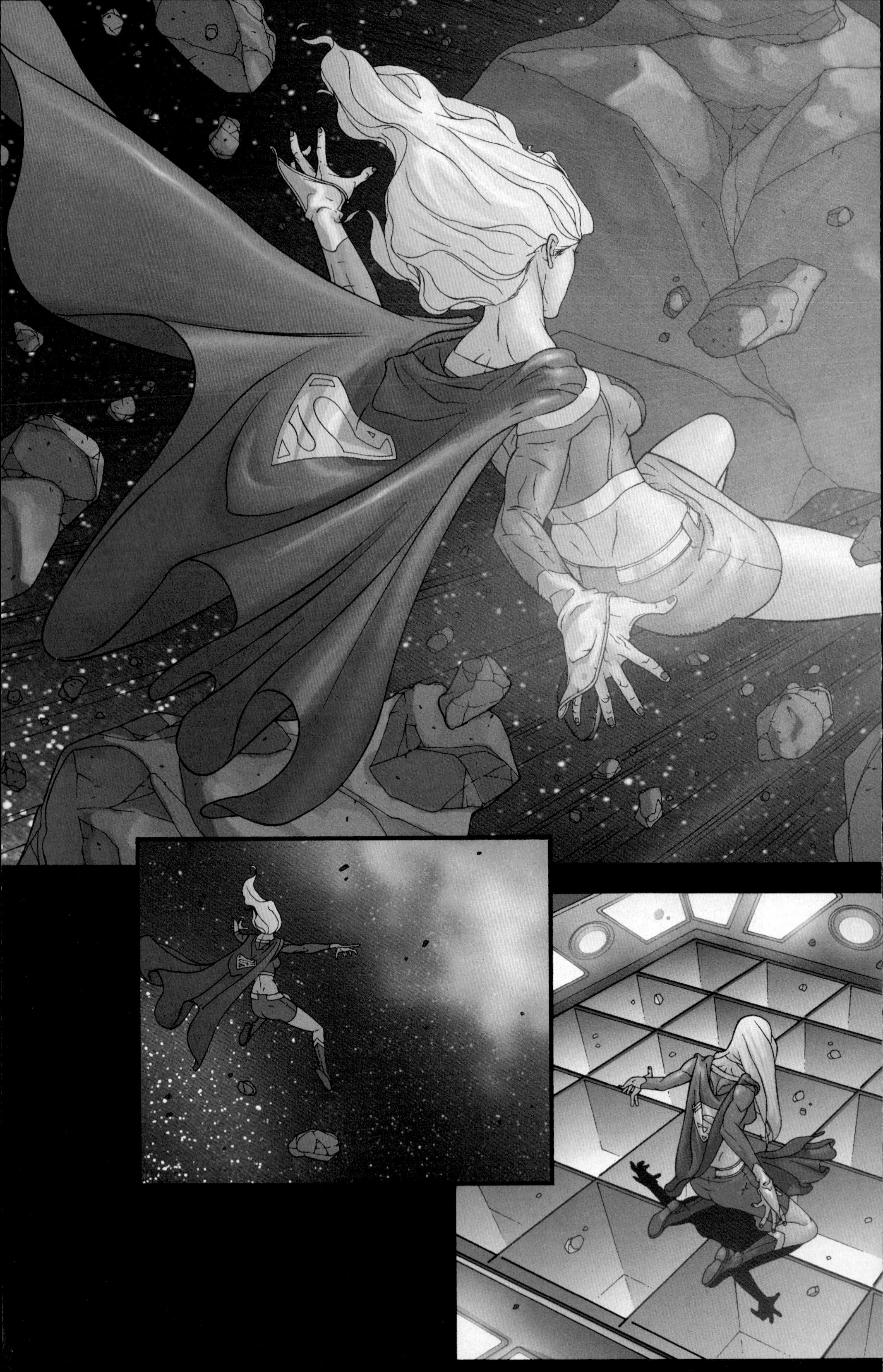

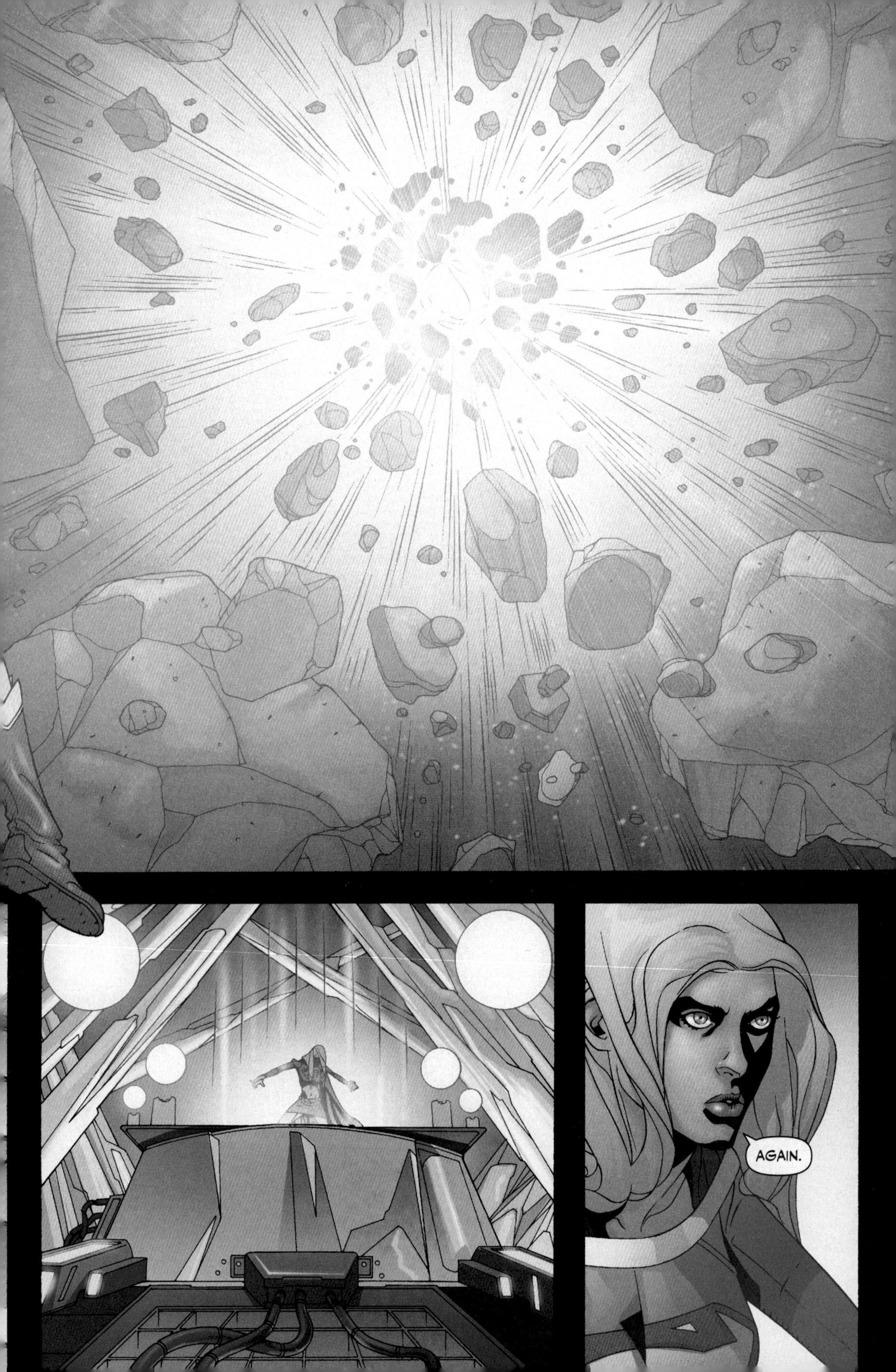
AGAIN.

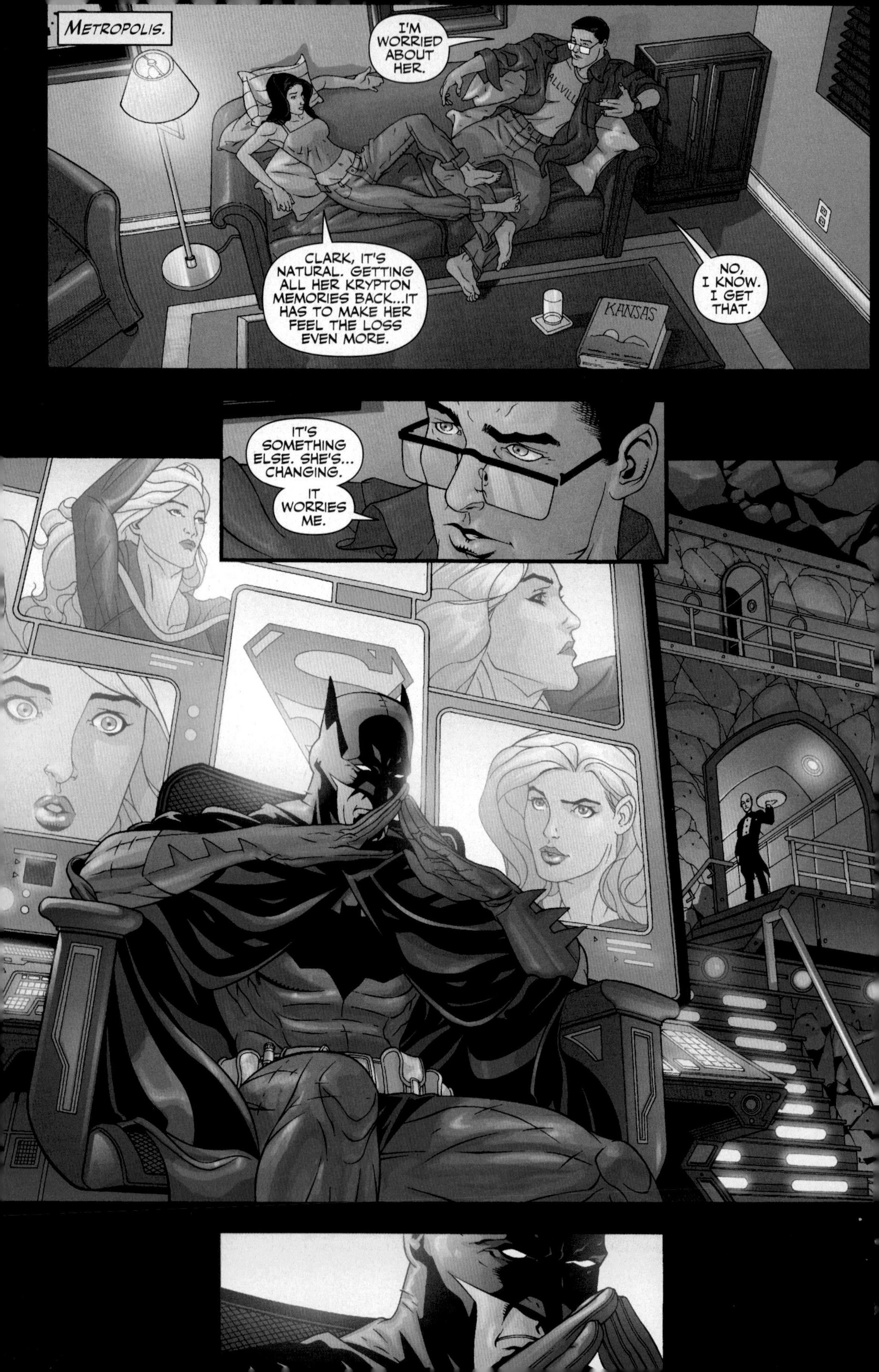
METROPOLIS.
I'M WORRIED ABOUT HER.
CLARK, IT'S NATURAL. GETTING ALL HER KRYPTON MEMORIES BACK...IT HAS TO MAKE HER FEEL THE LOSS EVEN MORE.
NO, I KNOW. I GET THAT.
KANSAS
IT'S SOMETHING ELSE. SHE'S... CHANGING.
IT WORRIES ME.

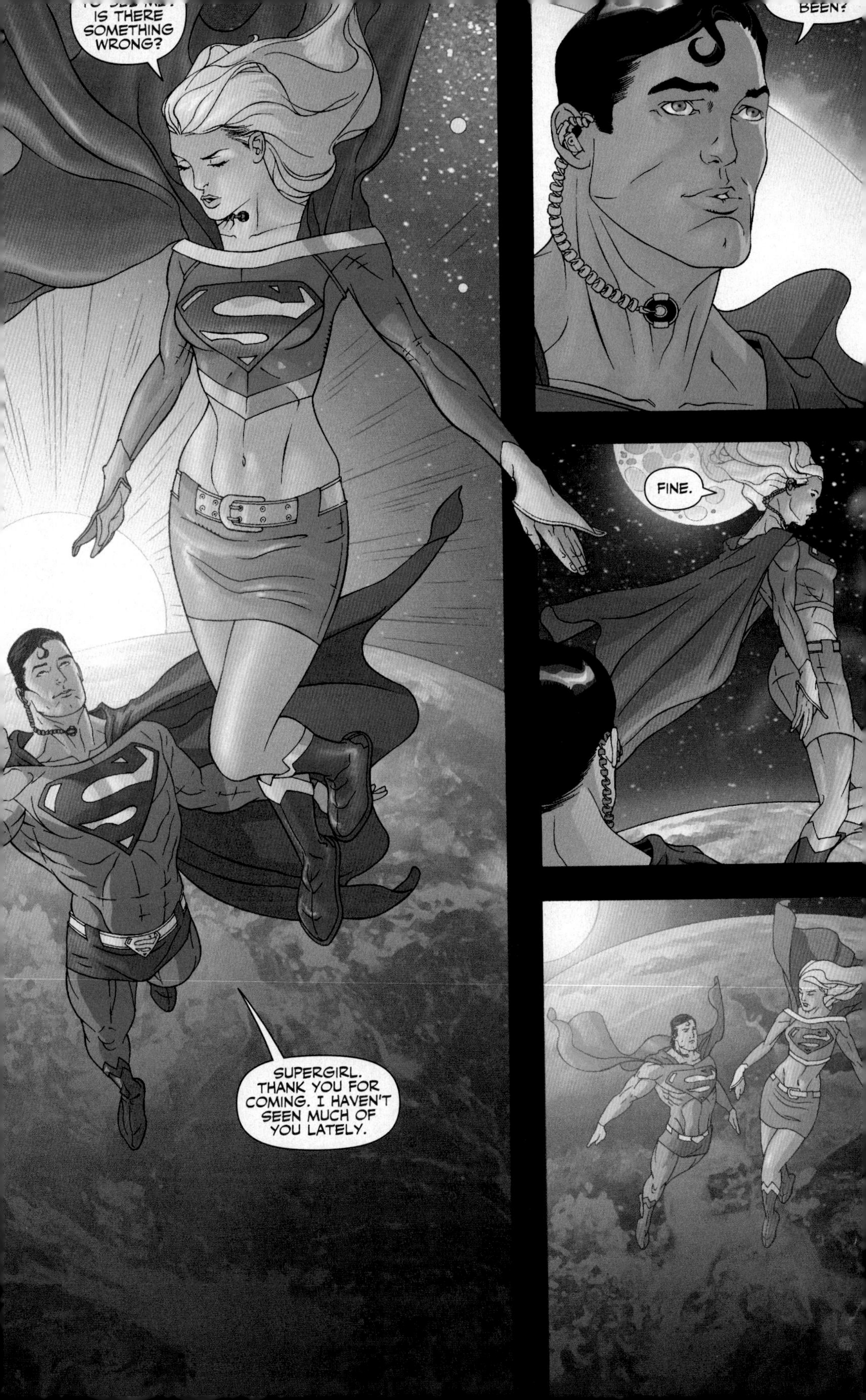
IS THERE SOMETHING WRONG?
SUPERGIRL. THANK YOU FOR COMING. I HAVEN'T SEEN MUCH OF YOU LATELY.
BEEN?
FINE.

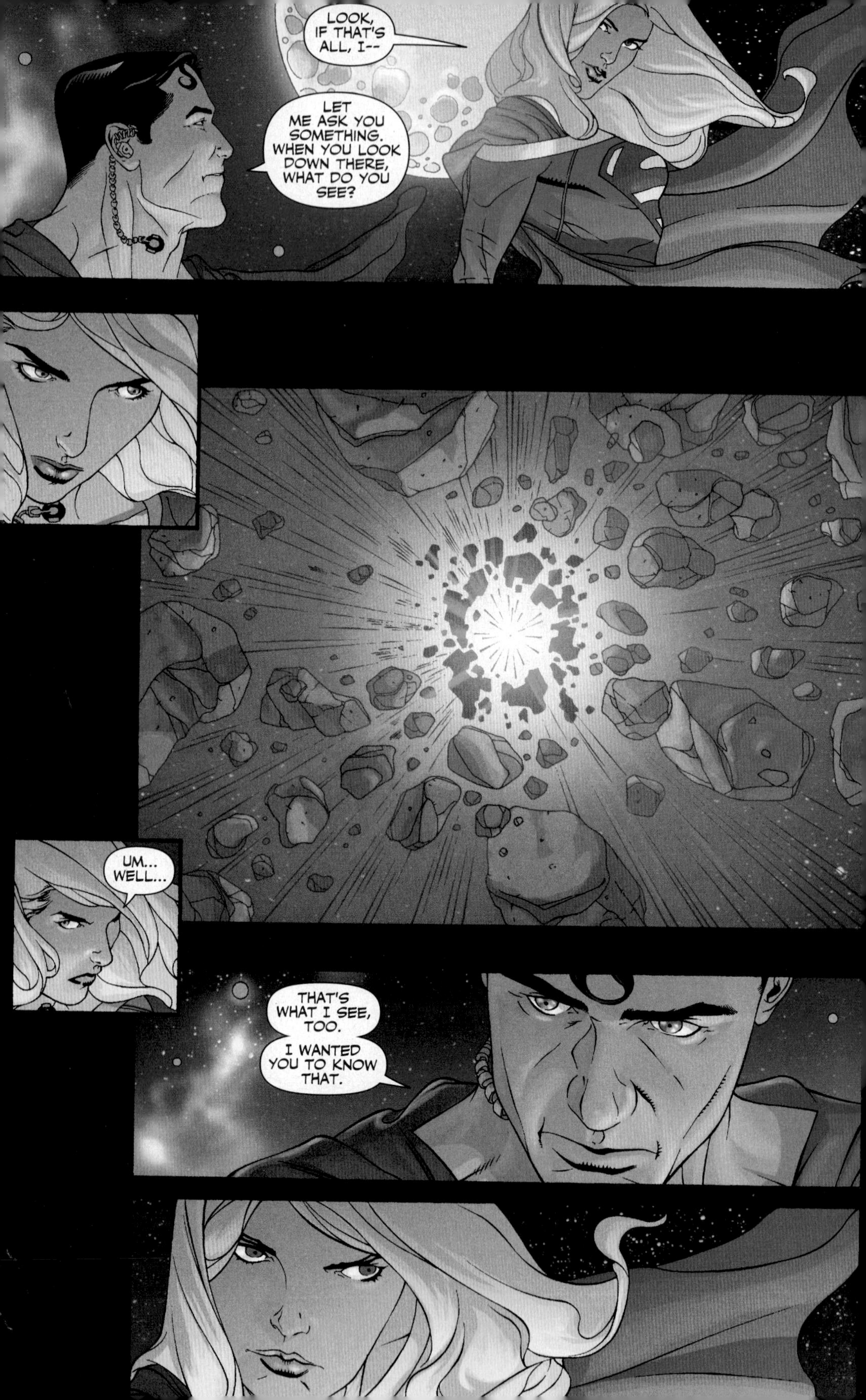
LOOK, IF THAT'S ALL, I--
LET ME ASK YOU SOMETHING. WHEN YOU LOOK DOWN THERE, WHAT DO YOU SEE?
UM... WELL...
THAT'S WHAT I SEE, TOO.
I WANTED YOU TO KNOW THAT.

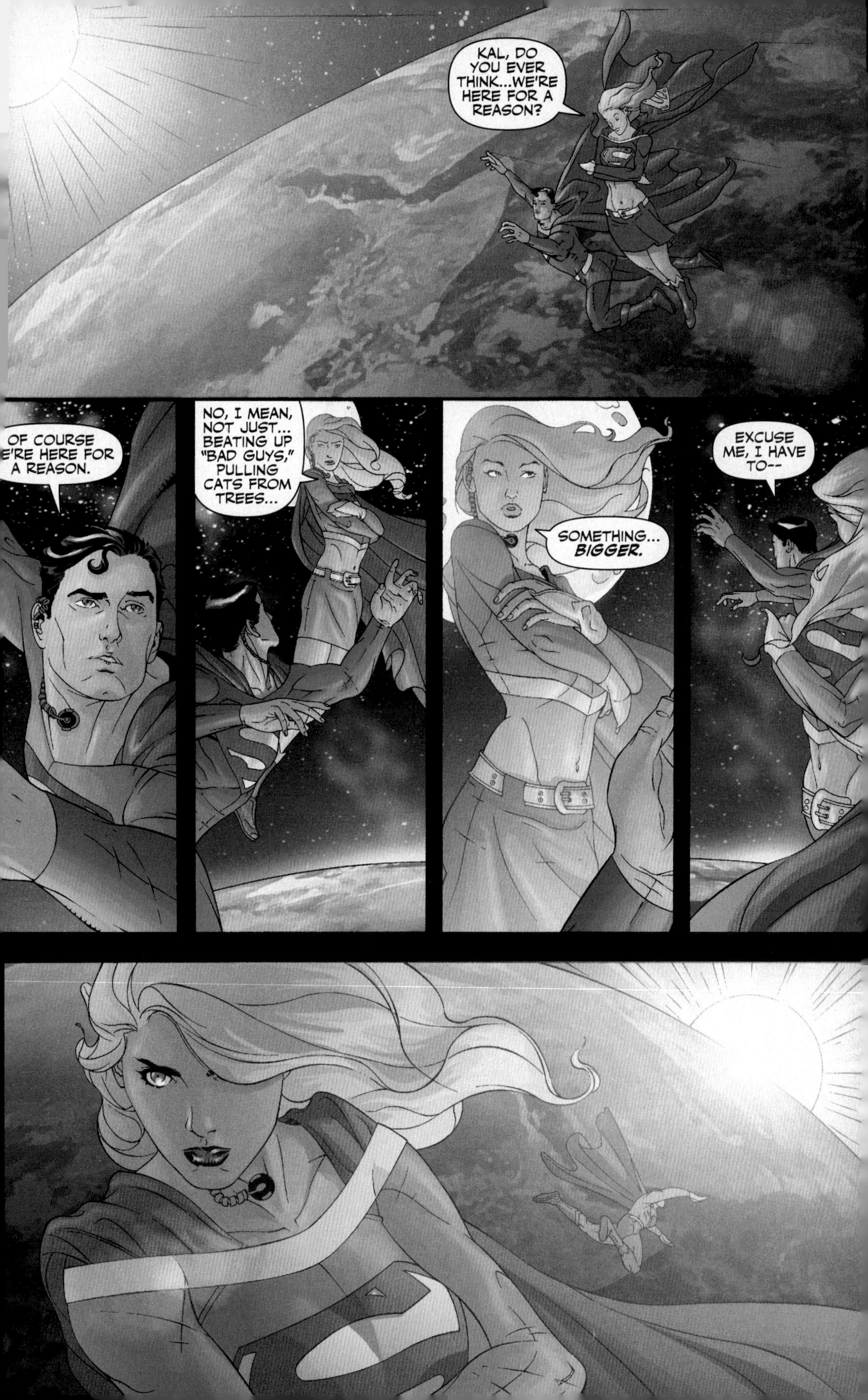
KAL, DO YOU EVER THINK...WE'RE HERE FOR A REASON?
OF COURSE E'RE HERE FOR A REASON.
NO, I MEAN, NOT JUST... BEATING UP "BAD GUYS," PULLING CATS FROM TREES...
SOMETHING... BIGGER.
EXCUSE ME, I HAVE TO--

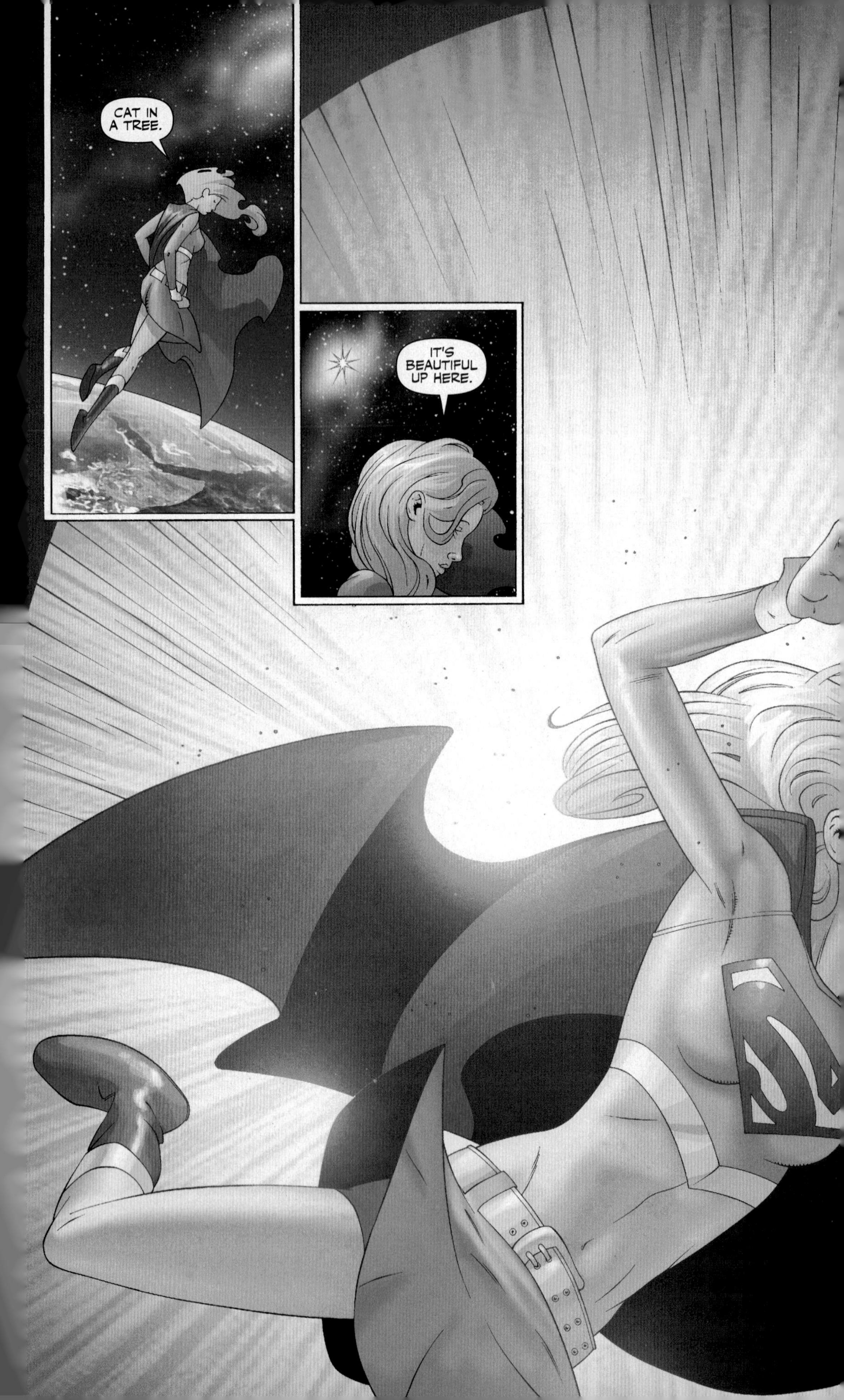
CAT IN A TREE.
IT'S BEAUTIFUL UP HERE.

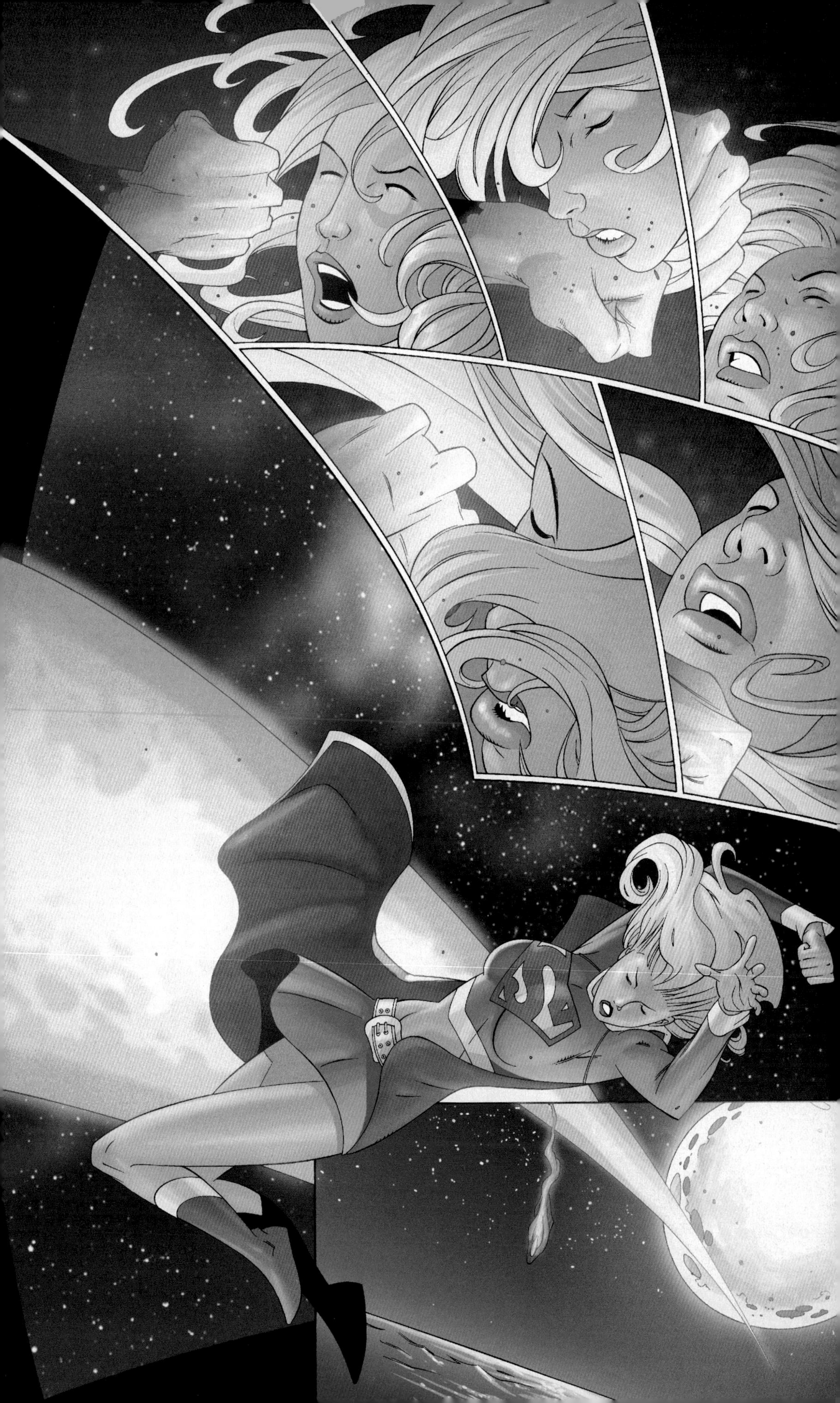

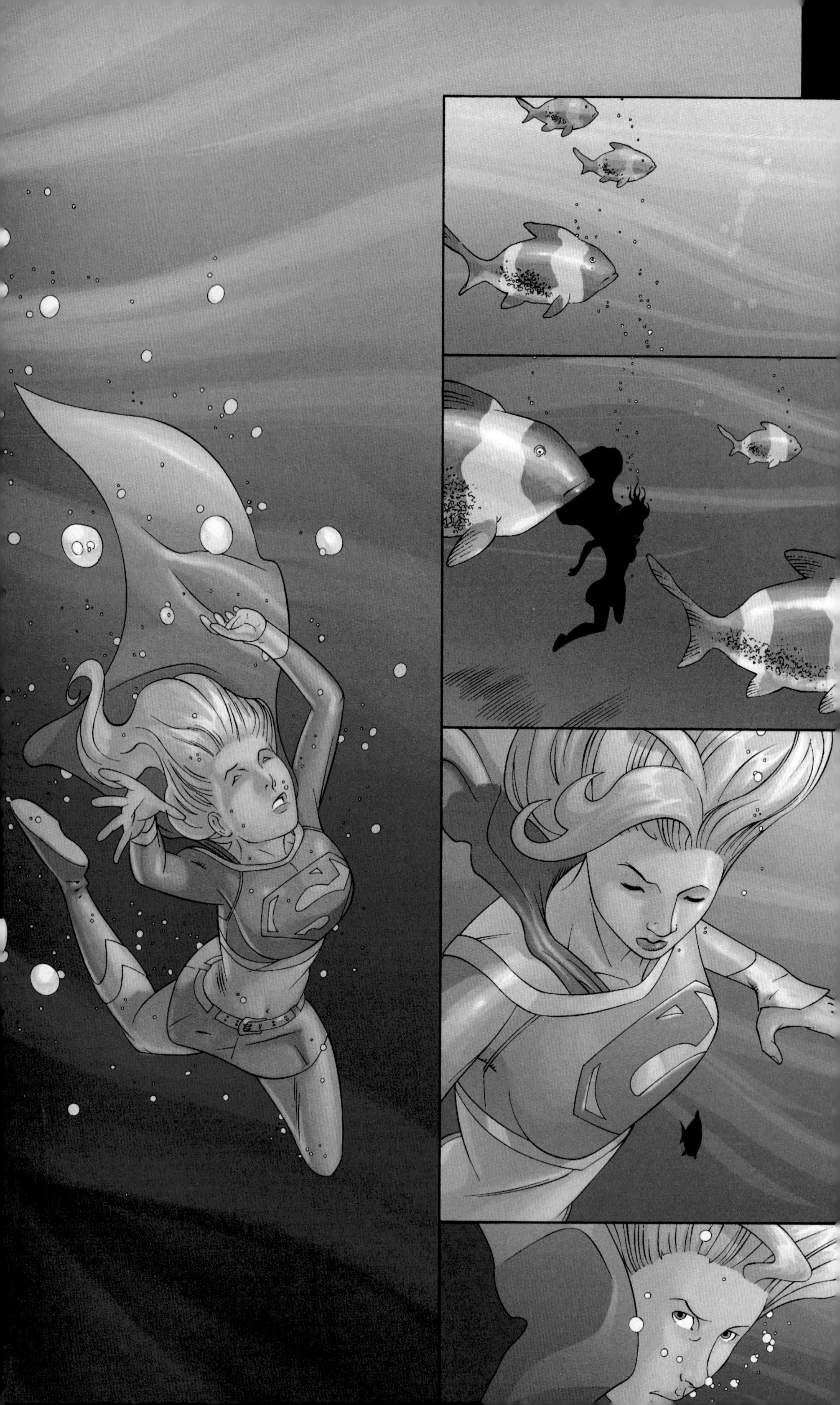

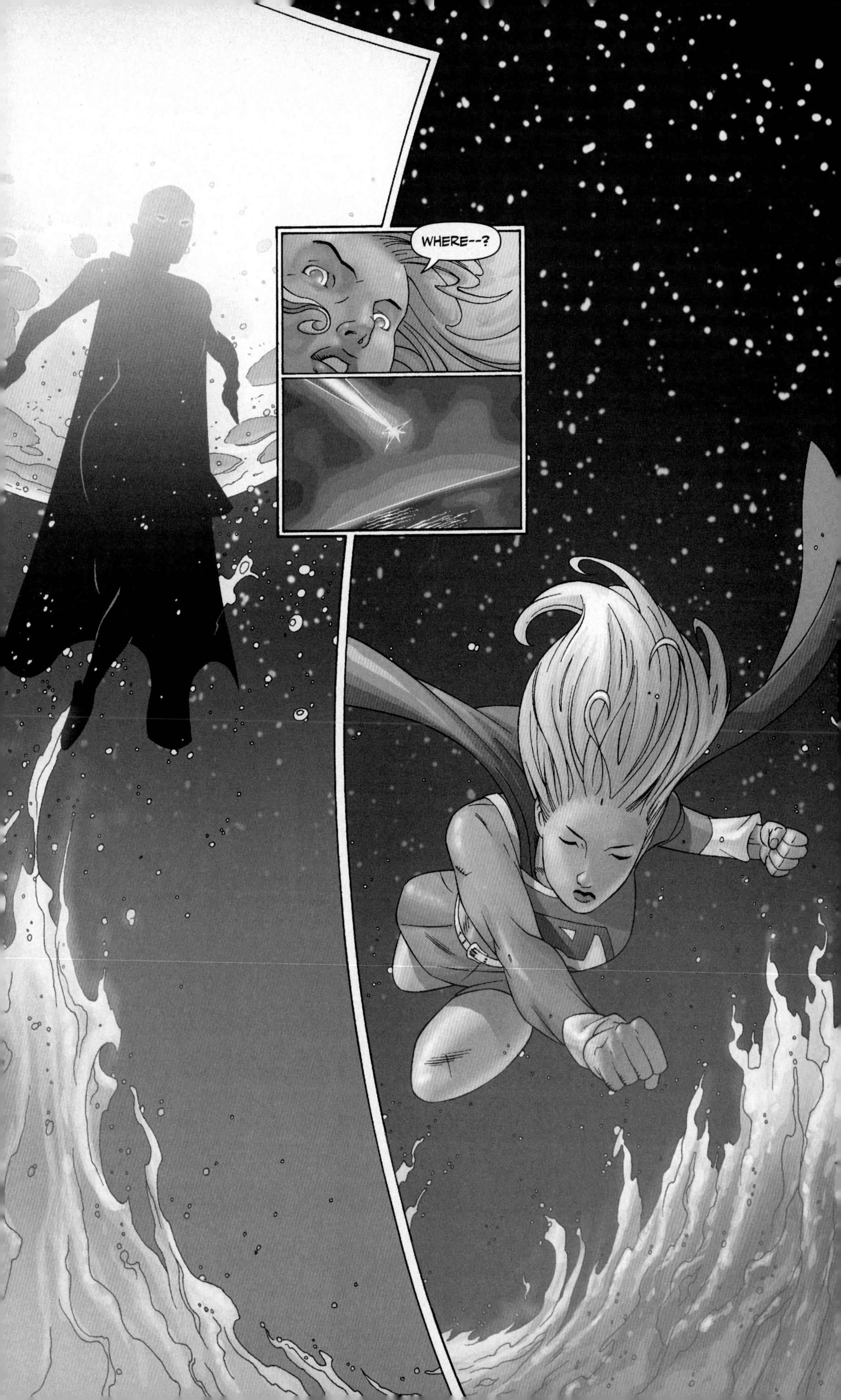
WHERE--?

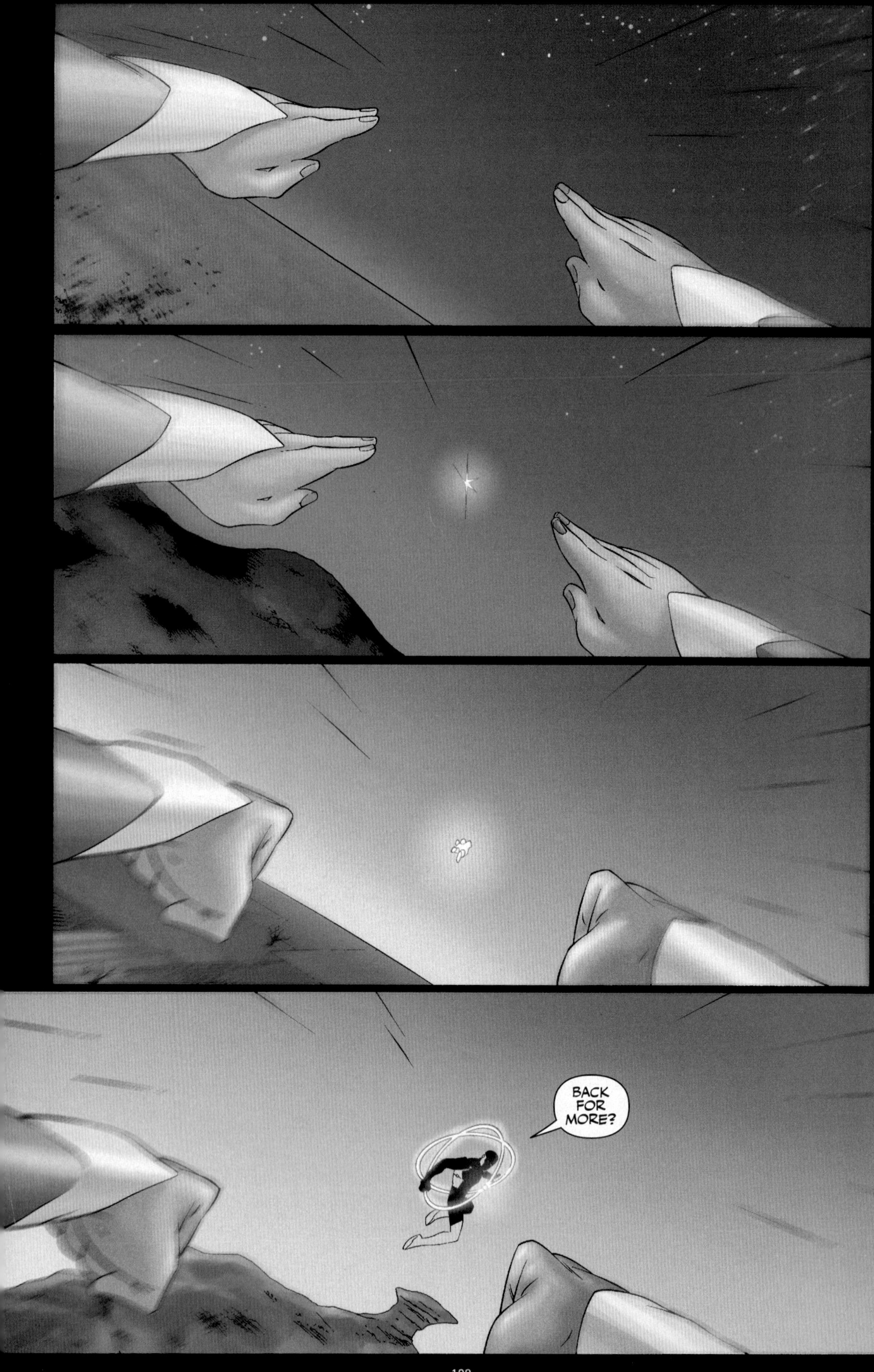
BACK FOR MORE?

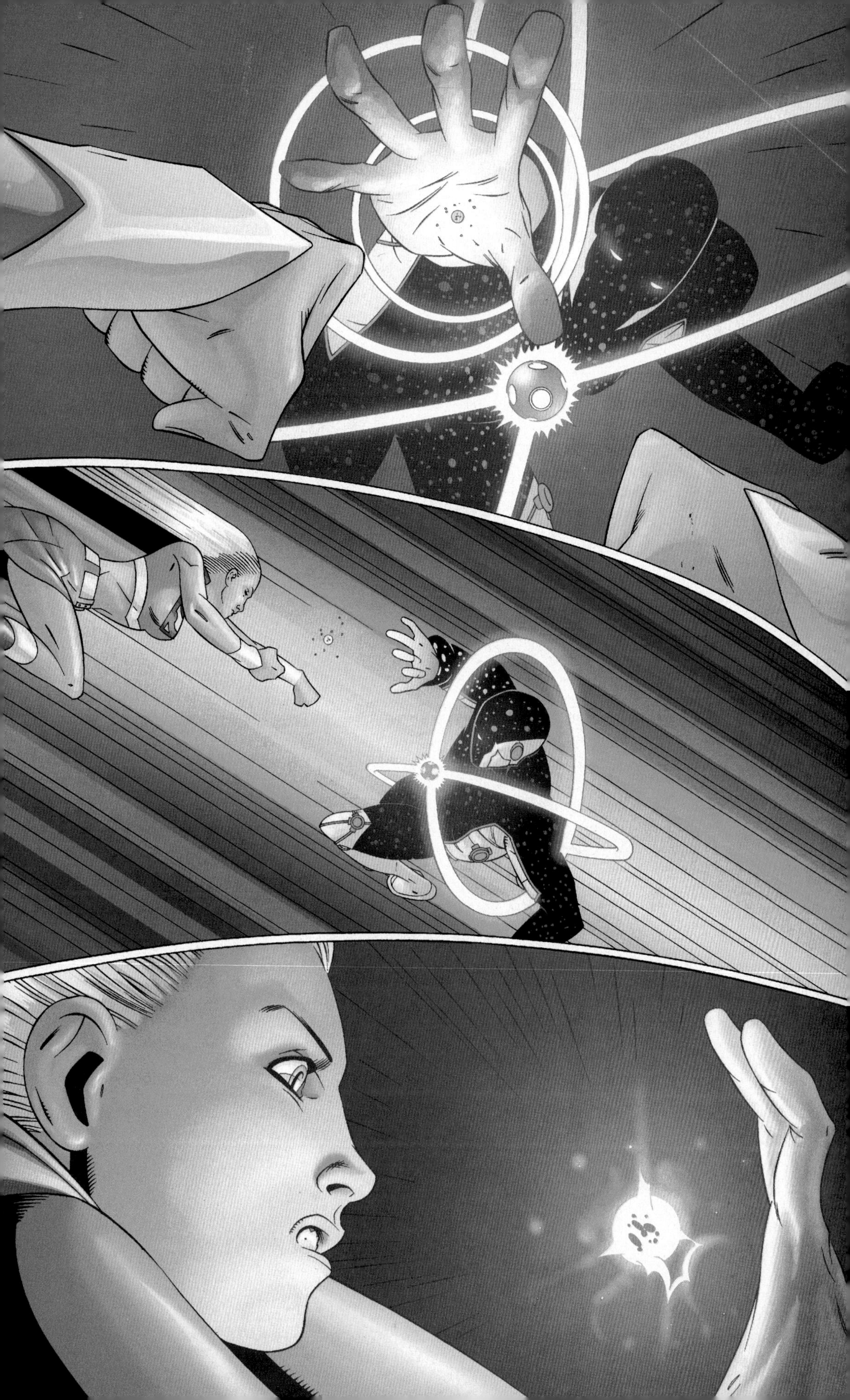

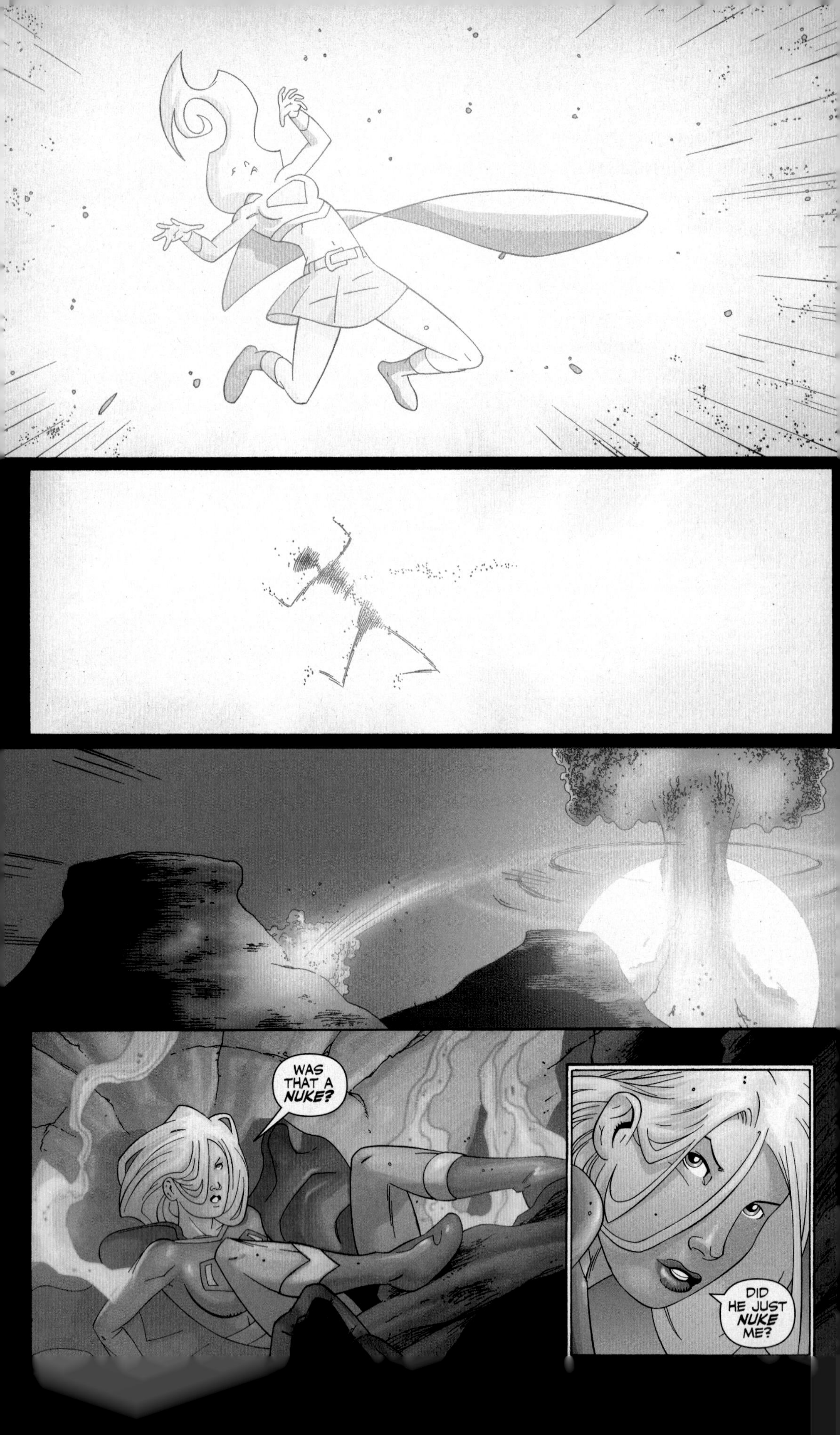
WAS THAT A NUKE?
DID HE JUST NUKE ME?

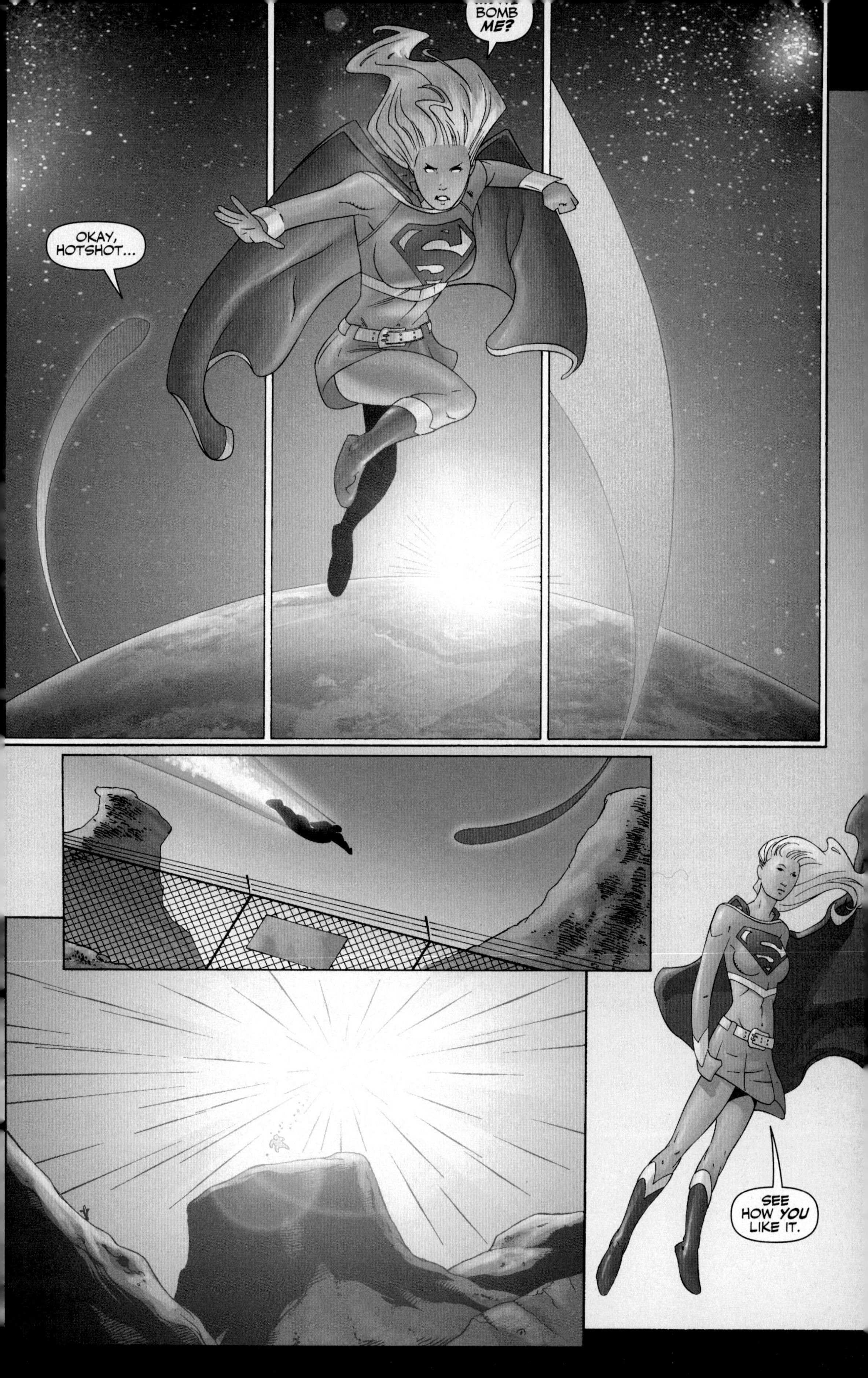
OKAY, HOTSHOT...
BOMB ME?
SEE HOW YOU LIKE IT.

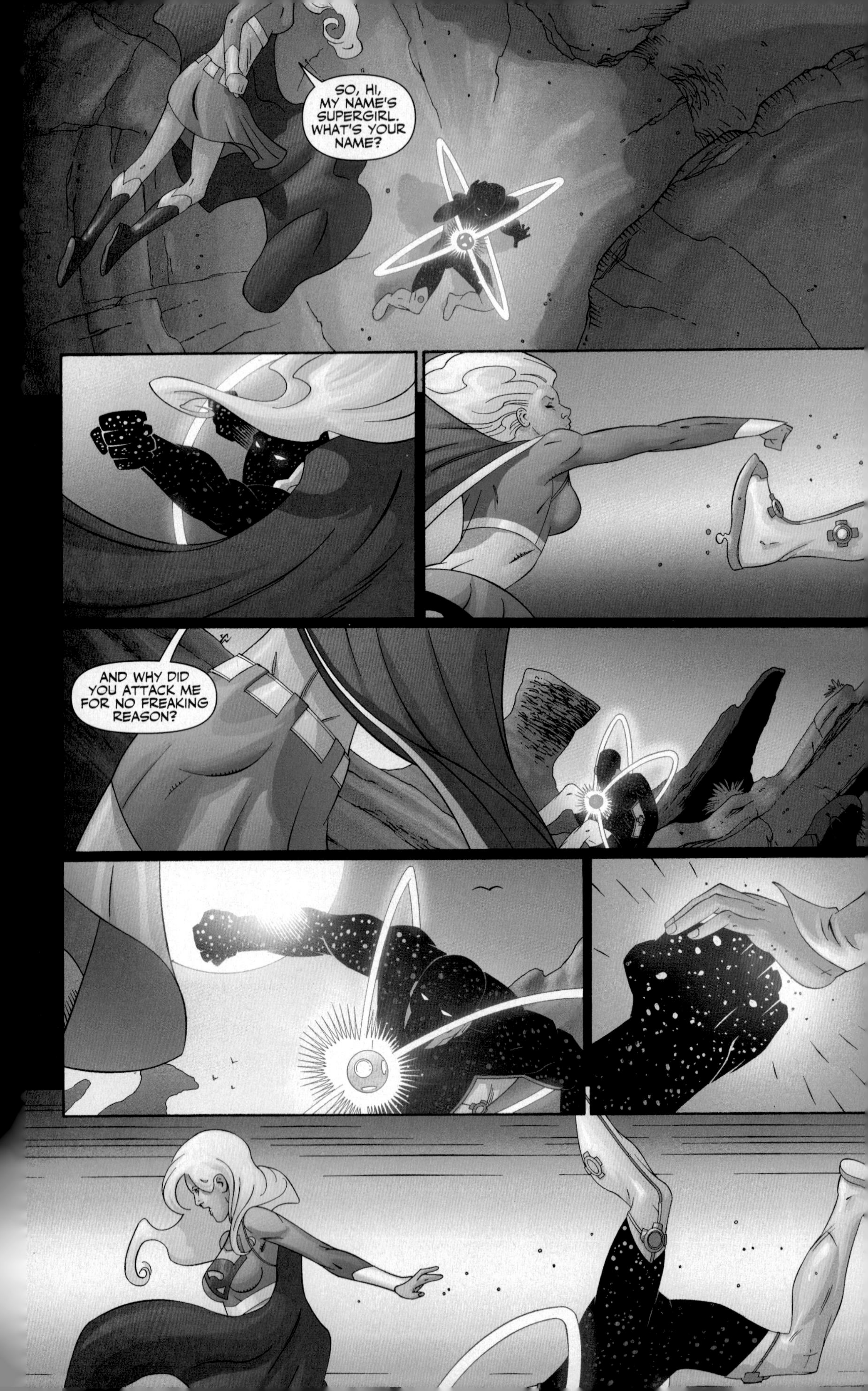
SO, HI, MY NAME'S SUPERGIRL. WHAT'S YOUR NAME?
AND WHY DID YOU ATTACK ME FOR NO FREAKING REASON?

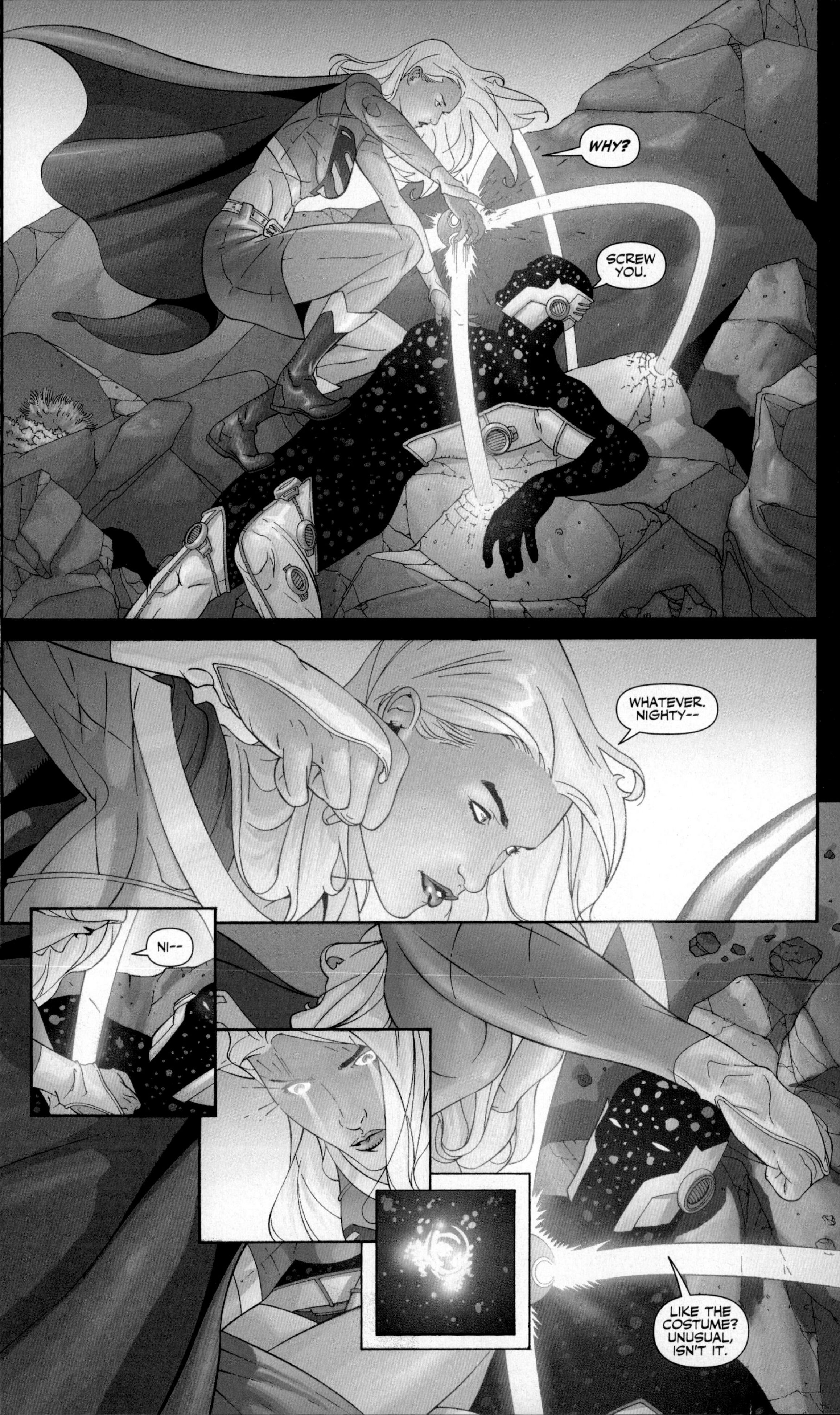
WHY?
SCREW YOU.
WHATEVER. NIGHTY--
NI--
LIKE THE COSTUME? UNUSUAL, ISN'T IT.

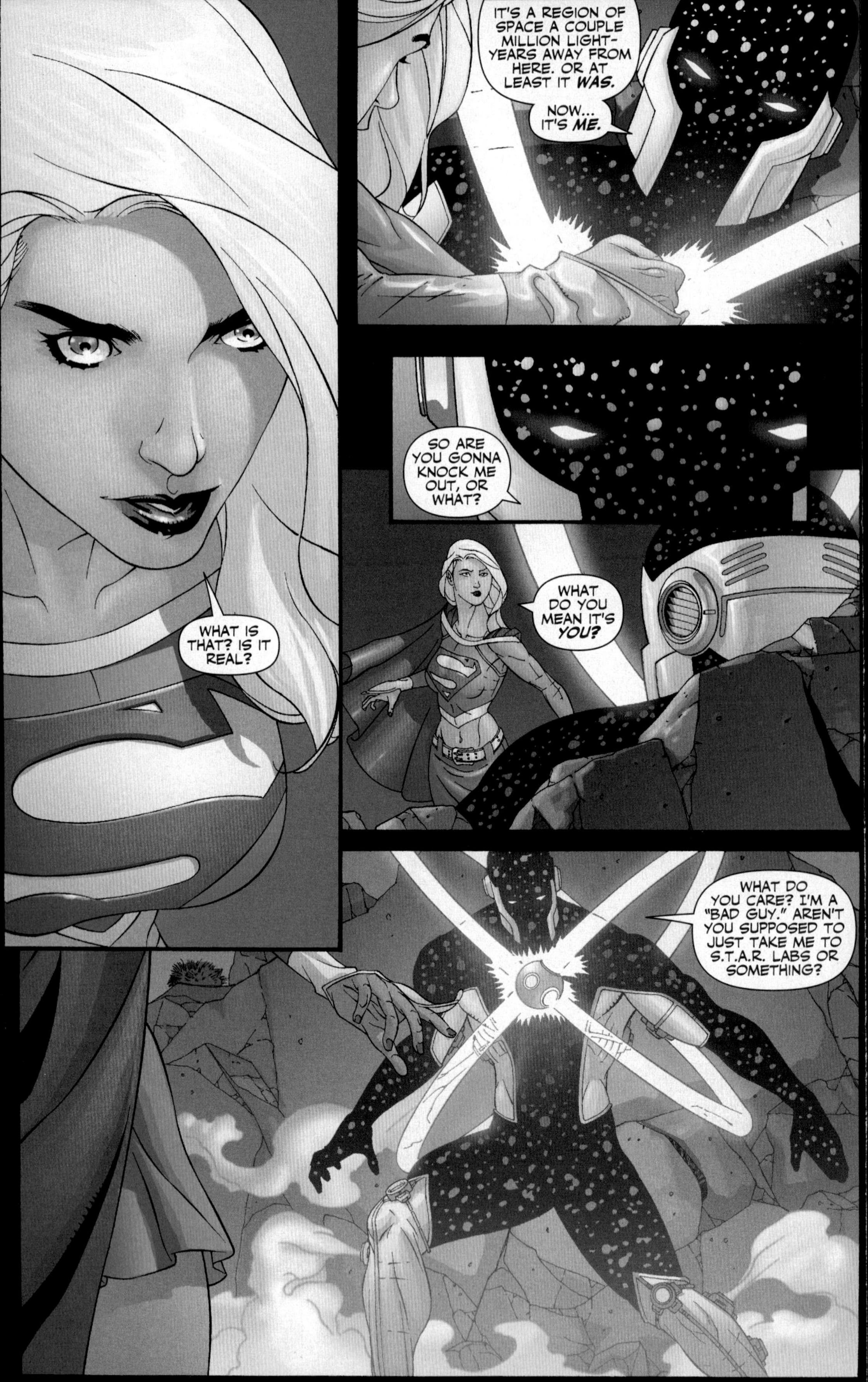

WHAT IS THAT? IS IT REAL?
IT'S A REGION OF SPACE A COUPLE MILLION LIGHT-YEARS AWAY FROM HERE. OR AT LEAST IT *WAS.*
NOW... IT'S *ME.*
SO ARE YOU GONNA KNOCK ME OUT, OR WHAT?
WHAT DO YOU MEAN IT'S *YOU?*
WHAT DO YOU CARE? I'M A "BAD GUY." AREN'T YOU SUPPOSED TO JUST TAKE ME TO S.T.A.R. LABS OR SOMETHING?

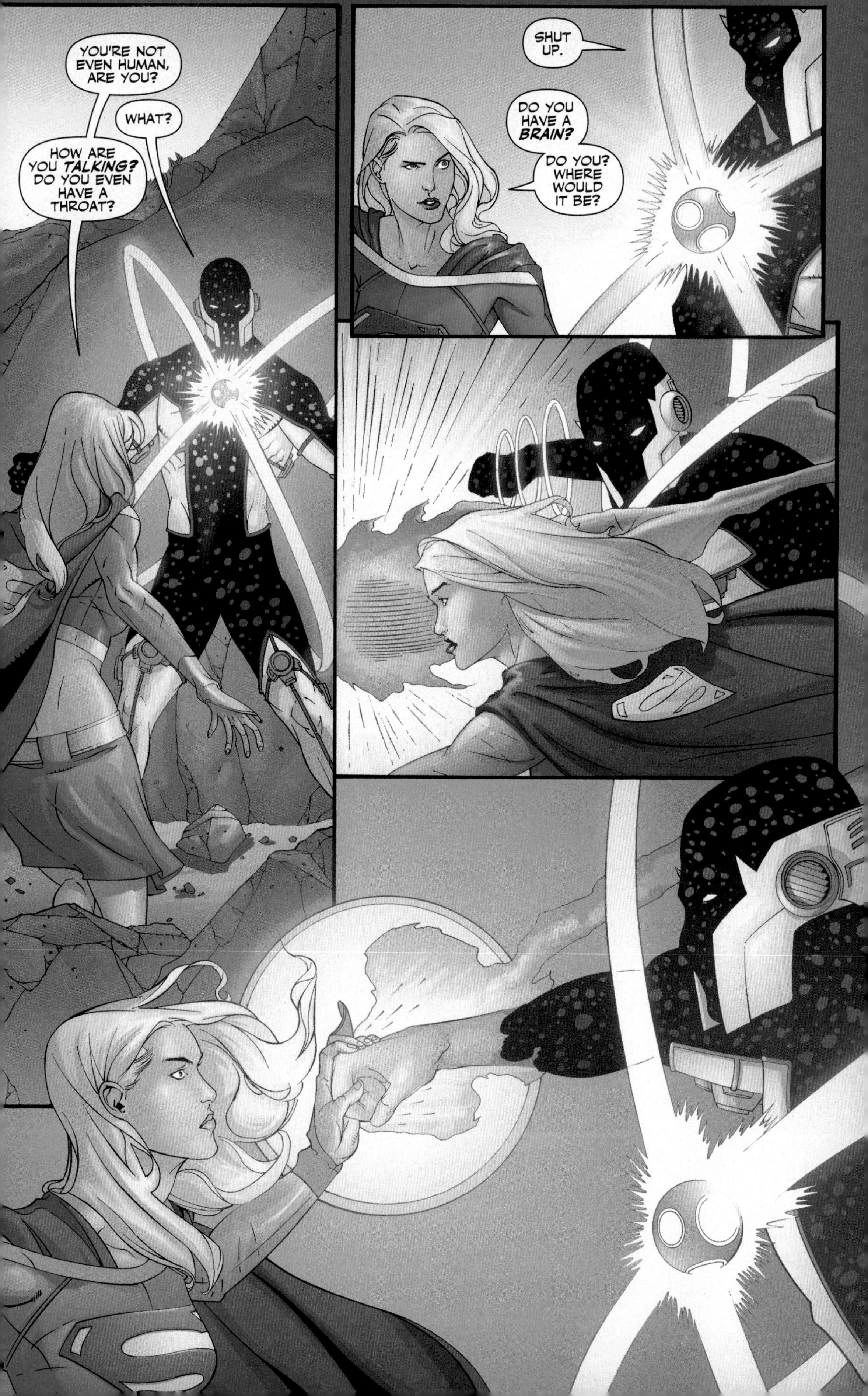
YOU'RE NOT EVEN HUMAN, ARE YOU?
WHAT?
HOW ARE YOU *TALKING?* DO YOU EVEN HAVE A THROAT?
SHUT UP.
DO YOU HAVE A *BRAIN?*
DO YOU? WHERE WOULD IT BE?

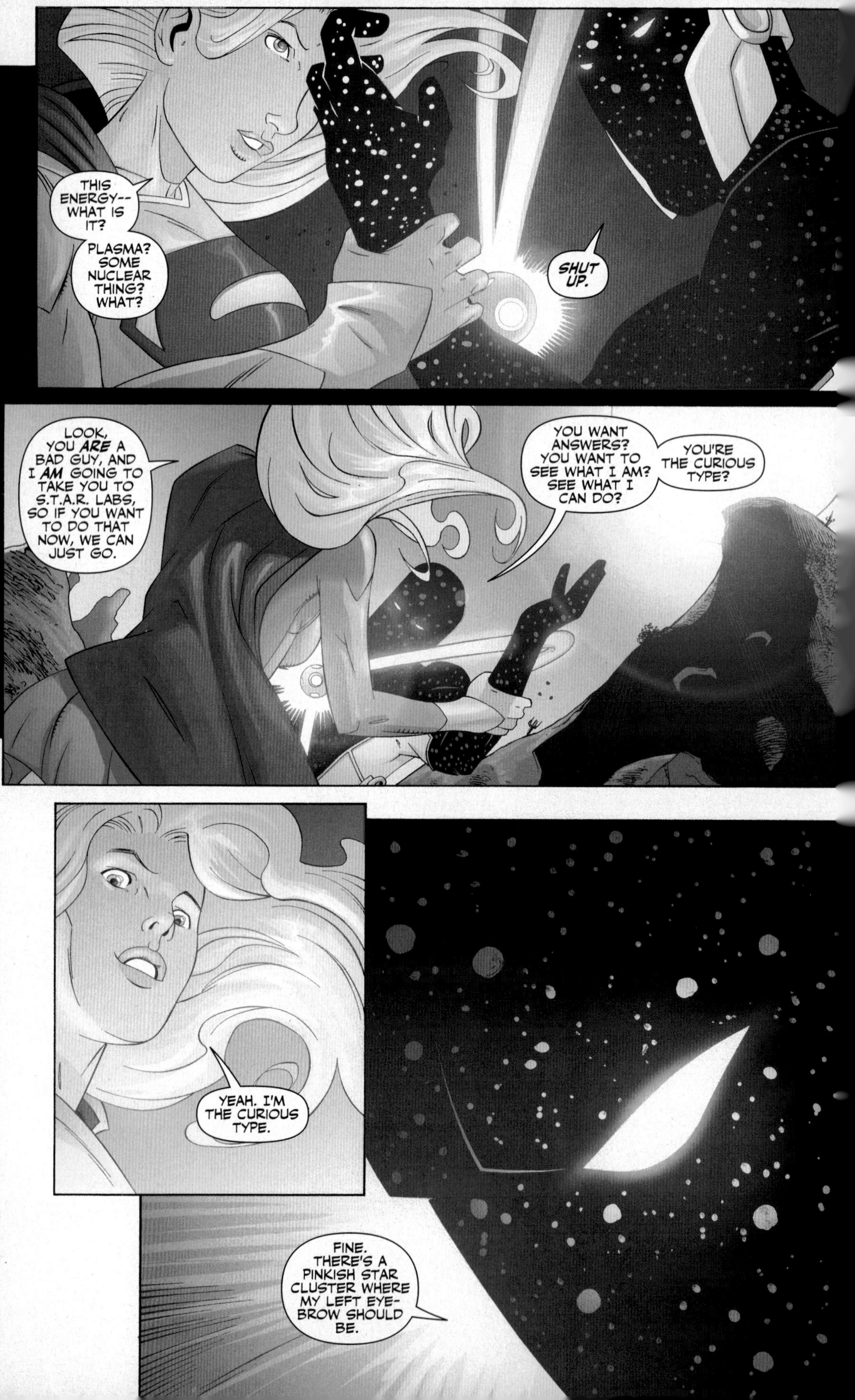
THIS ENERGY-- WHAT IS IT?
PLASMA? SOME NUCLEAR THING? WHAT?
SHUT UP.
LOOK, YOU ARE A BAD GUY, AND I AM GOING TO TAKE YOU TO S.T.A.R. LABS, SO IF YOU WANT TO DO THAT NOW, WE CAN JUST GO.
YOU WANT ANSWERS? YOU WANT TO SEE WHAT I AM? SEE WHAT I CAN DO?
YOU'RE THE CURIOUS TYPE?
YEAH. I'M THE CURIOUS TYPE.
FINE. THERE'S A PINKISH STAR CLUSTER WHERE MY LEFT EYE-BROW SHOULD BE.

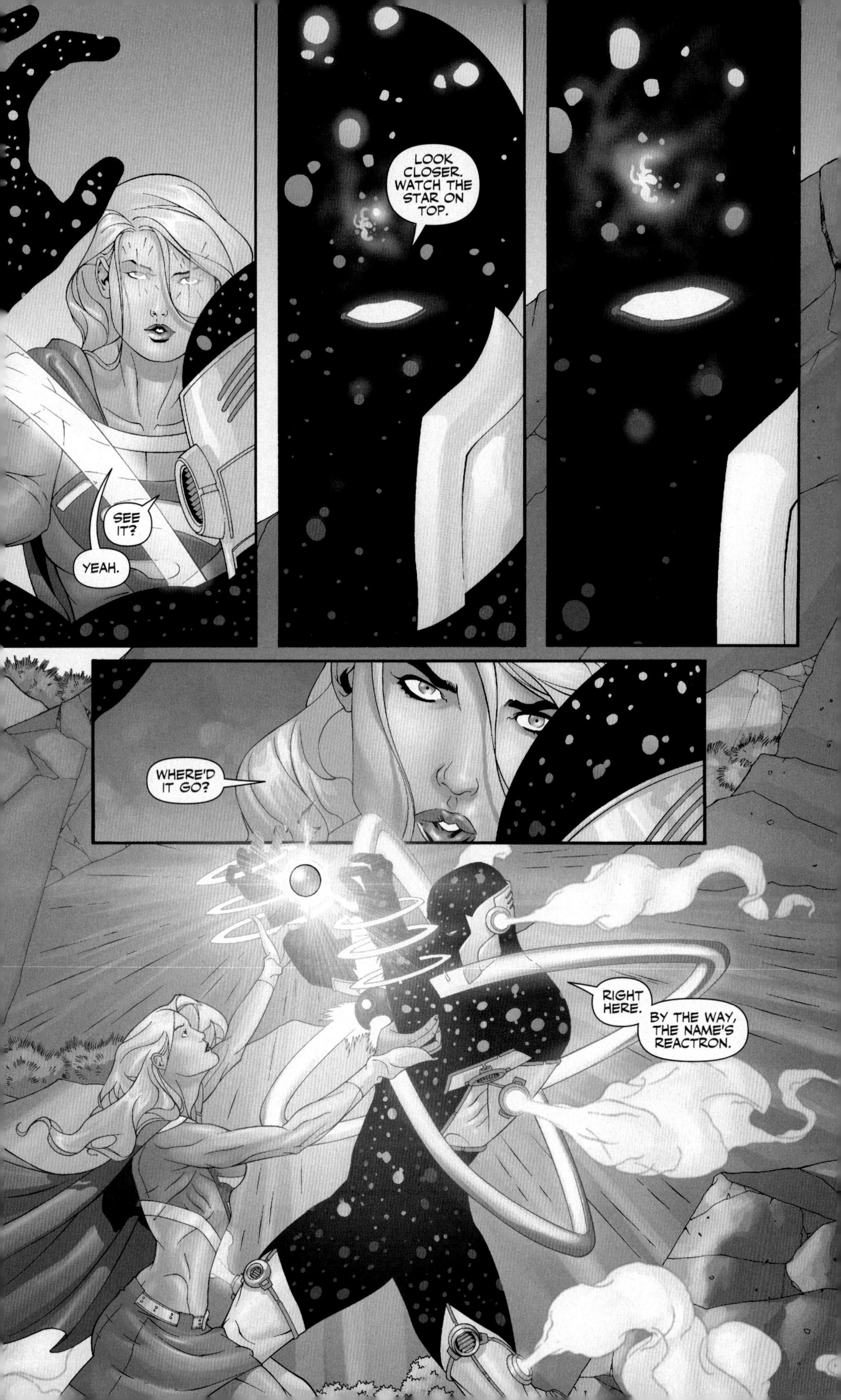
LOOK CLOSER. WATCH THE STAR ON TOP.
SEE IT?
YEAH.
WHERE'D IT GO?
RIGHT HERE.
BY THE WAY, THE NAME'S REACTRON.

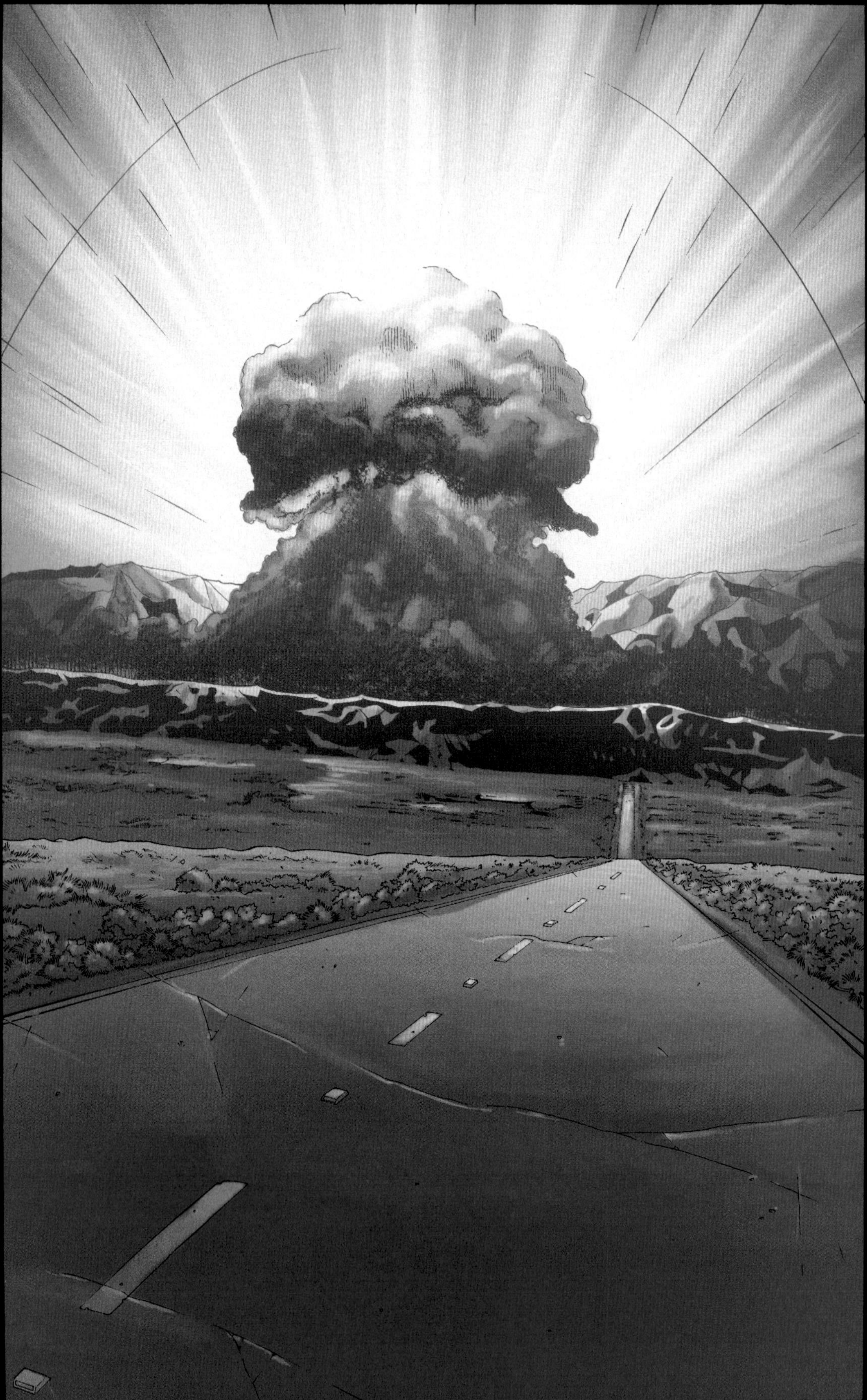

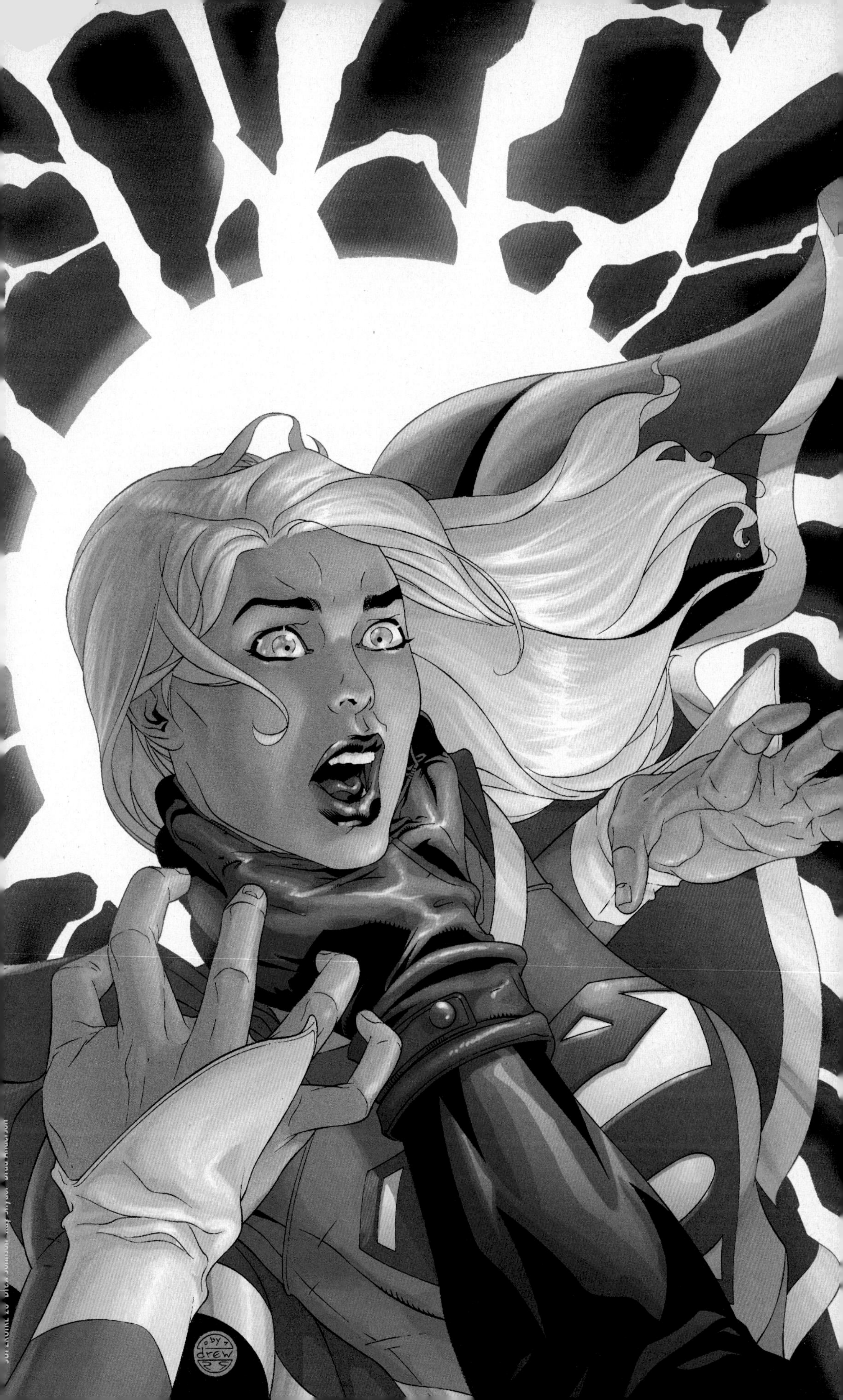

BREAK POINT

KELLEY PUCKETT WRITER
DREW JOHNSON LEE FERGUSON PENCILS
RAY SNYDER MARC DEERING INKS

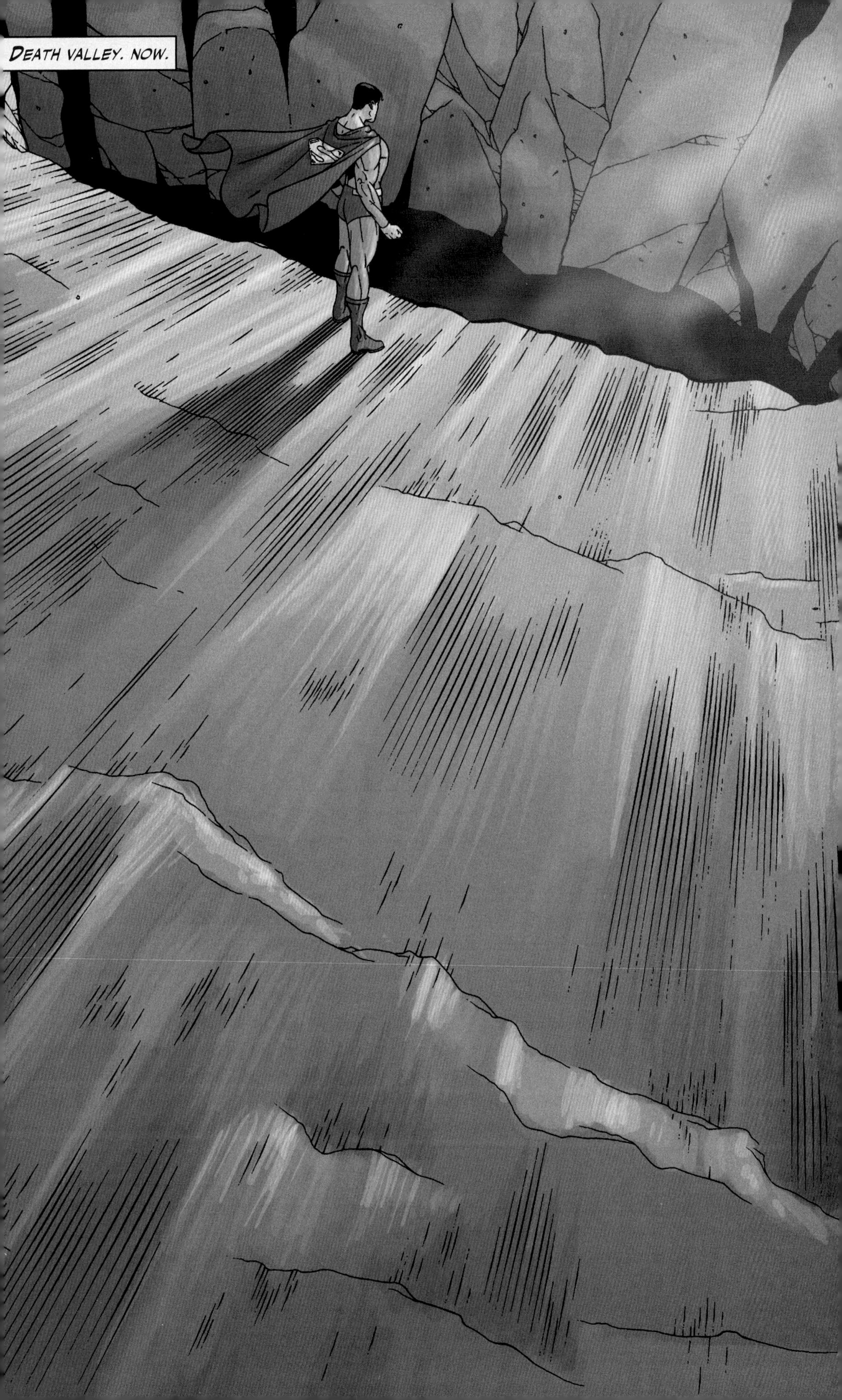
DEATH VALLEY. NOW.

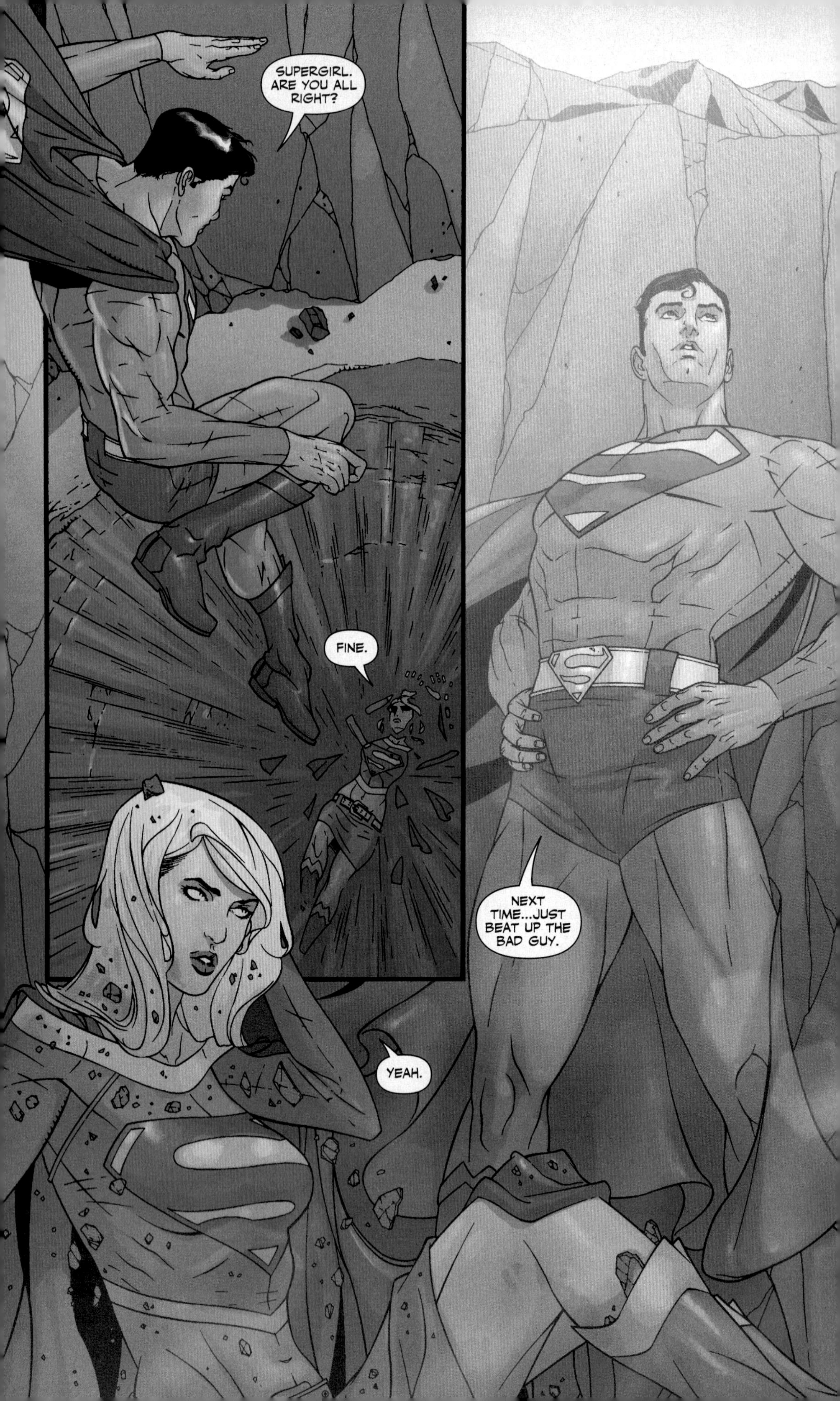
SUPERGIRL. ARE YOU ALL RIGHT?
FINE.
NEXT TIME...JUST BEAT UP THE BAD GUY.
YEAH.

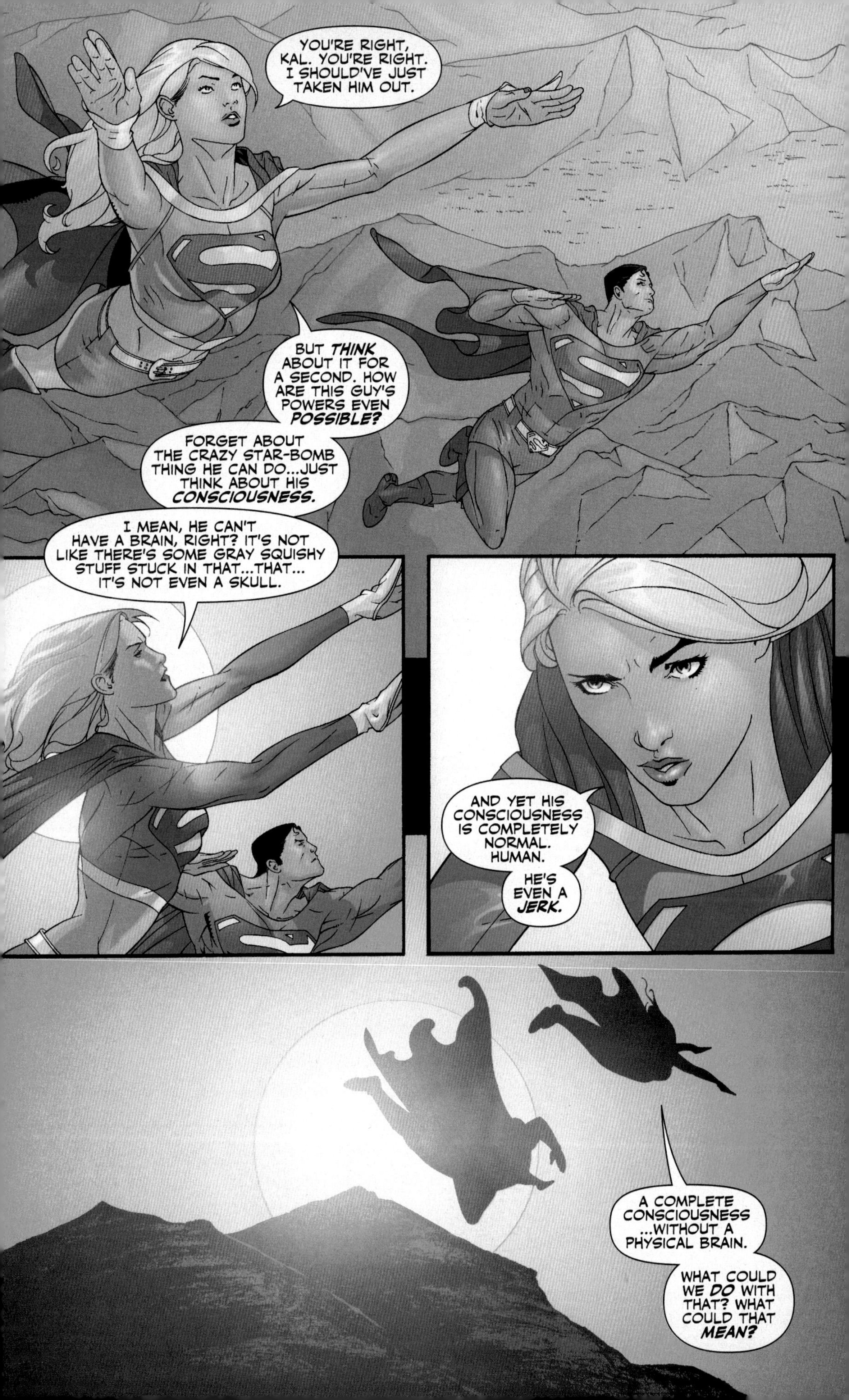

YOU'RE RIGHT, KAL. YOU'RE RIGHT. I SHOULD'VE JUST TAKEN HIM OUT.
BUT *THINK* ABOUT IT FOR A SECOND. HOW ARE THIS GUY'S POWERS EVEN *POSSIBLE?*
FORGET ABOUT THE CRAZY STAR-BOMB THING HE CAN DO...JUST THINK ABOUT HIS *CONSCIOUSNESS.*
I MEAN, HE CAN'T HAVE A BRAIN, RIGHT? IT'S NOT LIKE THERE'S SOME GRAY SQUISHY STUFF STUCK IN THAT...THAT... IT'S NOT EVEN A SKULL.
AND YET HIS CONSCIOUSNESS IS COMPLETELY NORMAL. HUMAN.
HE'S EVEN A *JERK.*
A COMPLETE CONSCIOUSNESS ...WITHOUT A PHYSICAL BRAIN.
WHAT COULD WE *DO* WITH THAT? WHAT COULD THAT *MEAN?*

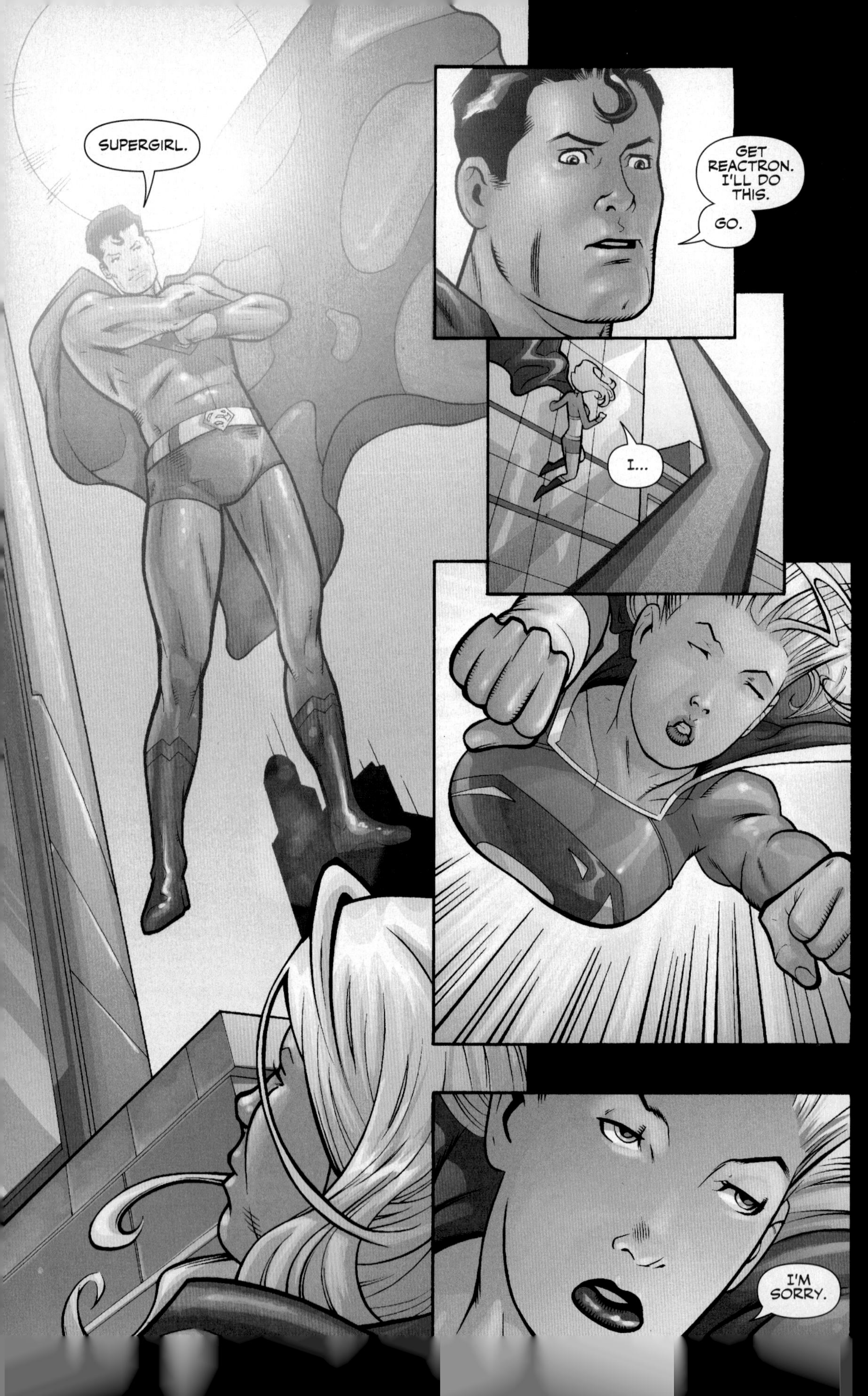
SUPERGIRL.
GET REACTRON. I'LL DO THIS.
GO.
I...
I'M SORRY.

"PAID"? WHAT DO YOU--?

A... BANK?

WAIT. LET ME GET THIS STRAIGHT.

YOU'RE... INVULNERABLE? PROBABLY CAN'T GET SICK, RIGHT? MAYBE *IMMORTAL*.

YOU HAVE *POWER*... BEYOND *IMAGINATION*...

AND YOU'RE USING IT...

...TO ROB A *BANK*?

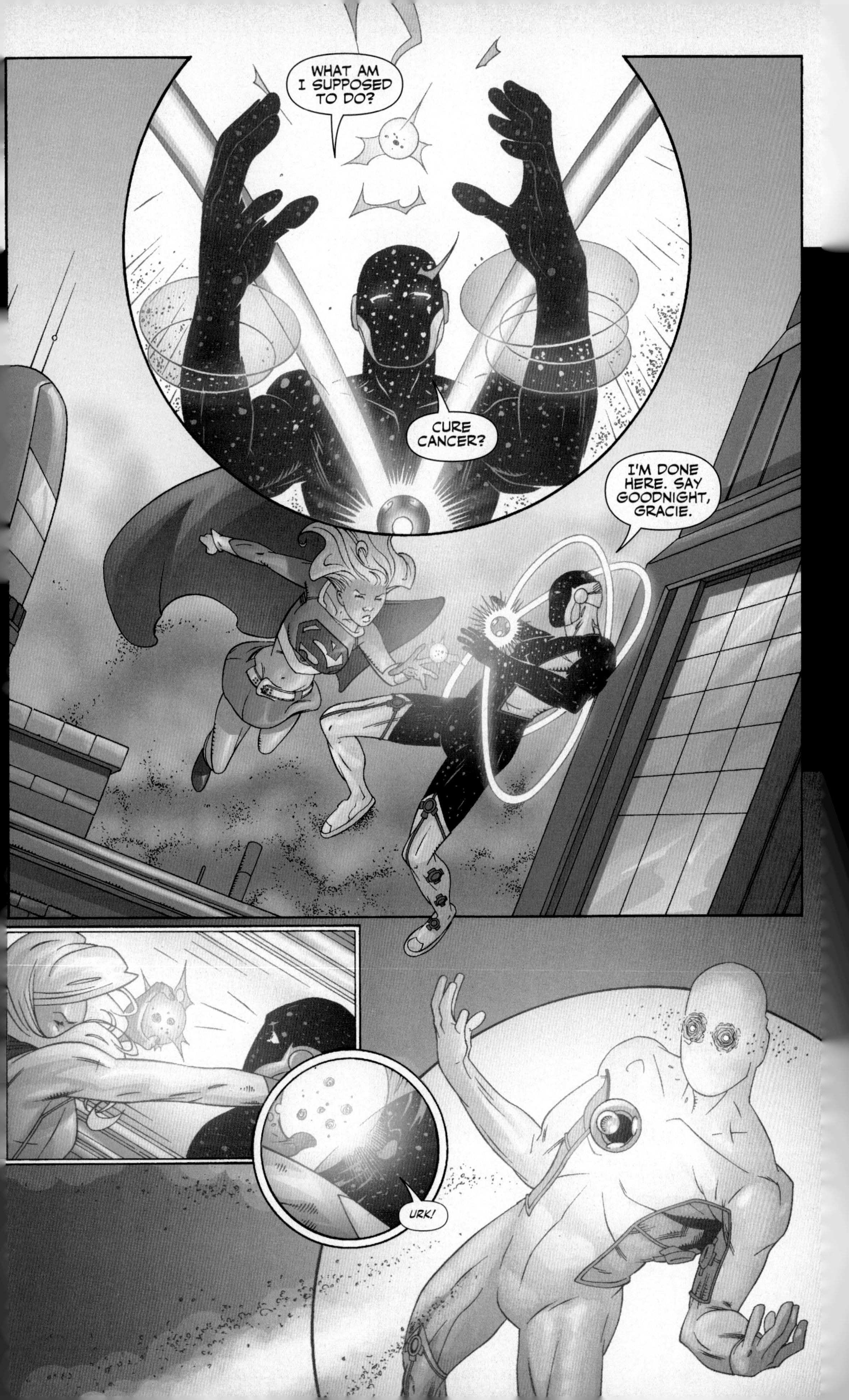
WHAT AM I SUPPOSED TO DO?
CURE CANCER?
I'M DONE HERE. SAY GOODNIGHT, GRACIE.
URK!

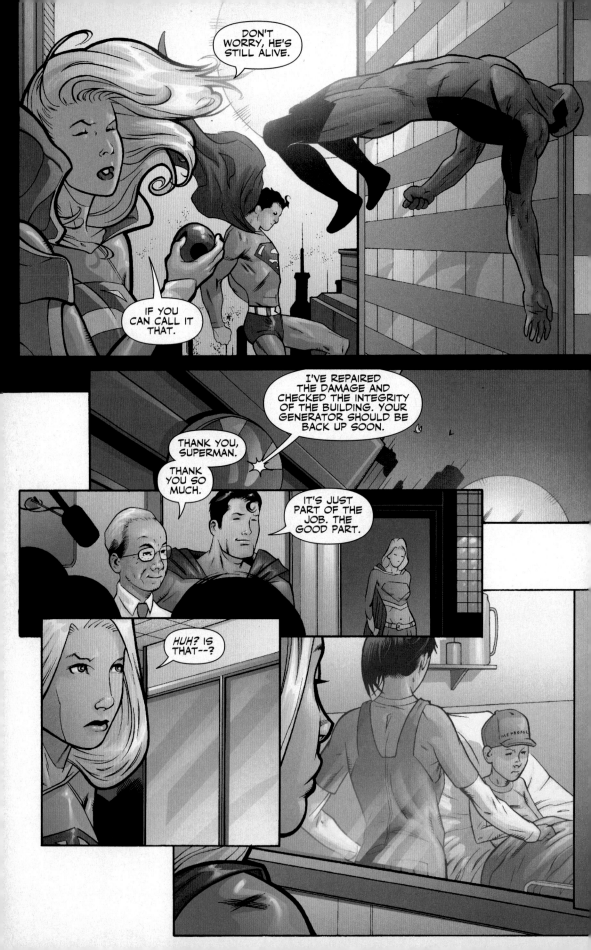

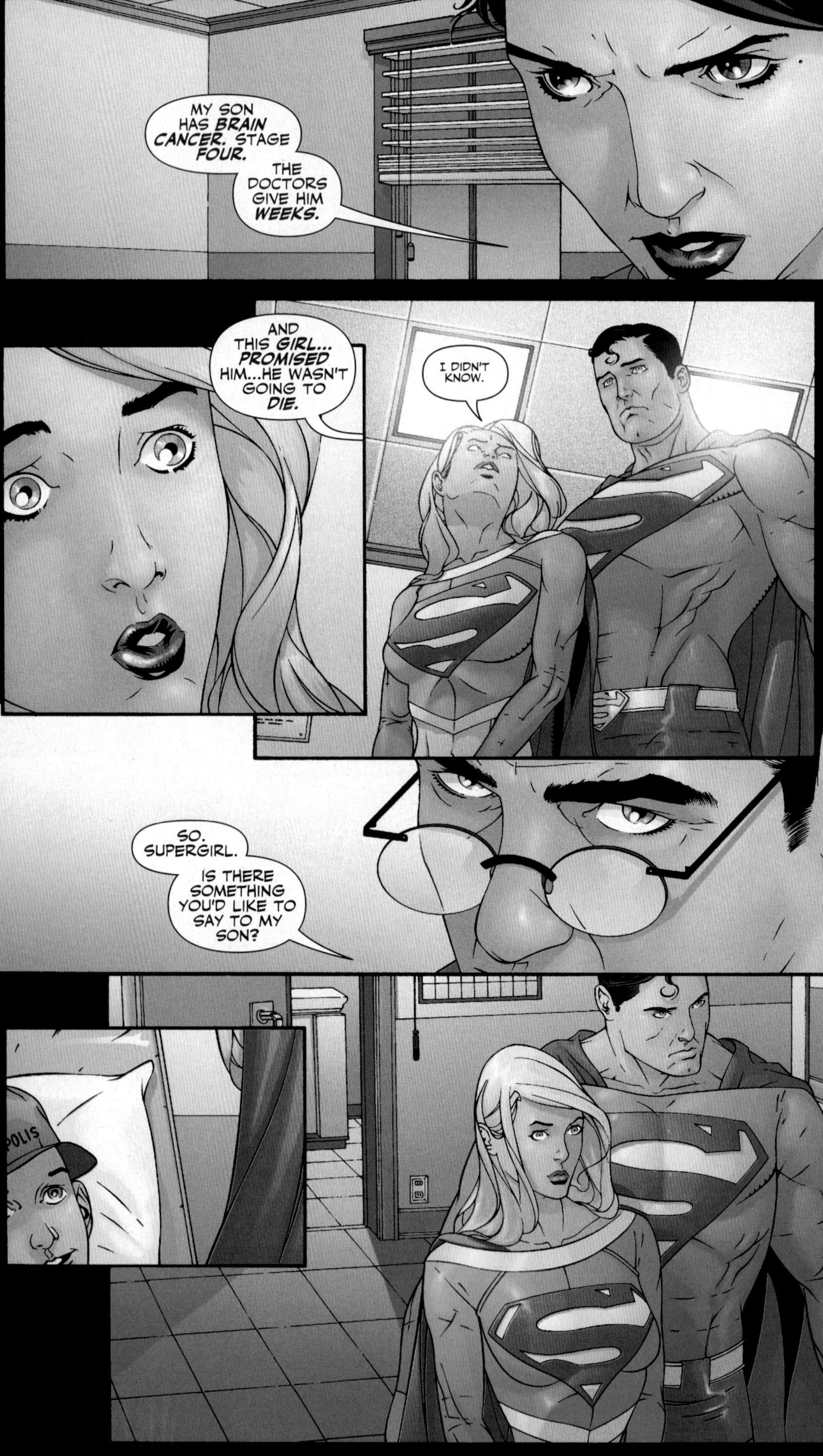
MY SON HAS BRAIN CANCER. STAGE FOUR.
THE DOCTORS GIVE HIM WEEKS.
AND THIS GIRL... PROMISED HIM...HE WASN'T GOING TO DIE.
I DIDN'T KNOW.
SO. SUPERGIRL.
IS THERE SOMETHING YOU'D LIKE TO SAY TO MY SON?
POLIS

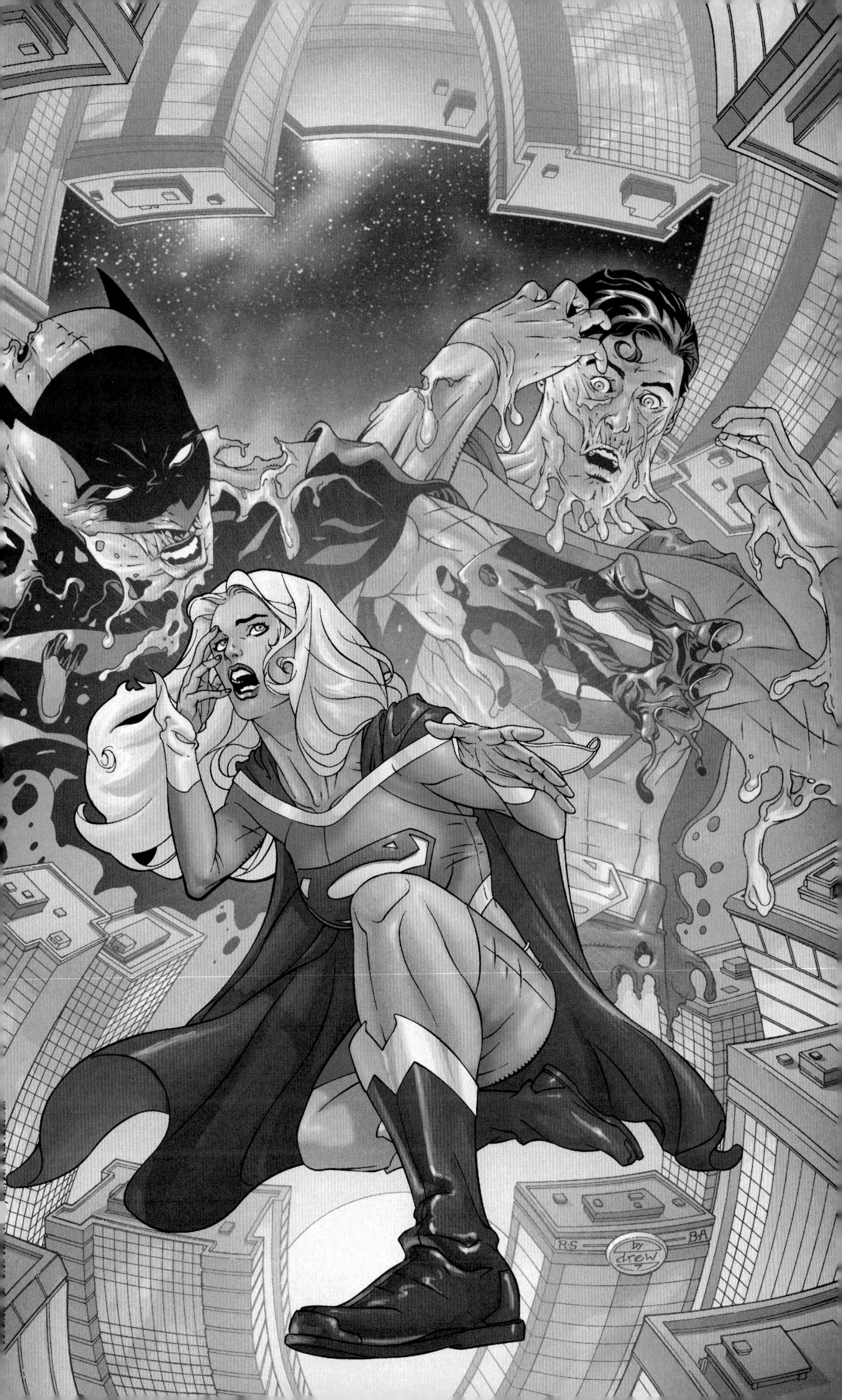
R·S
by drew
B·A

THE GIRL OF TOMORROW

KELLEY PUCKETT WRITER
RICK LEONARDI DREW JOHNSON PENCILS
DAN GREEN RAY SNYDER INKS

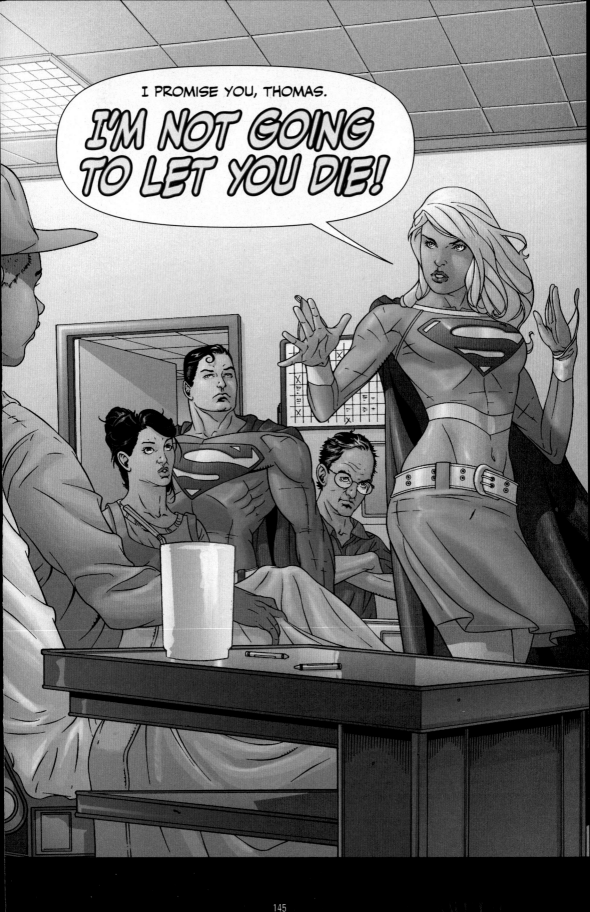

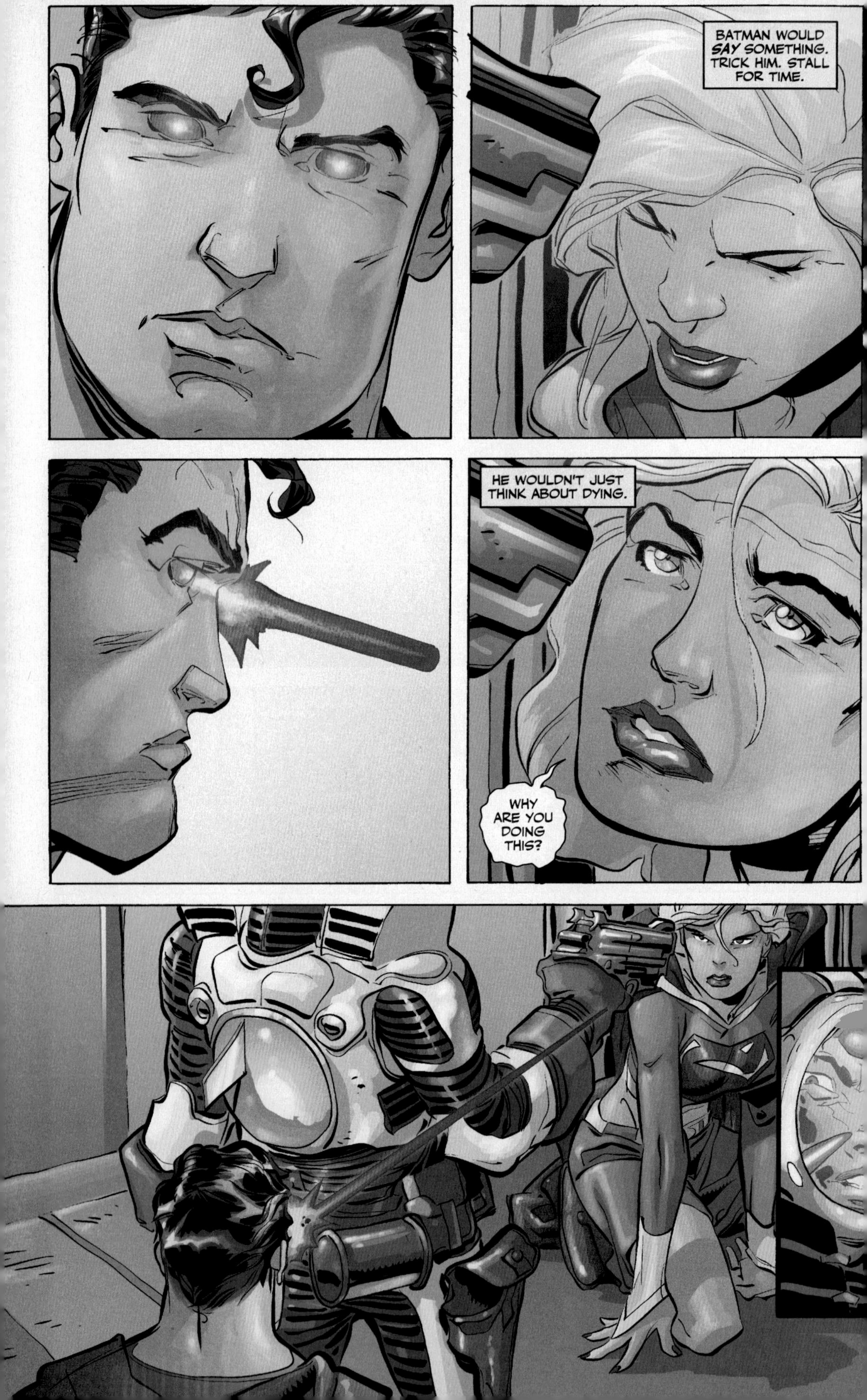
BATMAN WOULD SAY SOMETHING. TRICK HIM. STALL FOR TIME.
HE WOULDN'T JUST THINK ABOUT DYING.
WHY ARE YOU DOING THIS?

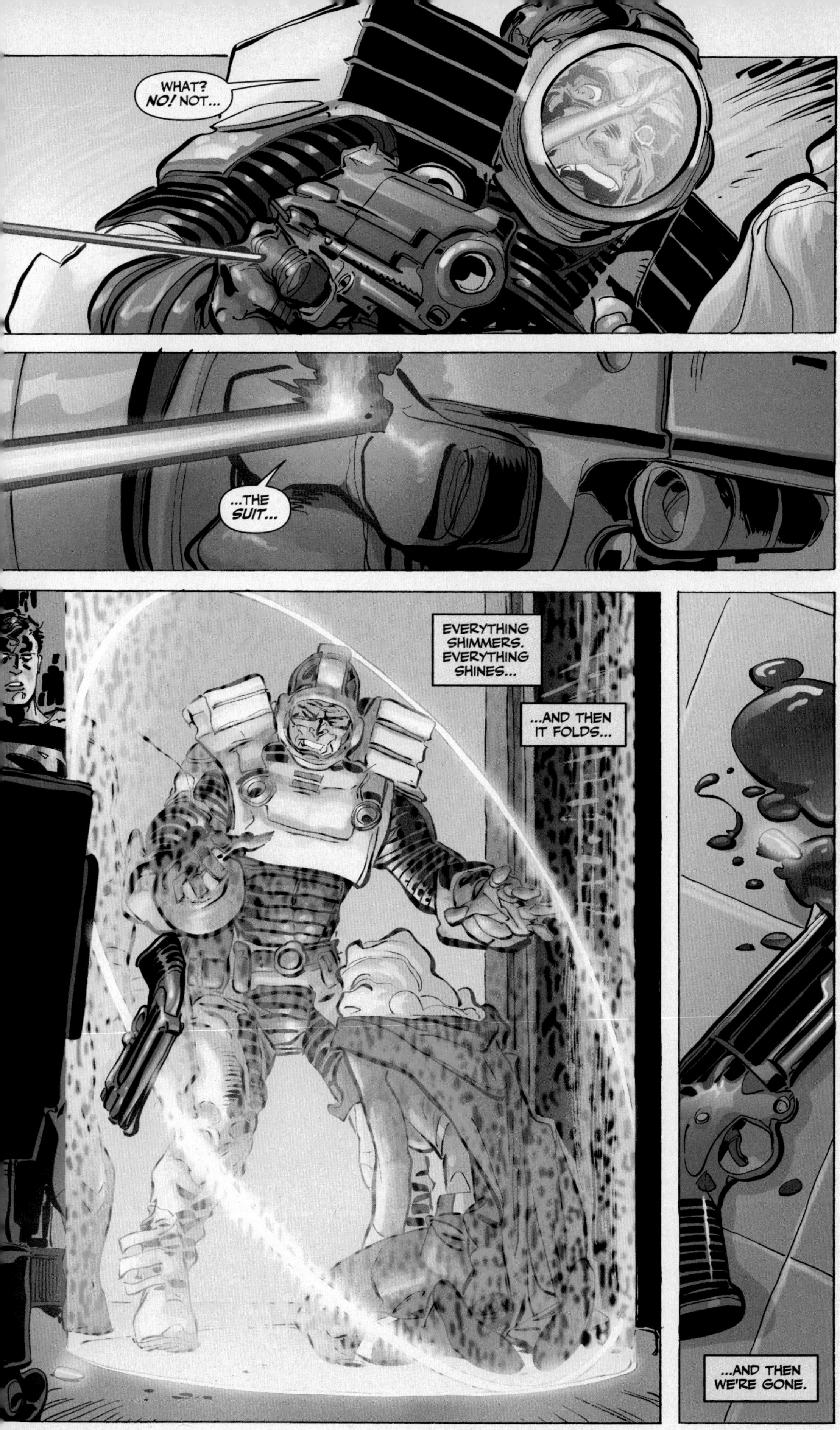
WHAT? NO! NOT...
...THE SUIT...
EVERYTHING SHIMMERS. EVERYTHING SHINES...
...AND THEN IT FOLDS...
...AND THEN WE'RE GONE.

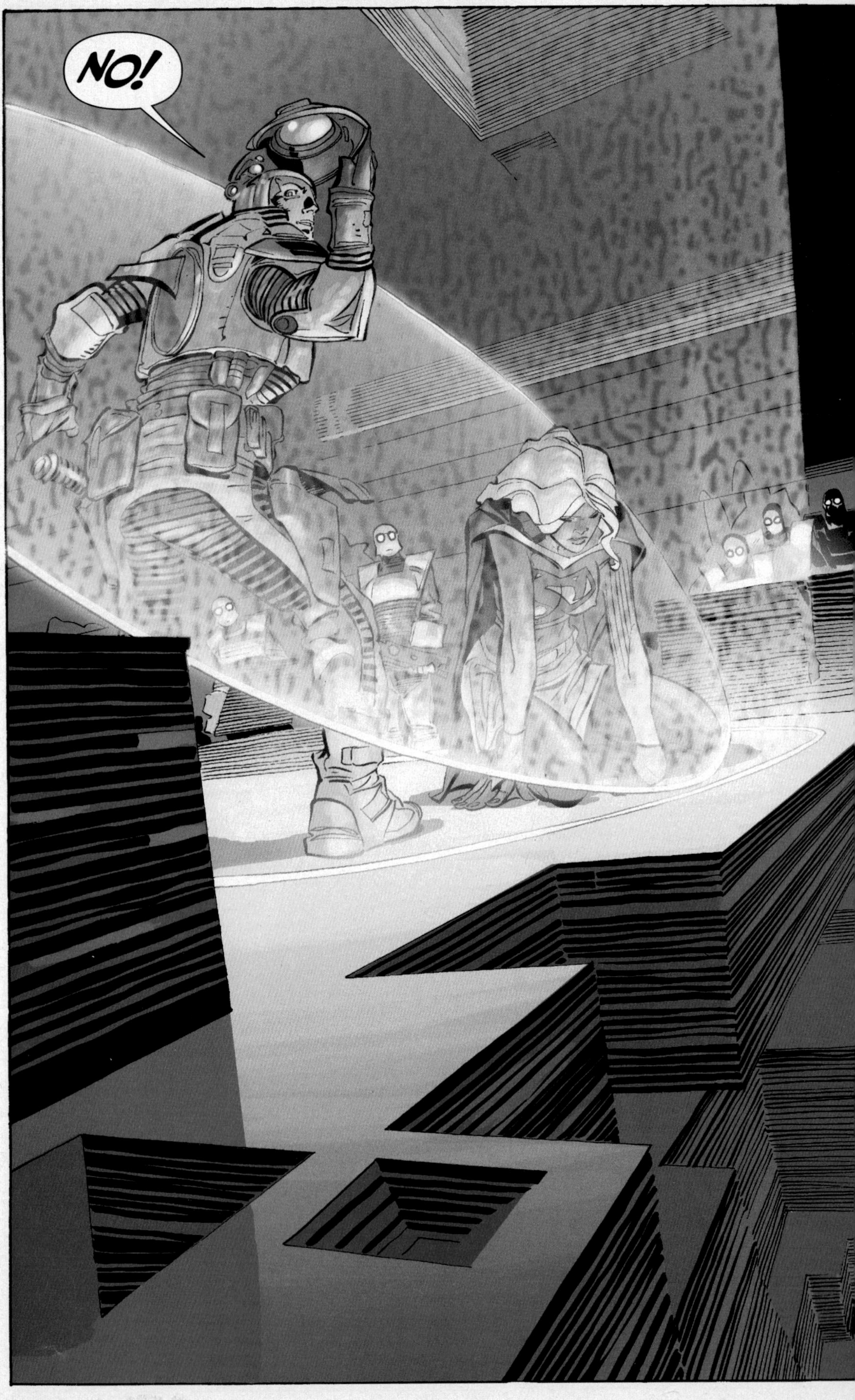
NO!

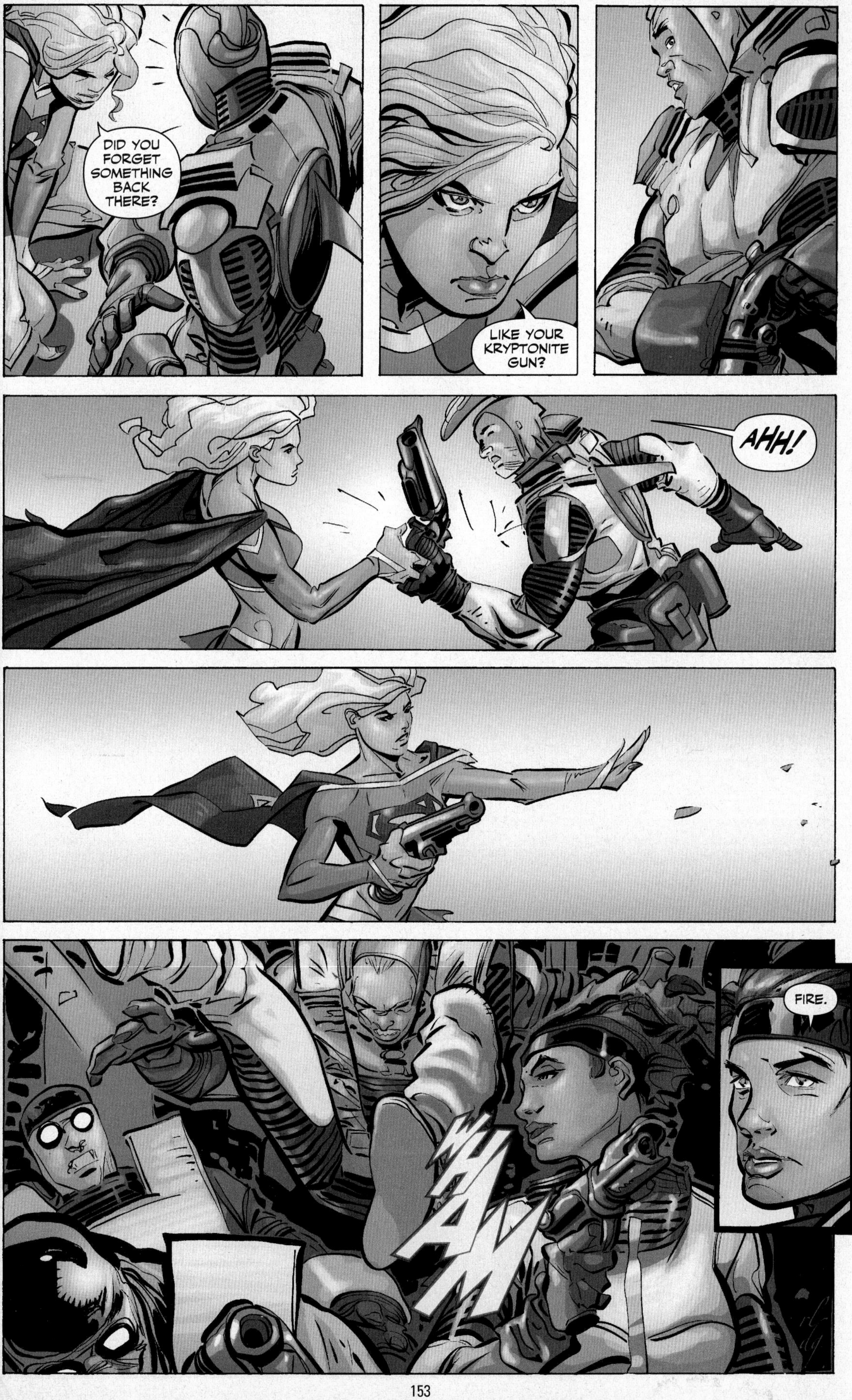

DID YOU FORGET SOMETHING BACK THERE?
LIKE YOUR KRYPTONITE GUN?
AHH!
FIRE.
WHAM

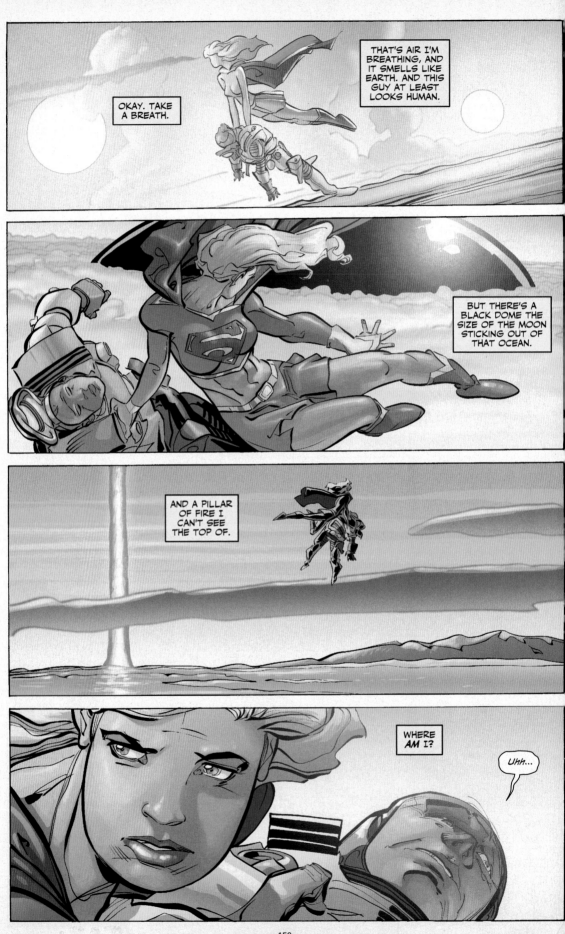

OKAY. TAKE A BREATH.

THAT'S AIR I'M BREATHING, AND IT SMELLS LIKE EARTH. AND THIS GUY AT LEAST LOOKS HUMAN.

BUT THERE'S A BLACK DOME THE SIZE OF THE MOON STICKING OUT OF THAT OCEAN.

AND A PILLAR OF FIRE I CAN'T SEE THE TOP OF.

WHERE AM I?

Uhh...

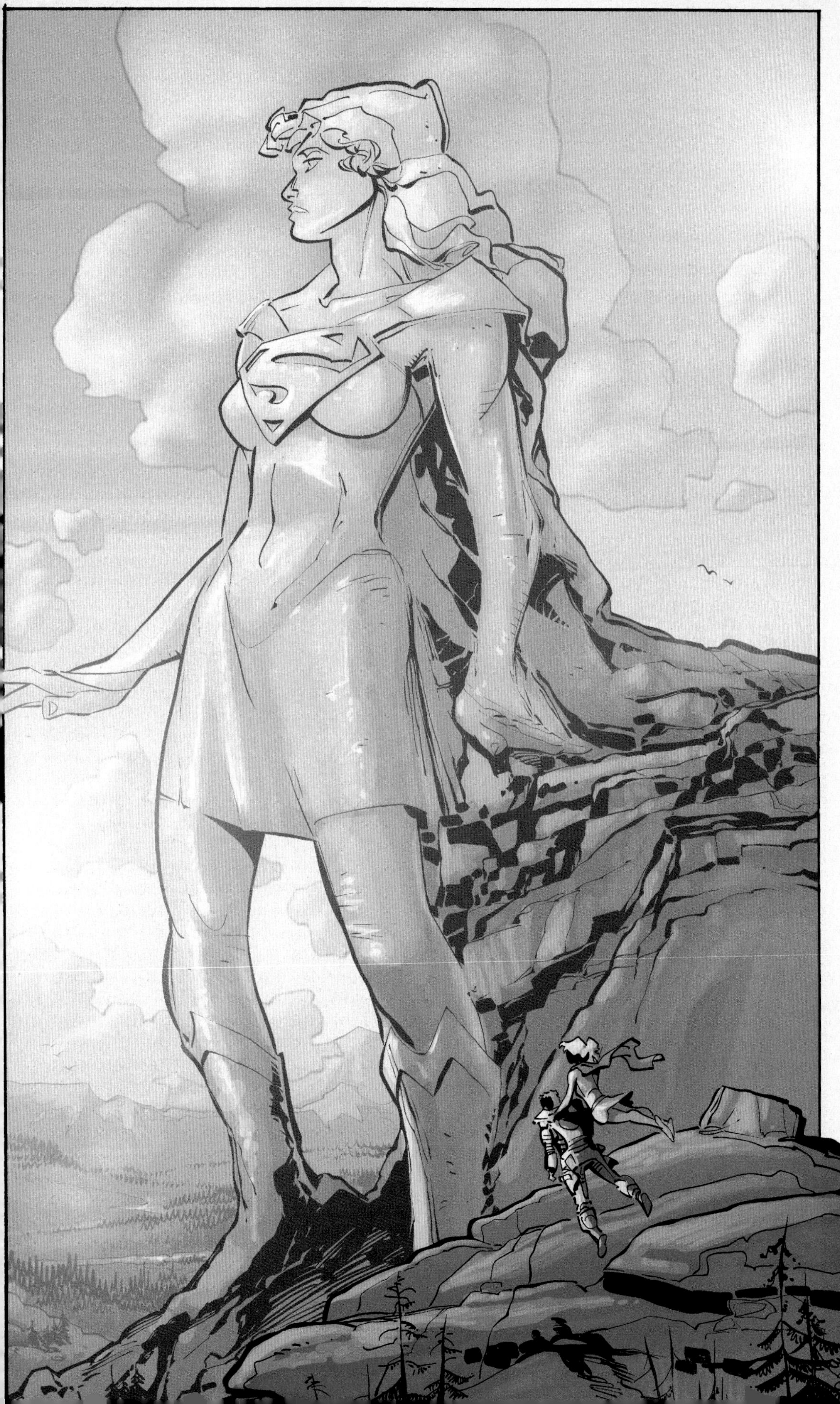

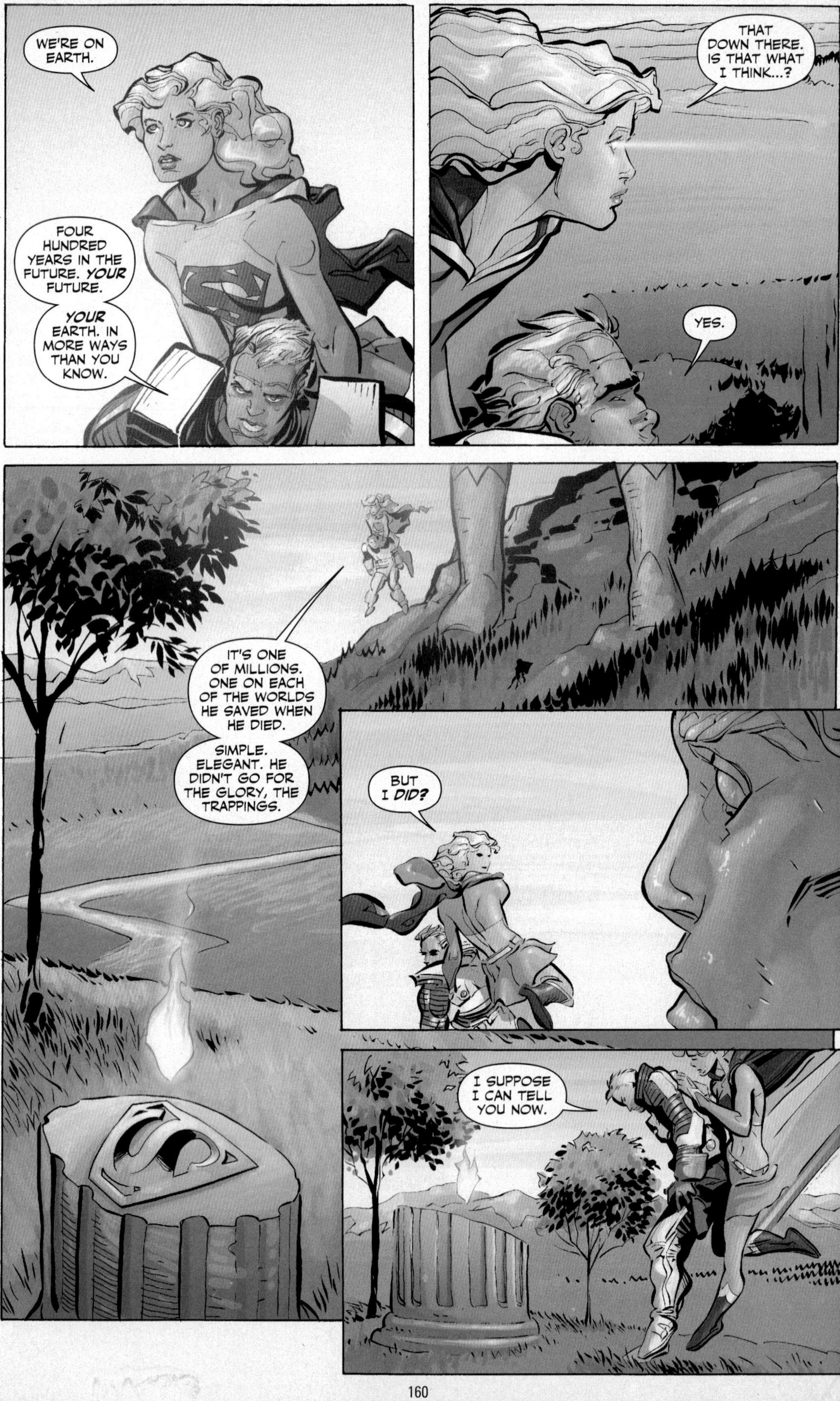
WE'RE ON EARTH.
FOUR HUNDRED YEARS IN THE FUTURE. YOUR FUTURE.
YOUR EARTH. IN MORE WAYS THAN YOU KNOW.
THAT DOWN THERE. IS THAT WHAT I THINK...?
YES.
IT'S ONE OF MILLIONS. ONE ON EACH OF THE WORLDS HE SAVED WHEN HE DIED.
SIMPLE. ELEGANT. HE DIDN'T GO FOR THE GLORY, THE TRAPPINGS.
BUT I DID?
I SUPPOSE I CAN TELL YOU NOW.

163

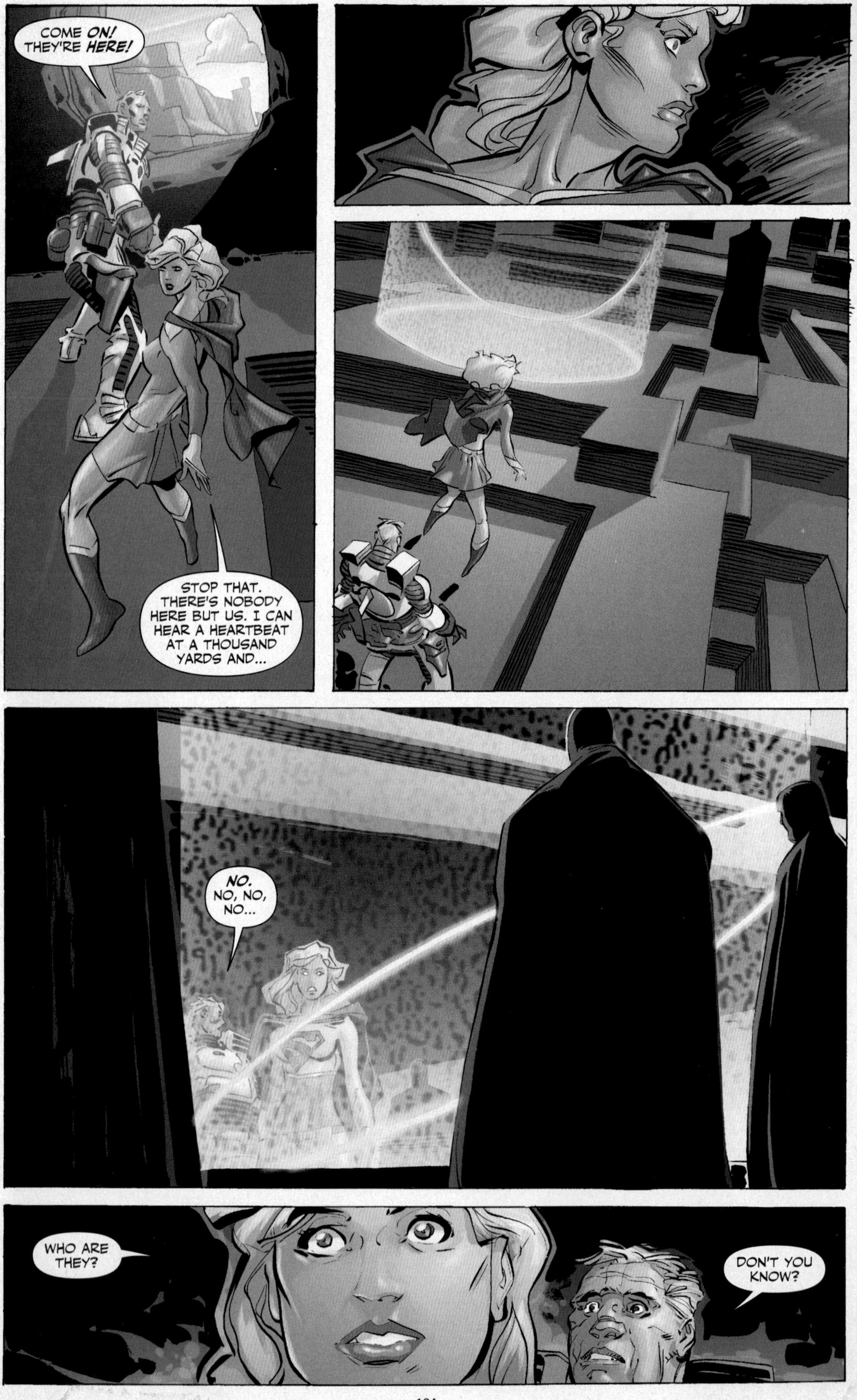
COME ON! THEY'RE HERE!
STOP THAT. THERE'S NOBODY HERE BUT US. I CAN HEAR A HEARTBEAT AT A THOUSAND YARDS AND...
NO. NO, NO, NO...
WHO ARE THEY?
DON'T YOU KNOW?

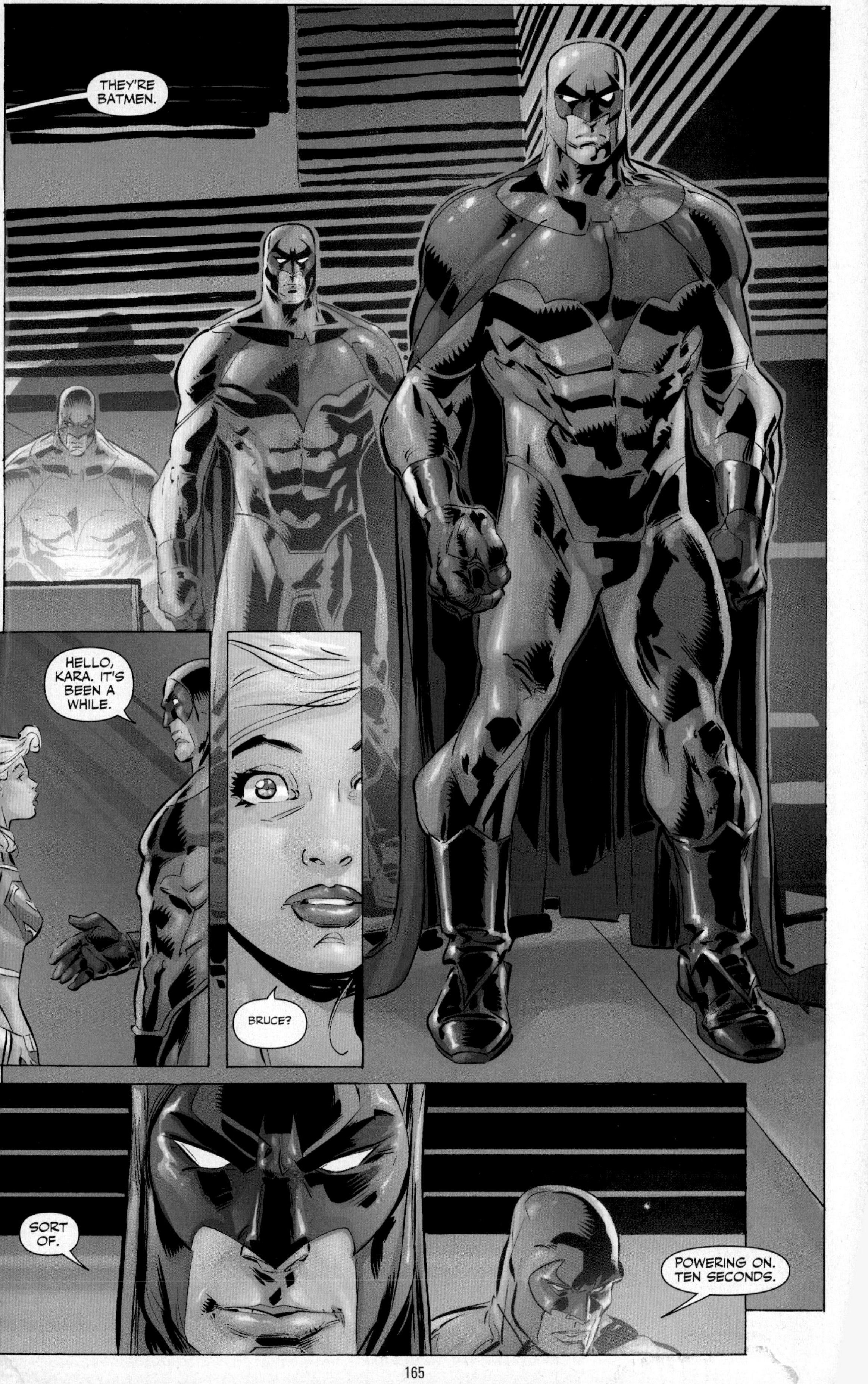
THEY'RE BATMEN.
HELLO, KARA. IT'S BEEN A WHILE.
BRUCE?
SORT OF.
POWERING ON. TEN SECONDS.

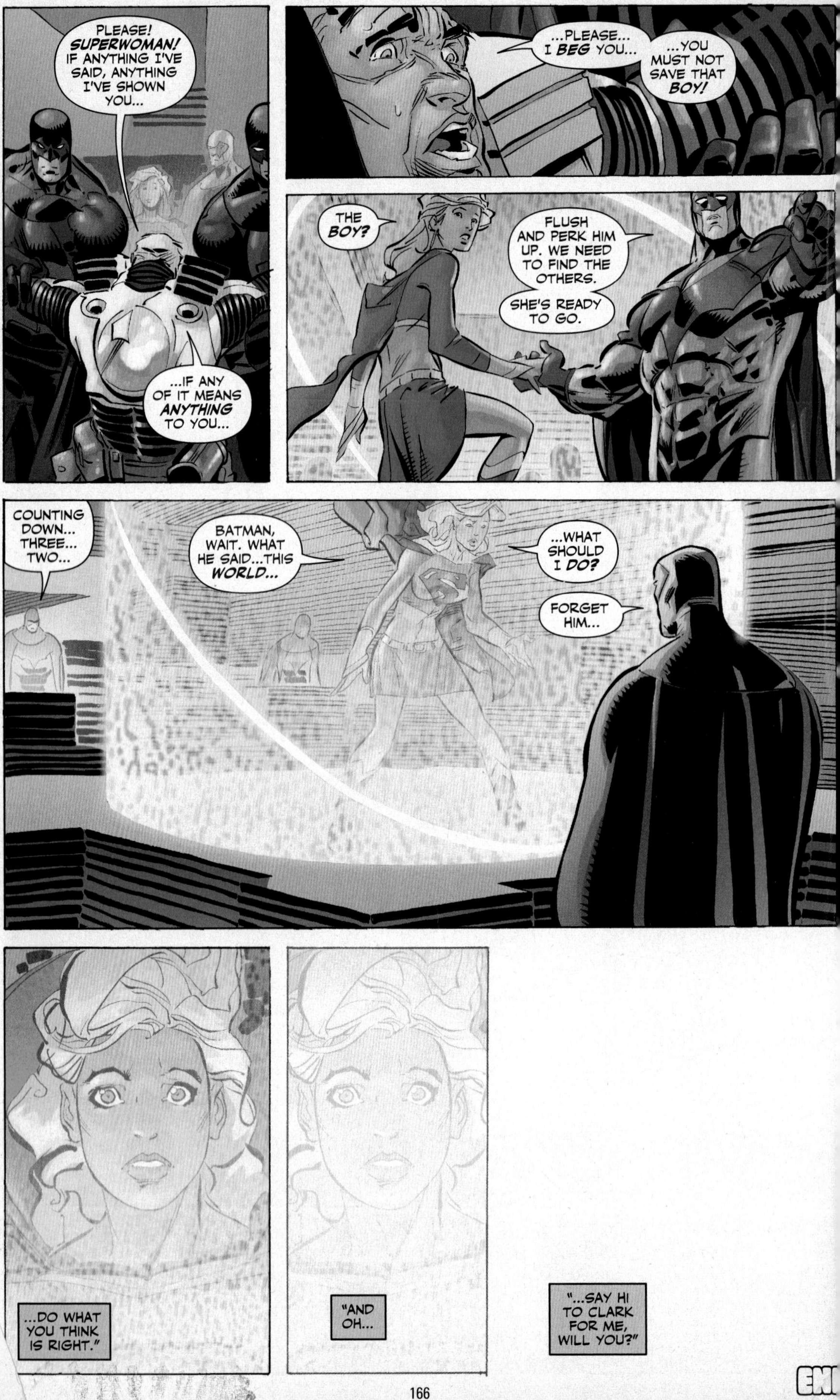

PLEASE! SUPERWOMAN! IF ANYTHING I'VE SAID, ANYTHING I'VE SHOWN YOU...
...IF ANY OF IT MEANS ANYTHING TO YOU...
...PLEASE... I BEG YOU...
...YOU MUST NOT SAVE THAT BOY!
THE BOY?
FLUSH AND PERK HIM UP. WE NEED TO FIND THE OTHERS.
SHE'S READY TO GO.
COUNTING DOWN... THREE... TWO...
BATMAN, WAIT. WHAT HE SAID...THIS WORLD...
...WHAT SHOULD I DO?
FORGET HIM...
...DO WHAT YOU THINK IS RIGHT."
"AND OH...
"...SAY HI TO CLARK FOR ME, WILL YOU?"

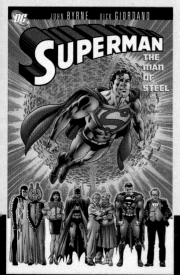

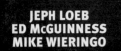